"Couples in which one partner has ADH in their relationships and may be prone to higher rates of divorce than are typical couples. That is why this book is so important. It is the only one currently available that focuses on the most intimate aspects of a loving relationship among couples and that is their sexual one. With great wit, candor, and sensitivity, Dr. Tuckman not only presents the results of the first large-scale survey of sexual relations in couples where ADHD exists and what problems they may be experiencing. Just as important, he tells you what to do about it. As with his other books on ADHD, readers will find here numerous recommendations for how to improve the quality of their relationship despite one or both members of a couple having adult ADHD. I highly recommend this book not only for couples, but for couple therapists, adult ADHD coaches, mental health professionals who work with adults with ADHD, and students in training in these disciplines as it is the only one currently available that deals with this topic exclusively and in such rich detail."

Russell A. Barkley, PhD, clinical professor of psychiatry, Virginia Treatment Center for Children and Virginia Commonwealth University School of Medicine, Richmond, VA

"In the very capable hands of Dr. Ari Tuckman, sex and ADHD finally get the attention it deserves! Whether you are a person with ADHD, or a partner of one, or just someone who finds themselves driven to distraction in this age of non-stop social media, there are incredibly valuable lessons in *ADHD After Dark* to help you get sexually focused."

Ian Kerner, PhD, sex therapist and best-selling author of *She Comes First*

"Many couples impacted by ADHD struggle, and their sex lives show it. So they rightly ask 'what will make our sex life better?!' Ari Tuckman, one of the top ADHD therapists in the world, knows. With research to back it up, he shares what strengthens the intimate lives of couples just like you. Read *ADHD After Dark*, and re-energize those intimate moments!"

Melissa Orlov, founder of www.adhdmarriage.com and author of the award-winning book, *The Couple's Guide to Thriving with ADHD*

"*Bravo!* for Ari Tuckman's *ADHD After Dark*. It's about time that someone asked real people to talk about real sex and real ADHD and that's what Ari did, and boy, did people ever talk! The result is this hugely valuable, engrossing, and fact-filled book. Both serious and celebratory, this unique book is a gem, the first of its kind, and a true find indeed!"
  Edward Hallowell, MD, author of *Delivered from Distraction*

"Dr. Ari Tuckman is a well-respected expert in the field of adult ADHD. He has the courage to write *ADHD After Dark* which advocates for awareness of possible effects of ADHD on sexuality and the couple relationship. He understands ADHD as an individual vulnerability, and urges the person and partner to be aware so that ADHD does not subvert sexuality. An important contribution to the ADHD community."
  Barry McCarthy, PhD, professor of psychology, American University, Washington, DC, and co-author of *Finding Your Sexual Voice: Celebrating Female Sexuality*

"*ADHD After Dark* exposes the devastating impact of ADHD on the sex lives of intimate partners. An online survey provided the data from an extraordinary number of individuals impacted by ADHD—directly or through an intimate relationship. Combining his experience as a systemically trained sex therapist with his proficiency in treating ADHD, the author shares an array of clinical interventions for couples affected by ADHD. Any therapist working with ADHD clients will find this book invaluable for improving sexual intimacy and relationship satisfaction."
  Nancy Gambescia, PhD, director, Postgraduate Program in Sex Therapy, Council for Relationships, Philadelphia, PA

"Tuckman's latest book addresses an important subject that is not often talked about: the impact of ADHD on people's sex and love lives. His work begins an important and much-needed conversation, and it offers practical advice and guidance to couples that can help them effectively navigate challenges and foster happier and healthier sex lives and relationships."
  Justin Lehmiller, PhD, author of the blog *Sex and Psychology* and the book *Tell Me What You Want: The Science of Sexual Desire and How It Can Help You Improve Your Sex Life*

"In this incredibly compelling book, Dr. Ari Tuckman adeptly combines original research about the sexual relationships, desires and habits of couples living with ADHD to help people find more happiness and connection. Written in a clear, friendly style, he's not afraid to tell it like it is: asking probing questions and providing honest, thoughtful, and even humorous insights into how spouses can create and maintain healthier, more satisfying intimacy. Useful 'Take Away Lessons' at the end of each chapter summarize important points and give readers practical steps to apply immediately. *ADHD After Dark* offers a positive, non-shaming approach to sexual relationships that is a much needed and significant contribution to the field of psychology. As a family therapist, I will definitely be referring to it and recommending it over and over again."

Sharon Saline, PsyD, author, *What your ADHD child wishes you knew: Working together to empower kids for success in school and life*

ADHD After Dark

This pioneering book explores the impact of ADHD on a couple's sex life and relationship. It explains how a better sex life will benefit your relationship (and vice versa) and why that's especially important for couples with one partner with ADHD.

Grounded in innovative research, *ADHD After Dark* draws on data from a survey of over 3000 adults in a couple where one partner has ADHD. Written from the author's unique perspective as both an expert in ADHD and a certified sex therapist, the book describes the many effects of ADHD on couples' sex lives and happiness, covering areas such as negotiating sexual differences, performance problems, low desire, porn, making time for sex, infidelity, and more. The book outlines key principles for a great sex life for couples with ADHD and offers strategies and treatment interventions where specific issues arise.

Written in a readable and entertaining style, *ADHD After Dark* offers clear information on sexuality and relationships and is full of valuable advice on how to improve both. This guide will be an essential read for adults with ADHD, as well as their partners or spouses, and therapists who work with ADHD clients and couples.

Ari Tuckman, PsyD, CST, is a certified sex therapist and psychologist specializing in the diagnosis and treatment of ADHD in children and adults. A prolific writer and international presenter, this is his fourth book on ADHD. He also hosts the popular podcast "More Attention, Less Deficit" for adults with ADHD.

ADHD After Dark

Better Sex Life, Better Relationship

Ari Tuckman

Routledge
Taylor & Francis Group

NEW YORK AND LONDON

First published 2020
by Routledge
52 Vanderbilt Avenue, New York, NY 10017

and by Routledge
2 Park Square, Milton Park, Abingdon, Oxon, OX14 4RN

*Routledge is an imprint of the Taylor & Francis Group, an informa
business*

Library of Congress Cataloging-in-Publication Data
A catalog record for this book has been requested

ISBN: 978-0-367-22392-2 (hbk)
ISBN: 978-0-367-22393-9 (pbk)
ISBN: 978-0-429-27467-1 (ebk)

Typeset in Optima
by Apex CoVantage, LLC

*To Heather, my smart and sexy wife who has
pushed me to become a better husband, father, and
person—not always when I wanted it, but always
when I needed it.*

Contents

Acknowledgments

I need to thank my friends from the world of ADHD who supported this project and helped spread the word about the survey: Melissa Orlov (ADHDmarriage.com), Eric Tivers (ADHD reWired podcast), ADDitudeMag.com, Rick Green (TotallyADD.com), Elaine Taylor-Klaus and Diane Dempster (ImpactADHD.com), Jeff Copper (Attention Talk Radio), Linda Roggli (ADDiva.net), Alan Brown (ADDcrusher.com), and others. They're the best.

I would like to thank Nancy Gambescia, PhD who ran the sex therapy training program at Council for Relationships. She is the perfect combination of clinical brilliance, empathic tenderness, and Philly attitude that any client or student would be lucky to have. Also, my couples therapy supervisor, Steve Betchen, PhD, who has an almost psychic ability to see through the messy complexities of a relationship to get to the heart of what is going on. They made the highly inconvenient half day in Philadelphia the best part of my week. I would also like to thank my classmates, in particular Darren Aboyoun, PhD, for their insights and friendship. Supervision with Martha Kauppi, LMFT has not only made me a better therapist, but her influence is woven throughout all the parts of the book that talk about how to improve your sex life and relationship. I would also like to thank Mike Giancola, LMFT for his insights on the porn chapter and Justin Lehmiller, PhD for suggesting the dating chapter.

I always believed in statistics, but mostly felt it was the sort of thing that was better when it happened to other people. But I did enjoy geeking out on this analysis, trying to see the patterns in the numbers and figure out what secrets they held. Thanks to my good friend, Nathan Coates, for showing me how to do a bunch of analyses in Excel, something that kept me busy for hours and hours. I would also like to thank Pete Ondish from the awesomely named Data Monster Consulting for cranking out some seriously scary stats and then explaining to me what the hell it all meant (twice).

And last but definitely not least, I want to thank the 3000+ people who gave their time to fill out a ridiculously long survey and share their honest feelings. I take that generosity very seriously and hope that you feel that the lessons in this book are worth your investment.

Introduction: Good Sex is Extra Important for Couples With ADHD

So, what's in a title? Why ADHD after dark?

First, it's a reference to sex and other fun, naughty activities that happen under cover of darkness. Or at least out of public sight (usually). But there is also a second meaning: that ADHD is at its worst when you're in the dark about it. As in, you don't even know that that is what is making your life harder, whether it's your own ADHD or your romantic partner's. There are lots of really helpful books out there on how to work on your ADHD and make various aspects of your life better (I've written a few of them). There are even some books on how to make your relationship better which are also really helpful. What seems to be painfully absent is a book on how ADHD can impact a couple's sex life and how to make that part better—and the rest of your relationship, too.

When I've presented on ADHD and sex, I've joked that this is a topic that no one is talking about, by which I mean the people standing at the front of the room—probably most of the people in

> *What would make your sex life better for you?*
> Having had some over the past three decades would have been nice. I have had to accept a sexless relationship for a very long time.
> *What would make your sex life better for your partner?*
> Beats me.
> *Is there anything else that you would like us to know?*
> We have lived with undiagnosed ADHD for over 37 years. The diagnosis answered a thousand questions and decades of confusion for me. It is a very painful situation. He is still in denial of the impact his ADD behavior has had on me over the years. I do not understand hyposexuality. I am a sexual being. I thought most people were. Why does nobody talk about this aspect of humanity and the ADHD individual? It's too late for me, but there might be somebody else out there wondering if there is any hope.
> *Non-ADHD woman, 66, married, been together 21+ years*

the audience have talked about it a lot. Just as learning about how ADHD impacts time management, for example, can be helpful, so too can learning about how it impacts your sex life and relationship. These seem like way too important topics to have been neglected up to this point.

If you feel like you have been wandering around in the dark too long, it's time to shine some light on the subject. And if you feel like you have been alone too long in these struggles, take heart in the fact that a lot in this book is based on the results of an online survey I created—you have more than 3000 people by your side who know what it's like when one partner in a couple has ADHD.

Sex is Important

Sex feels good and we have a biological drive to seek it out. These are both true, but sex is much more than that, especially when it occurs within a relationship—and especially when it occurs within a long-term relationship that is full of stresses, big and small. I won't go so far as to say that it is the glue that holds couples together, but it is one of the glues.

Sex is a chance to spend some time together, to connect, to recharge. To have some fun and seek some perhaps too-absent pleasure. To play and let the imagination run wild. To flirt. To be passionate. To let loose a part of yourself that doesn't come out enough under the civilizing influence of daily demands. To share your most intimate desires with your partner and to be amazed by your partner's.

There are many ways that couples connect and draw each other closer to counter the frustrations that push them apart. Sex is one of the few that simultaneously works at the physical, emotional, and intellectual levels. It's easy to let sex fade over time, gradually crowded out by other demands of time and energy, or to be the victim of ill will or performance problems. I would make the case that sex is way too important to let it wither away and instead encourage you to put in the effort to keep its special place in your day and in your relationship.

The Double-Edged Sword of Sex

If sex is important to you and it's going well, then there is a lot of good that can come from having great sex together. But if things aren't going well sexually and it is important to you that they do, then this can be a significant source of disappointment, frustration, and resentment. Of course, most couples have times when their sex life wanes or when there are ongoing disagreements, but if they can overcome these setbacks, then both their sex life and relationship can become better than they were before.

> It's upsetting and humiliating feeling that my husband doesn't want to have sex with me. He says he is attracted to me and wants to have it; he just forgets about it. That makes no sense to me at all. It negatively impacts my self-esteem.
> *Non-ADHD woman, married, been together 11–20 years*

We all know that ADHD can make it harder for both romantic partners to feel happy in the relationship (which is why you're reading this). Couples who already have enough other things to fight over don't need to also disagree about sex. I don't want bad sex to be the final nail in the coffin for your relationship.

So there is a lot on the line when it comes to sex and it cuts both ways. Let's use good sexual connection as a way to keep couples together and work on everything that will make the relationship better.

The simple goal of this book is to help you and your partner have better sex (whatever that means to you both) so that there is more positive energy in the relationship. Think of it as giving you extra emotional fuel to then better deal with all the other stresses of daily life.

The deeper goal is to help you and you partner work on all the big and little things that go into creating a truly great sex life. This process will make you happier with each other in other nonsexual ways as well. While there is plenty to talk about that is just about the mechanics of sex, if your sex is happening within a relationship, then both you and your partner will each need to work on certain things for the other person to feel more interested in being sexually vulnerable—which is what it takes to keep sex exciting. In fact, that desire to keep sex interesting is part of what drives ongoing relationship growth.

How to Read This Book

This book very much has a progression of topics from one chapter to the next, but you can also feel free to jump around and read what is most relevant at that time. Also, each chapter ends with the most important and useful take away lessons. But, so that you have a road map, here is the general layout.

We begin with *Section I: The Lay of the Land: Research Results*. Before I could write this book, I had to do some basic research because it turns out that there was no hard data on the sex lives of couples where one person has ADHD. Don't take it personally—sex research overall is woefully underfunded. Of course, there is all the general good advice, but does it all still apply when one person has ADHD? To answer this question, I created the ADHD Relationship Sex Survey and somehow got 3000 people to fill it out. As it turns out, some of the generic advice I had been giving clients and audiences at presentations was wrong or not helpful. I was actually really happy to see that—this is why we do research. Now we know better and you will get the best advice we have at this time. I present the research data with the goal of making it useful to readers, so it won't feel like a stats class, but if it still gives you flashbacks, you can skim or skip ahead.

Then we move on to *Section II: Principles of Great Sex Lives.* In addition to lots of information specific to couples where one person has ADHD, I have also included chapters on general sexuality and how to make your sex life better, angled towards couples with ADHD. Despite our cultural obsession with sex, there is still a lot of incorrect information out there—and a lot of lack of information. You will probably find some interesting and useful tidbits in these chapters, since odds are that some of it applies to your situation. There's way more here than in your high school health class textbook, so it's worth a look, no matter how much of a sex genius you are.

Finally, in *Section III: Overcome Specific Issues,* I include chapters on specific sexual problems since they are more common than you might think—and probably more treatable than you might think. So, if there is something getting in the way of your sex life, these chapters are for you. If you're suffering, then definitely read them.

I also include a number of appendices that include the ADHD Relationship Sex Survey so you and your partner can take it for yourself; provider directories; and other worthy books.

Some Disclaimers

This book is mostly written for straight couples. That wasn't the original plan, but I got too few responses to the survey from people in same-sex relationships to be able to do any meaningful analysis. So that is a project for another time, but it is my hope that there will still be helpful lessons in this book for readers of every orientation.

Even if you are in a straight relationship, you will find that some of the research findings and lessons apply very well to you and your relationship, whereas others don't. That's OK. No couple will fit everything in any book, so take from it the lessons that seem helpful to you and your relationship at this time.

Most of the respondents to the survey were ages 30–59 and living together in committed relationships (dating, engaged, or married). This isn't that surprising: that is where things get more complicated for all couples. Add ADHD (or anything else, including kids) into the mix and things get even more complicated. So these are the people who are most motivated to look for help which is how they found my survey and were willing to spend the time to fill it out—and probably why you're reading this now. There's a good parallel there—the research subjects match the readers. Having said that, this book is also helpful for dating couples who are contemplating moving in together and/or getting married, who were a smaller part of the survey respondents. It's always better to learn some good lessons from those who have come before you. By working on some of these things now, you can create a better foundation for your relationship. In that vein, the final chapter offers advice for singles who are looking to couple up.

Section I
The Lay of the Land: Research Results

Introduction: Better Sex Through Statistics: The ADHD Relationship Sex Survey

There has been some good work done on helping mixed couples (where one romantic partner has ADHD and one doesn't) improve their relationship. Melissa Orlov, Gina Pera, Susan Tschudi, and Ned Hallowell have written books and articles, presented at conferences, streamed webinars, etc. and they do a great job of it. There's certainly no shortage of relationship topics to talk about and there isn't enough time in the day to cover them all. But sex tends to only get mentioned in passing. It may be that I'm too interested, but isn't sex one of the big parts of romantic relationships? Sure, there's also all that other stuff, like creating a shared dream, raising kids, paying the bills, and fighting over who didn't load the dishwasher, but isn't sex one of the things that makes romantic relationships unique?

I decided to start talking about this important topic because nobody else was. And by nobody else, I mean the people who write books and present on ADHD. The couples talk about it plenty. Given what I know about relationships and sex in general, plus what we know about how ADHD affects relationships, I felt pretty prepared. Unfortunately, the lack of hard data meant that I was limited to doing a lot of theorizing and extrapolating (i.e., making shit up). While this is fun and easy, I felt a responsibility to do better than that—after all, there is a lot of unhappiness here for couples who are struggling.

The ADHD Relationship Sex Survey

Somehow or other, I hit on the idea of doing a survey to find out how these couples feel about their relationships and sex lives, with the goal of getting some actual data so we could make better recommendations. I started thinking about all the things that I wanted to know and then went crazy and came up with seventy-two questions (once you add in the sub-questions). For an online survey. Where participants aren't getting reimbursed. And they're doing it in the middle of their busy lives. For people who get bored easily. . . . Brilliant.

Amazingly, more than 3000 people filled it out, most of them all the way to the end. I think what this shows is that people are interested in this topic. *Really* interested. So it was still a crazy idea, but people liked it, for which I am eternally grateful. Participation was completely anonymous, but I did thank participants by doing a two-hour webinar sharing the results before I shared that data anywhere else. That only seems right.

Part of the success in recruiting participants came from my good friends in the world of ADHD who spread the word about the survey: Melissa Orlov (ADHDmarriage.com), Eric Tivers (ADHD reWired podcast), ADDitudeMag.com, Rick Green (TotallyADD. com), Elaine Taylor-Klaus and Diane Dempster (ImpactADHD. com), Jeff Copper (Attention Talk Radio), Linda Roggli (ADDiva.net), Alan Brown (ADDcrusher.com), and others. We all owe these great people some thanks. And they have fantastic material you should check out anyway.

The questions covered demographic information (age, duration of relationship, etc.), ADHD treatment effort and effectiveness, relationship satisfaction, and a lot of questions about sexual satisfaction, activities, barriers, etc.

Take the Survey Yourself

I designed the survey not only to collect data, but also with the hope that the people taking it would find it helpful as an opportunity to spark some new thinking about their own sex life and relationship. My hope was that both partners would take the survey and then discuss their answers, both the similarities and differences. This can be a helpful entry into some bigger conversations. You and your partner can take it yourself—check out Appendix A on p. 345.

Nice Numbers!

I was lucky enough to get a lot of people to respond to the survey. Of course, it's easier to get lucky when you have a bunch of awesome friends putting the word out about the survey. I have data from more than 3000 respondents, many of whom made it all the way through all seventy-two questions, giving us more than 200,000 data points. So that is *a lot* of data. This is good news for all of us because it enables us to do a lot more analysis of the results and gives us more faith that what we found actually means something.

As is often the case with surveys, I got a lot more women and, as you might expect, more people with ADHD than without. The breakdown (at one point when I downloaded the data) looks like this:

- 1263 ADHD women
- 1051 Non-ADHD women
- 673 ADHD men
- 196 Non-ADHD men

Non-ADHD men are predictably the smallest group of respondents. Ideally, we would have gotten a more balanced mix of respondents, but I did keep in mind that we need to consider gender whenever we compared ADHD vs non, just to make sure that any differences weren't actually just gender effects. I always compared men with ADHD to those without and women with ADHD to those without, rather than doing all ADHD versus all non.

Although there were eighteen-year-olds and those over sixty who took the survey, most of the respondents were in their thirties, forties, and fifties. In addition, most of the respondents were married. This combination of age and relationship status may reflect the tendency that those who are younger are less likely to have as many shared responsibilities (e.g., kids, mortgage, etc.) and therefore don't feel the effects of ADHD as much and are therefore less invested in seeking information on ADHD or taking the survey. Meanwhile, those who are sixty and above are less likely to have been diagnosed with ADHD, even if they have it, so they are also less likely to take the survey.

I am very cognizant of the fact that the impact of ADHD (or whatever) very much depends on the person's circumstances. For example, working a dumb job over the summer while living at home is very different from working full time while raising two toddlers. A person's age influences the kinds of situations they are in which then affects their relationship and romantic partner. When life is easy, we can be more forgiving of a romantic partner's quirks; when the demands pile up, we have less patience available. Generally, life gets more complicated as we get older, at least until the kids move out and perhaps the finances get more established. Also, when partners' lives are more intertwined (e.g., mortgage and kids), they expect more from each other and get angrier if the partner falls short of their expectations. Therefore, ADHD will become more obvious as a relationship progresses from casual dating to co-parenting. Most of the respondents had been together for at least six years, meaning more committed relationships. So this also impacted potential respondents' motivation to take the survey.

I Only Care if it's Useful

One of the implications of having so many respondents is that it is easy to find differences that are highly statistically significant, but otherwise meaningless. For example, if men with ADHD were to rate treatment as being 1% more effective than women with ADHD did, you could show that to be a significant difference if you have a large enough sample size. But who cares about 1%? So throughout the data analysis, I am focusing on the things that actually matter, the stuff that you can do something with. With seventy-two questions, there's plenty of worthwhile data to talk about. If I don't talk about something, then it's most likely that it didn't come up as a big enough difference. Or it didn't occur to me.

Also, you may be relieved to know that when I share the survey results in the chapters that make up the rest of this section, I'm not just sharing a bunch of boring stats. In addition to the boring stats, I also include lessons learned and implications for what to do with that information to make your relationship and sex life better. This isn't a journal article and there won't be a test at the end—it's about making people's lives better.

Some Minor and Major Number Crunching

The good news about having so much data is that there is a lot that you can do with it. This means findings that are not only interesting, but also useful.

Types of Comparisons

Survey data can be analyzed in a number of ways. For example, we can take a single question and find out how respondents answered it. For example, on average, how frequently would respondents want to have sex? Or what percentage of respondents would want to have sex at least once per week? This is easy to do and yields some interesting data, but it's only the beginning. It's much more interesting—and useful—to compare the answers to two questions, for example by adding in gender. How often would men versus women want to have sex? And it gets even better when we look at three questions, for example by adding in ADHD status—what is the average desired sexual frequency for men with ADHD, men without ADHD, women with ADHD, and women without ADHD? Now we're getting somewhere. We can also look at things like, how did those with the highest sexual satisfaction rate treatment effectiveness compared to those with the lowest sexual satisfaction? With seventy-two questions, we can do all sorts of comparisons and pull out all sorts of information.

But wait, there's more! In addition to this relatively simple analysis which I did, self-proclaimed data romancer Pete Ondish did some hardcore deep analysis of the data and cranked out a bunch of seriously scary-looking stats tables. For example, he took all the data and crunched it to find out which were the most important at predicting respondents' relationship satisfaction.

Four Kinds of People, Two Kinds of Couples

Throughout the analysis, I looked not only at ADHD versus non-ADHD, but also at men versus women, because gender can have a large effect on most of the questions that I asked—sometimes even larger than the ADHD effect. This makes for four different kinds of people that we looked at in the analysis:

- ADHD women
- Non-ADHD women
- ADHD men
- Non-ADHD men

Those four kinds of people then get into two kinds of heterosexual couples:

- ADHD woman with a non-ADHD man
- ADHD man with a non-ADHD woman

Not surprisingly, there can be some pretty big differences between the kinds of answers provided by those four kinds of people. Also, not surprisingly, it can make a big difference which person in the couple has ADHD in terms of how it affects the relationship. Although ADHD is ADHD, the expectations for men and women in society and in relationships are different. Gender affects what we expect of ourselves and what we expect of our partners. So there is the direct effect of ADHD, the direct effect of gender, and then the interaction effect between the two. See what I mean about lots of interesting analysis options?

Speaking of which, I limited the survey to couples where only one partner has ADHD. As with the gay and lesbian couples, double-ADHD couples are a project for another day.

Descriptive and Suggestive Results

All this analysis leads to two different kinds of results. Some of it is *descriptive* of the similarities and differences among the people who took the survey—how are these couples doing? What are the differences between people with ADHD versus those without? What about men and women? The goal here is to help us better understand how people in these mixed couples do as individuals and together. These are the descriptive results and my slogan for them is, "This is interesting!" Sometimes just knowing about similarities and differences is therapeutic by itself. These results will be covered in *Chapter 2: How ADHD Impacts Sex and Relationships.*

The second kind of analysis is what I am calling *suggestive*— what are the happiest folks doing differently from the least happy? What can we learn from the happiest folks? The goal here is to help us focus on the things that seem to make the most difference for these couples, so that all couples can find more happiness. My slogan for these suggestive results is, "This is worth investing in!" If you're looking to make changes, these are the places to start. Emulate the best. These results will be shared in the two chapters after that: *Chapter 3: Make the Most of Treatment* and *Chapter 4: Role Models: What Can We Learn from the Happiest Couples?*

The survey results are then interwoven though the rest of the book also.

Remember, Everybody's Got Something

As you read the results from the survey, you will see a lot of differences between the ADHD partners and the non-ADHD partners— and also between men and women. You may feel disheartened and that the differences between you and your partner are too big to bridge. I have two thoughts for you: First, group averages can be useful, but they don't tell us about individuals, so focus instead on how these averages help you and your partner understand each other better—if they don't, then move on to the next chapters. Second, we need differences in our relationships—we need a partner who complements us and brings something different to the party.

ADHD can definitely affect both people in the relationship and how they relate to each other. However, so does everything else about who you each are, including where you grew up, how your parents raised you, your various strengths and weaknesses, lessons learned from previous relationships, your favorite TV shows, etc. You and your partner will complement each other in some ways and drive each other crazy in others. ADHD will be part of this—it may at times be the most obvious problem in the relationship, but it is never the only problem. No couple is ever that lucky to only have one area of disagreement. Seriously.

Don't let ADHD become the easy scapegoat, because it's still only part of what is going on there and over-focusing on one part makes it easier to ignore other important parts. Other couples may not have the struggles that come with ADHD, but they have other struggles—some similar to yours and some different. If ADHD is a part of your relationship, you will need to deal with it, and some other stuff too, but there is plenty of happiness to be found if you both do it well.

It's All Good

You'll figure this out even if I don't say it, but I take the position that when it comes to sex and relationships, there are many, many ways to be happy. You and your partner need to figure out what works for you. As long as it occurs between two consenting adults and both

> In our particular case, I do not believe my ADHD is a factor. Constant therapy (personal and couples) over the last several years have uncovered a sometimes, near crippling, mix of anxieties/insecurities working against my partner.
> *ADHD man, 57, married, been together 21+ years*

people are operating in good faith, then it's all good by me. This includes the kinkiest, craziest stuff that doesn't even have a porn site for it yet, as well as the most straight-laced vanilla sex with the lights off. I don't get to vote on your sex life. I certainly have my own opinions and preferences, as well as clinical experience and knowledge about what tends to work better for most couples, but you and your partner (or even partners) need to make your own decisions about whether a particular recommendation fits your life at this time and is therefore helpful. It's OK if some of my ideas aren't; just take the ones that are.

Cut to the Chase: Give Me the Important Lessons!

At the end of each chapter in this section, I will include a brief summary of the Take Away Lessons from the data. In other words, the lessons learned from the data that you can apply to improve your relationship. If you're impatient (or bored) with the data you can skip to the end of the chapter and then explain it to your romantic partner by saying, "Our relationship and your happiness is so important to me that I just couldn't wait another second to learn how to make it better."

1

In Their Own Words

The goal of a survey is to get a bunch of numbers to crunch and thereby create some clarity out of messy confusion. Unfortunately, you're limited to the questions you asked and how you asked them. Therefore, it's helpful to also ask some open-ended (fill in the blank) questions, to see what you may have missed.

At the very end of the survey, I asked three open-ended questions:

- What would make your sex life better for *you*?
- What would make your sex life better for *your partner*?
- Is there anything else that you would like us to know?

In case I didn't already know why this survey and book were important, the comments really made it clear that way too many people are suffering much more than they need to be. Lots of pain, disappointment, anger, resentment, disconnection, and rejected desire. Some people haven't had sex in years or decades—some feel really badly about this, some have resigned themselves to it, some don't miss it, and a few are happy about it. And, contrary to the stereotypes, it's not just the guys and the young folks who miss that sex—there are also lots of women who do, including some in their seventies. And then there were those who wrote about how amazing and important their sex life was. When it comes to sex, there is a lot to lose and gain.

Survey respondents were clearly invested in this topic and took the time to write out 5046 comments—after filling out a survey of seventy-two questions. They still felt they had something important to add. To their credit, I got almost the same number of comments about what would make sex better for themselves versus for their partner (1713 versus 1653), so most of these folks are equally interested in their partner's satisfaction. This is not only generous but also wise, since it's hard to get more or better sex for yourself if your partner isn't also enjoying it. Their comments are full of brilliant, insightful, funny, poignant, and bravely vulnerable quotes that I wish I could share, but I promised confidentiality and I need to honor everything they have given me. Therefore, I sent out a second request for quotes with explicit permission to use in the book and those are scattered throughout in text boxes.

Many of the comments spoke about how ADHD was impacting the couple's relationship and/or sex life and a lot of them lamented the potentially preventable struggles if the diagnosis had come earlier. But equally noteworthy was that there are lots of other relationship and sexual issues going on here that have little or nothing to do with ADHD and are directly affecting the respondents' relationship and sex life. These other topics, including how ADHD can interweave among them, are covered in the second half of the book, so that you are fully armed to make things better.

Many of the respondents complained about mismatched sexual appetites in terms of desired frequency and activities. Many wanted a better relationship and sex life, but felt powerless to overcome the obstacles. Many felt judged by their partner for their desires and wished they could share more of who they are sexually and also know their partner more fully and honestly. They wanted more communication about how to make their relationship and sex life better. Too many people said that they had no idea what would make sex better for their partner because their partner wouldn't tell them, even when asked directly. Or perhaps the topic was never broached and both partners avoided those potentially uncomfortable conversations. Needless to say, silence rarely makes a bad situation better.

As is common with couples, many of the comments reflected interlocking patterns, where each partner's actions stopped the other from giving them what they want. We can get in our own and each other's way. For example, someone would say that they wanted more nonsexual affection in order to feel more interested in sex but that their partner just wanted more sex. Hmm, seems like they each have the key to giving the other what they want and thereby getting more of what they themselves want. I know, it's not that simple, but in some ways it is. . . .

There were a number of comments from respondents with small and dissatisfying sex lives saying that they had much better sex with previous partners and also with this partner at other times in the relationship. It's easy to fall into the mindset that the current situation won't change (at least for the better) because this is just who we each are, but then lose sight of the fact that this is not how we have each always been. A couple's sex life is really affected by the context and can change if they put in the effort to do so—although that may involve working on some aspects of the relationship that feel pretty distantly connected to your sex life.

Respondents also spoke about various health concerns, medication side effects, and menopause decreasing libido and/or making sex uncomfortable, all of which contributed to difficulties with sexual performance and/or pleasure. There were also other sexual dysfunctions, like erectile disorder, premature ejaculation, and painful intercourse. This severely limited or ended some folks' sex life, but others worked around it—which is a really good lesson for all of us

We both need to make it more of a priority. Also—create mood together instead of realizing late one morning after sleeping in, oh, I was thinking about making love, but now it's too late, isn't it? With ADHD it's probably a combination of now or not now timing and balancing energy levels. But that doesn't make it better or easier!

Non-ADHD woman, 59, married, been together 21+ years

to be flexible about how we approach our goals and how we define success. This includes how respondents dealt with infidelity—for some it was a death blow and others limped along with the damage, but some found a way to rise above this painful setback and rebuild their relationship into something even better.

Many of the women felt badly about their weight or attractiveness, but so did some of the men. Interestingly, many people felt that their partner's weight was more of a problem for their partner than it was for them and that the self-consciousness put much more of a damper on their sex life than the weight itself did.

Lots of the women wanted more sleep and time for everything, especially if they had young children. Sex became one of the first casualties when sleep and time were in short supply. They wanted more help from their male partners and felt that they would have more energy for and interest in sex if they felt less overwhelmed. The non-ADHD women wanted a partner who carried more of his own weight, whereas the ADHD women needed more help because they had their own struggles with staying on top of everything. All of these loose ends made it harder for the women to mentally shift gears and get into the mood for sex. Many of the women said that a babysitter would dramatically improve their relationship and sex life—can we call this couples therapy and submit it to insurance?

If they did start fooling around, the women, especially the ADHD women, felt more distracted than the guys. This could be external factors, like outside noises or being worried about being walked in on, but also internal thoughts (to-do list, other demands in life, etc.). External factors might be more easily addressed—as my sex therapy professor would emphatically state, "Put a lock on your bedroom door!" Quieting internal chatter can be more difficult, but can also be addressed. Their male partners would notice that the women were sometimes not mentally present during sex. It seems like perhaps guys were more likely than women to hyperfocus during sex.

Finally, too many respondents of all kinds complained of having a partner who would ignore their sexual initiations, but would expect a positive response when they initiated. Needless to say, selfishness and insensitivity almost always cast a long shadow in a relationship.

I should also say that there were also lots of respondents who were very happy with their relationship and sex life. Some of these folks have been together for decades but are still going hot and

> *What would make your sex life better for you?*
> I wish I could be more present. Sometimes I get distracted. It's not for his lack of trying!
> *What would make your sex life better for your partner?*
> I think sometimes he picks up on the fact that I seem some- place else.
>
> *ADHD woman, 46, engaged and living together, been together 6–10 years*

heavy and spoke about the many relationship benefits of a great sex life. Interestingly, even the folks who were very satisfied still had some things that they wished were different—we all have things to work on and improvement should always be an option.

Let's now look at some of the findings that were specific to each of our four types of respondents. Perhaps notice if any of these sound familiar.

Non-ADHD Women

Many of these women want more sex with a generous partner who is affectionate, interested, and connected in both sexual and nonsexual ways. They would like their partners to step up more and handle more of the demands of daily life so it isn't so imbalanced. Having a partner who feels like a child is a total turn-off, as is a volatile temper. They want a partner who is able to discuss and work on problems effectively. By contrast, guys who blindly ignore problems but then expect these women to eagerly jump into bed are only turning their women off even more. The worst are the guys who won't deal with their ADHD, are reactive when confronted, and are generally selfish in bed and elsewhere—in these cases, ADHD may be the least of the problems. A bunch of women concede that they need to ask more for what they want—and perhaps tolerate their partner reacting badly or challenge him if he shuts down and ignores her.

Many of these women are so fed up that they feel done with sex, perhaps in general or perhaps just with this partner. Some of them would indeed still like to have a good relationship and sex life, but

What would make your sex life better for you?
More romantic dates and times leading up to sex. More attention towards me and less distraction. Him focusing on our home and relationship more.
What would make your sex life better for your partner?
Me not being so frustrated and happier. Showing him appreciation more.

Non-ADHD woman, 56, married,
been together 11–20 years

feel resigned to their fate and are unhappily settling for what they have. Some have partners who don't seem all that interested in sex in general, whereas others have partners who seem to use porn as an escape from dealing with what is going on in their sex life and relationship. A surprising number of women complained about their male partners not taking care of their health and/or hygiene and that this was a turn-off for them.

Many of them also felt that their partner was too distracted during sex and in general. They wanted more nonsexual touch and affection through the day, not just once the clothes started dropping. Some better initiations would also result in more acceptances. Once things did start rolling, they wanted more foreplay—for its own sake but also to help the women better transition mentally and physically into a sexual mindset. All of this requires some planning ahead and then awareness in the moment.

ADHD Women

Lots of the women with ADHD complained about struggling to keep up with all the many demands on their time and energy and not feeling supported by their partners. Adding insult to injury, many felt criticized for the ways that ADHD impacted their ability to stay on top of everything which had a predictable effect on their desire to have sex with their partner. They wanted both more physical help and emotional support, especially if they felt that they had a disproportionate share of child care and housework. Some also wished their partner was able to take feedback and requests better, sexually and otherwise, so they could work more as a team. Some insightfully admitted that they need to ask more for what they want, even (or especially) if their partner responds badly or ignores them.

Put it all together, those who were unhappy felt that there were too many strains on the relationship and not enough closeness or affection. They wanted more nonsexual touch that didn't contain an obligation to take it all the way to intercourse. They wanted more foreplay—for its own sake but also to help them better transition mentally and physically into the experience. More so than the non-ADHD women, they struggled to clear their minds before and during sex, so it was all the more important to invest the time and energy to get into the right mindset for sex. Some of them found that distractibility could interfere with reaching orgasm—however, many of them still enjoyed the experience even if they didn't get all the way there. Some of them also found that their ADHD made it harder for them to consistently follow through on treatments for sexual problems which impacted their sexual performance and pleasure.

Non-ADHD Men

Many of these guys wanted their female partners with ADHD to be more involved in the relationship in general and more affectionate in nonsexual ways. This involved more prioritizing of time together, including the time and energy for sex, so it doesn't become the last thing to happen and the first thing to be squeezed out. They recognized that their partner's distractibility and struggles with time management during the day ultimately impacted how much time was available for sex. They also found that their partners were more likely

> *What would make your sex life better for you?*
> Quantity for starters. We are super busy with work and teenagers. So tiredness is a huge factor. I am consistently putting myself to bed before my husband tucks the kids in.
> *ADHD woman, 42, married, been together 21+ years*

> 32 years and I still find myself challenging if it is an illness or intentional.
> *Non-ADHD man, 62, married, been together 21+ years*

to be distracted during sex which interferes with her enjoyment, making the experience less enjoyable for him as well. Some also reported that their partner wasn't sufficiently attentive to his needs during sex.

ADHD Men

Many of these guys were acutely aware of their partner's frustrations with the impact of his ADHD and how that negatively impacted her interest in sex and general affection. They felt disappointed, hurt, and angry about this distance between them. Many of them recognized how their ADHD affected their partner and knew that they should help out more, but struggled with being consistent about it. They also wanted more empathy, understanding, and kindness from their partner about what living with ADHD is like for them. Many didn't know what to do to improve the relationship or felt that they can't please their partner, that it will never be enough.

In Conclusion

I really appreciate that so many respondents felt strongly enough about this topic that they took the extra time to share their thoughts directly. This color commentary fleshed out what the other survey questions found and confirmed some of my assumptions. Every individual and couple is unique, but I really want to get this right. Sex and relationship happiness are way too important to just guess at.

> *What would make your sex life better for your partner?*
> I honestly don't know at this point.
> *ADHD man, 56, married, been together 11–20 years*

2

How ADHD Impacts Sex and Relationships

There has been research about sex (what people are doing and how often, problems that arise, etc.) and there has been research about ADHD, but before this survey, there hasn't been any significant

Whenever I talk about sex in this book, I am using a broad definition, not just the narrow definition of intercourse. My instructions in the survey included: "When we use the term 'sexual activity,' we are using the term broadly to include any form of physical erotic activity. This includes kissing, touching, oral sex, intercourse, using sex toys, and any other activity that one or both of you considers sexual. It may or may not result in orgasm." Not only is this more representative of what most couples are doing, but it also enables us to get a broader picture of what is going on in these relationships. Defining sex broadly also promotes a more satisfying sex life.

> I wish I had known about how ADHD affects sex lives early on in my relationship. . . . It would have saved me a lot of pain and confusion knowing that there are predictable patterns of hyperfocus wearing off, etc.
>
> *Non-ADHD woman, 36, married,*
> *been together 6–10 years*

research on how ADHD affects a person's sexuality or couple's sex life. This seems like kind of an important area of adult life, no? Not to be snarky, but is the divorce rate low enough that we don't need to worry about this?

The good news is that the survey looked at all sorts of different elements of respondents' sex lives so we now have some data on this important area. I will summarize those findings in this chapter.

Surprising Findings

As I was writing the survey, there were certain questions that I just *knew* how people would respond. I would have bet some serious money on how the results were going to come out. Fortunately, I didn't actually bet any of that money, because there were four questions where I was totally wrong. This is actually a really good thing and is the reason we do research—not only to fill in what we don't already know, but also to show us where what we think we know is actually incorrect.

So let's start this chapter with the four things that I got totally wrong because they're really interesting.

First, before the survey, I would recommend that people with ADHD have sex when their medication is effective since it should (theoretically) help them be more present, less distracted, more attuned to their partner's experience, and less impulsive. In theory, this makes sense. As it turns out, most of the people who took the survey hadn't read the theory. Of those who had sex when medication was active, 41% said that medication had no effect on their enjoyment of a sexual encounter. The rest were evenly spread across the various response options ranging from a large negative effect to a large positive effect, with about 3–5% of people endorsing each option—they pretty much cancel each other out, at least on average, so it isn't a useful sweeping generalization to recommend it to everyone. For most people, ADHD medication doesn't do much for their sex life, at least while they're having sex. If you are in that minority who feels like it helps, then have sex while it's working. If you're in the minority who feels like it makes things worse, then don't.

I also asked respondents about their desires for both variety and novelty in their sexual experiences. I really believed those with ADHD would want more of both, since folks with ADHD tend to get bored with repetition. Fortunately, it turns out that sex isn't very repetitive. That seems like good news, right? I talk about this in more detail in the section on *Sexual Variety*, but for now, suffice to say that overall there wasn't much difference between those with and without ADHD, except that ADHD men had a somewhat higher desire for a larger repertoire of sexual activities than the non-ADHD men.

It also turns out that people with ADHD don't talk more during sex—boring math class, yes; sex, no. It's possible that those with more of the hyperactive/impulsive symptoms might be bigger talkers than those with just the inattentive symptoms, but I didn't ask people to specify, so I wouldn't be able to pick this up in the data. Regardless, if you and your partner enjoy talking during sex, then go for it. It can be a fun way to add another layer to the experience, add some playful teasing, stay in synch with your partner, and possibly bring back a distracted partner.

There were plenty of other surprising and interesting findings in the data which I will cover in the rest of this chapter, as well as throughout the book. These four findings were the most surprising and therefore deserving of special mention. The lesson here is to allow yourself to be surprised and to be willing to question some of what you know to be true—because maybe it's less true than you think. As much as it feels good to have our preconceived notions validated, it's perhaps more useful to challenge some of those beliefs if we want to improve our relationships.

From Bad to Worse?

Those who rated ADHD as having a large negative effect on their sex life also tended to rate almost all aspects of their sex life and relationship more negatively. This leads to at least two possible interpretations. The first and more obvious one is that when someone feels that ADHD has a large negative effect on their sex life, then it can really make a mess of things and affect many aspects of their sex life and relationship. That's possible, but in relationships, it's usually the case that one aspect is influenced by other aspects and in turn also influences other aspects. It's rare that the influence only goes one direction.

This brings us to the more nuanced interpretation which is that when a person is unhappy in their sex life and relationship, then ADHD can be seen as an obvious cause of that unhappiness. This isn't to say that ADHD isn't contributing, but it isn't the only driver of that dissatisfaction. These unhappy folks probably see lots of aspects about the relationship negatively and that negative mood makes them round things down, rather than up. There is also the possibility of a self-reinforcing process where feeling negative about the relationship leads to a tendency to be angry or disengaged and therefore for both partners to use less productive problem-solving. So bad goes to worse.

If you feel really down on your sex life and/or relationship, whether or not you see ADHD as a major driver of that unhappiness, I would encourage you to keep an open mind and to look for the ways that you and your partner each reinforce those problematic interactions. Don't let ADHD be the scapegoat that everything gets blamed on, even if it is an obvious part. After all, couples without ADHD still have issues to work on, so work on other issues, too. Changing one piece often leads to changes in other pieces, if you let it. Of course, if you didn't have at least some optimism, you wouldn't be reading this, so invest the necessary energy to make things better. Most of this book is actually about helping you do the work to make things better in your sex life and relationship overall.

Early is Easy

One clear finding in the survey was that most people tended to be pretty satisfied in their relationship during the first year. I suppose this makes sense in that if someone is unhappy in that first year, there probably isn't a second year.

Unfortunately, most people rated their current relationship satisfaction as lower, on average somewhere around neither satisfied nor dissatisfied. For all couples, as the years move on, life tends to get more complicated and the demands increase, which makes for fewer fun, easy times together. There also tends to be more to fight about, like kids and money, and both partners are more invested in the outcomes of those disagreements than they were in where they were going to dinner on those first dates. We also expect much more of our partners when we've been together for a while, so their actions affect us more. When one of those partners has ADHD, especially if there were some years or decades before it was diagnosed and treated, then that can exacerbate the typical struggles that other couples also wrestle with.

Of course, just because something is common doesn't mean that we should go down without a fight. It's not necessarily that relationship satisfaction inevitably declines so much as that it can take more intentional effort to create and sustain that happiness with each other than it did in the beginning. It's easy in the busyness of life to allow the relationship to slide into last place on the priorities list, right after organizing the sock drawer. So it takes some intentional effort to keep feeding the relationship.

This is true for all couples, but may be especially important when it comes to meeting the non-ADHD partners' needs. According to the survey, the non-ADHD partners felt less satisfied in the relationship over the current month than the ADHD partners did. This was especially true for the non-ADHD women, who had the lowest current relationship satisfaction compared to women with ADHD and men with or without ADHD. This certainly fits what I see in my office, as well as other aspects of the survey that we will discuss throughout the book. Perhaps the non-ADHD women and men expect more out of their relationships, but it seems like they feel that their partner's ADHD has more of a negative effect on the relationship than the ADHD partners do. These more negative feelings about the relationship should be taken seriously and addressed. Treatment goals should probably also include specific elements in the relationship, not just work or school functioning. For example, medication can be dosed so that its benefit extends past the exit sign at work and also includes evenings and weekends at home. (Unless you have a butler who can take care of all that stuff.)

Early is Easy in Bed, Too

Just as everyone tended to be rather satisfied with the relationship in that first year, most people tended to be rather satisfied with their sex life in that first year. And again similarly, most are less satisfied with their current sex life, with the non-ADHD partners being less satisfied than the ADHD partners, especially the non-ADHD women who were the least satisfied. This all then fits with the finding that non-ADHD partners of both genders felt that ADHD adds more barriers to sexual activity than those with ADHD did. So it appears that the non-ADHD partners attribute at least some of their decline in sexual satisfaction to their partners' ADHD. This seems like a pretty good reason for both partners to work on that ADHD.

Interestingly, the ADHD women were the most satisfied with their current relationship and sex life. So there is obviously a big interaction between ADHD and gender—it makes a big difference which person in the relationship has ADHD. Even if ADHD is ADHD, men and women have very different expectations for themselves and their partners, so how it plays out in life may be different.

When you look at these group averages and see that many people aren't very satisfied in their sex lives, it tells us a few things. First, if you're pretty satisfied, then congratulations—you and your partner are obviously doing a bunch of good stuff. Second, if you're less satisfied than you would like to be, then you're not alone. Perhaps that's comforting—but isn't a reason to resign yourself to it. Third, this dissatisfaction is too important to ignore—which is the whole premise of this survey and this book. I want more couples feeling good about their relationship and sex life. It's good for them, it's good for their kids, and at least in some small way, it's good for society. We're not messing around here.

So work on whatever it is that is taking away from your relationship and sex life. Seeing a direct connection between insufficiently managed ADHD, for example, and a less satisfying sex life can be a great motivator for some people to work on their ADHD. This is

> This may not be ADHD related, but we have a very good sex life for the first six years of marriage (including her initiating sex and being a willing participant), then she got pregnant. After the baby was born, she never initiated sex again. Any intimacy was initiated by me and at best she was an unenthusiastic participant, at worst her response was a NO. At some point I gave up and we haven't had sex in years.
>
> *ADHD man, 60, married, been together 21+ years*

probably more motivating than insisting that they should come to find the quiet joys of a perfectly clear countertop.

Sexual Frequency

If there's one thing I have learned from *Men's Health* and *Cosmo*, it's that you can't do a sex survey without asking people how often they have sex. But before I bust out those numbers, let's keep a few things in mind. First, sexual frequency can change a lot over time in a relationship—it can not only decrease with time, but also increase, depending on the week, month, or year. Variability is pretty typical. Sometimes these changes are directly related to sex; often they have nothing to do with sex (like work stress) but influence it nonetheless. Second, don't feel bad if you're having less sex than others are having (or too smug if you're having more). The important thing is that you and your partner are having about as much sex as you would like—for some this is a lot, for others this is a lot less. While quantity matters, quality is often more important, as is the relationship context. Good sex is more important than more sex—lots of mediocre sex isn't very satisfying.

In case you're interested to see what others are up to, check out Table 2.1 with the sexual frequencies for all respondents.

When the woman in the couple has ADHD, they have sex on average every 5.0 days versus every 6.25 days when the man has ADHD. This translates into seventy-two versus fifty-eight times per year. This isn't a huge difference, but it is probably one that you

Table 2.1 Sexual Frequencies

Frequency	Number	Percent	Cumu-lative Percent
Not within the last six months	330	12.0	12.0
Within the last six months	258	9.4	21.3
Once this month	443	16.1	37.4
2–3 days/mo	550	19.9	57.3
1 day/wk	461	16.7	74.0
2–3 days/wk	454	16.5	90.5
4–6 days/wk	168	6.1	96.6
Daily	94	3.4	100.0
Total	2758	100.0	

can feel, especially if your desired frequency is much higher. This is just one of many examples of how gender had as big an effect on respondents' answers as ADHD did.

Desired Sexual Frequency

As it turns out, most people want to have a lot more sex with their partner than they are having. Like, *a lot*. The overall average, including all respondents, was every 2.1 days or 172 times per year. That is almost three times more sex than the average of how much sex people are actually having. Wow, that's a lot of unmet desire. That's also a big part of the rationale for this book, to help couples have better sex lives which then also improves their relationship overall. This unmet need can be a good motivator to work on all of those things that detract from both.

Although overall most respondents want more sex, it's interesting to see the patterns in how much sex, on average, our four different kinds of respondents want. The simplest way to show these comparisons is in Table 2.2, followed by some thoughts on the implications of these differences.

Table 2.2 Relative Desired Sexual Frequencies

Men: 188x/yr every 1.9 days	>>	Women: 162x/yr every 2.3 days
ADHD women: 176x/yr every 2.1 days	>>	*Non-ADHD women*: 143x/yr every 2.6 days
ADHD men: 191x/yr every 1.9 days	>	*Non-ADHD men*: 179x/yr every 2 days
ADHD women: 176x/yr every 2.1 days	=	*Non-ADHD men*: 179x/yr every 2 days
ADHD men: 191x/yr every 1.9 days	>>	*Non-ADHD women*: 143x/yr every 2.6 days

A number of interesting findings come out of these numbers. First, it's already well known in the research that men tend to want more sex than women and this survey supports that, although the difference is nowhere near as big as common wisdom would have you believe. Related to this, it is important to remember that this difference is at the level of group averages—there are plenty of couples where the woman has a stronger libido (one figure I heard was 30%). As always, what matters most is what happens in your own relationship, but you may want to take a look at any implicit assumptions you and your partner have about gender's effect on sexual desire.

Perhaps more interesting is the findings on how ADHD affects desired sexual frequency, something that we didn't have any previous research on, except for all the couples out there who have been involved in a lifetime of case studies on the topic. I decided to not calculate the simple average of all respondents with ADHD versus those without because I didn't have the same number of men and women and that would skew the results. But if we look at the genders separately, we can see that ADHD has a much bigger influence on women's desired sexual frequency than it does on men's. In total though, I would say that those with ADHD tend to have stronger libidos.

Since sex, using the term broadly, tends to happen with another person (we'll talk about masturbation next), we also need to look at how the couples match up. Couples with closely matched libidos tend to have less to disagree about than couples with larger differences. It's amazing how the average for ADHD women and non-ADHD men were almost identical. If this is true in your relationship, then that's probably a good thing. This similarity may be one of the reasons why these couples have more sex than the couples where it's the man who has ADHD.

By contrast, the ADHD men had the highest desired frequency whereas the non-ADHD women had the lowest. In couples with this significant difference, it's easy to fall into a chase dynamic where the higher desire partner is often eyeing the lower desire partner for signs of being interested in sex, whereas the lower desire partner is often feeling scrutinized. The one feels disappointed, the other pressured. The whole messy process can be a desire killer that spills over into other parts of the relationship. If you and your partner have a big difference in desired frequency, then check out the section in *Chapter 7: Respectful Communication and Negotiation.*

Masturbation to Make Up the Difference?

Since our partners are not always available or in the mood, masturbation is an easy way to have a good time by yourself. Let's see what the numbers from the survey look like, in Table 2.3.

For both genders, those with ADHD masturbated more than those without. As with the desired sexual frequency, this was truer for the women than the men. However, there was a much larger difference between the men and women. While this may somewhat reflect

Table 2.3 Masturbation Frequency

ADHD women: 60x/yr every 6.1 days	>>	Non-ADHD women: 42x/yr every 8.7 days
ADHD men: 143x/yr every 2.6 days	>>	Non-ADHD men: 105x/yr every 3.5 days
ADHD women: 60x/yr every 6.1 days	<<	Non-ADHD men: 105x/yr every 3.5 days
ADHD men: 143x/yr every 2.6 days	>>>	Non-ADHD women: 42x/yr every 8.7 days

differences in libido, it is also true that it is still much more socially acceptable for men to masturbate than it is for women—although fortunately that is changing. Women may have times when they would be interested in masturbating, but feel like they shouldn't, feel guilty about taking the time to enjoy themselves, or feel like they should direct that sexual desire towards their partner, even if he isn't available.

When we look at the difference between the partners in the two types of couples, we again see that a woman who has ADHD is likely to be more similar to her non-ADHD male partner in her masturbation frequency, compared to the difference between a man with ADHD and his non-ADHD female partner. As we will discuss in *Chapter 7: Respectful Communication and Negotiation*, masturbation can be a good way to deal with differences in desired sexual frequency. Related to that, check out Table 2.4.

It is amazing how, for the men, the total sexual frequency almost exactly matches their desired sexual frequency. This tells us that, on average, the men in the survey used masturbation as a way to make up the difference between actual and desired sexual frequency and get the amount of sex (or at least orgasms) that they wanted.

Table 2.4 Total Actual Sexual Frequency Versus Desired Sexual Frequency

	Sexual Freq./Yr		Masturbation Freq./Yr		Total Sexual Freq./Yr		Desired Sexual Freq/Yr
ADHD Men	58	+	143	=	201	vs.	191
Non-ADHD Men	72	+	105	=	177	vs.	179
ADHD Women	72	+	60	=	132	vs.	176
Non-ADHD Women	58	+	42	=	100	vs.	143

By contrast, the women's total sexual frequency fell far short of their desired sexual frequency—they were not using masturbation to make up as much of the difference. There can be a lot of reasons for this and it obviously all depends on the individual but, after consulting with some colleagues, a number of possibilities come to mind. First, it is probably still true that women in general don't feel as comfortable allowing themselves to masturbate as men do. There may be more guilt there or just the feeling that that is something that women shouldn't do (except perhaps when they really need to). If you are a woman with a partner with a higher desired sexual frequency than you, then there may be some spoken or unspoken pressure to not "use up" any horniness on your own, since your partner will then miss out on some action.

From a more logistical perspective, there are also the matters of available time and privacy. While this is absolutely not true for everyone, generally men can masturbate to orgasm more easily and quickly than women can. For example, a man can easily rub one out in the shower and no one will be the wiser. If a woman needs (or desires) a vibrator and a bit more time to use it, there may be fewer opportunities where she has enough time and privacy to feel comfortable masturbating, for fear of being discovered. Plus, moms might get more interruptions from kids than dads do.

Finally, there is also the issue of spontaneous versus responsive desire. I will talk about this more in *Chapter 9: Sex 101 (and 201, and 301 . . .)* , but basically those people with more spontaneous desire tend to feel horny easily, whereas those with more responsive desire tend to need more external stimulation in order to light that spark of sexual desire. As with all human traits that lie along a continuum, it is all normal and what is best is always in the eye of the beholder. Once things get going, people at both ends of this spectrum can have just as good a time, but some people get that initial spark more easily than others. Broadly speaking, more men tend to lean towards the spontaneous desire side of the spectrum, so they feel horny more quickly and then allow themselves to gratify that desire by seeking out their partner or taking care of business on their own. By contrast, more women tend to lean more towards the responsive desire side of the spectrum. They can love sex as much as their male partners or more, but they are less likely to suddenly want sex. This then may also mean that they are less likely to suddenly feel like masturbating.

If you would like to have more sex (or orgasms) but don't use masturbation to make up that difference, then perhaps it is worth spending some time exploring why that is or what is getting in the way. I am not suggesting that you should have to make up the difference, but it may be interesting to think about why you don't, especially if you would kind of like to. You may also want to check out *Chapter 10: Taking Some Personal Time: Masturbation.*

Sexual Barriers and Masturbation Frequency

Some people don't want their partner to masturbate because it feels like a criticism of their partnered sexual activities or that it reflects dissatisfaction with their partner. I thought it would be useful to see what the data has to say about that. In the survey, I listed twenty-five possible barriers to more frequent and/or enjoyable sexual activity and asked respondents to rate how much each barrier applied to them. Since people can use masturbation as a way of coping with sexual difficulties or disappointments with their partner, I wanted to see if there were certain barriers that had a larger impact on how often people masturbate. This might prove helpful if some people want to address those barriers and convert some of that masturbation into partnered activities. So I looked to see if there was a relationship between respondents' masturbation frequency and any of those potential barriers—in other words, are high masturbation frequencies related to high ratings for any of the barriers? Do any of the barriers result in much more masturbation?

For the men with and without ADHD, none of the barriers were related to their masturbation frequency. In other words, overall, the men aren't masturbating because of problems with their partner or sex life. Any one individual may be affected by one or more of these barriers, but we can't say that that is true across the board. It may be helpful to point out here that, on average, men were *not* masturbating more because of any of these barriers:

- I don't feel that the sex will be satisfying, so I don't even bother
- I am no longer sexually attracted to my partner

- Sex has become kind of predictable and boring
- My partner does not understand my sexual needs or can't please me sexually
- I feel uncomfortable sharing my sexual desires with my partner

Perhaps their partners will find this heartening and also give everyone less reason to worry or feel bad about masturbation. Obviously, you may still want to talk with your partner about it if you feel it is an issue between the two of you.

For the women, both with and without ADHD, there were four barriers that were found to be related to how often they masturbated—but none of them were the ones just previously listed which should be heartening for their partners as well. For three of these barriers, the more they rated it as a barrier, the less they masturbated:

- I am disinterested in sex in general, not just with this partner
- I am too tired to have sex
- It can be difficult to switch gears from other demands and be sexual

All of these make sense and reflect a general decline in sexual interest or, perhaps more broadly, a greater life stress. One of those barriers went the opposite way. The more of a barrier it was, the more the women masturbated:

- My partner acts disinterested in having sex with me, even when I ask

This one also makes sense. The women are basically using masturbation to make up for the partnered activities they aren't getting, but more so when their partner is disinterested, rather than as an add-on to an at least OK sex life.

As before, if you feel that any particular sexual barrier is having a negative effect on your sex life, whether shared or solo, then it's probably worth talking with your partner about it.

I will talk more about all of the barriers later, in the sections *Sexual Barriers and Porn Use* and *Barriers to a More Satisfying Sex Life*.

Porn Use Frequency

I asked respondents how often they looked at porn (alone or with their partner, to orgasm or not). It should be noted that this is a pretty broad question and can include everything from a few minutes of casually flipping through pictures to an extended porn binge. Given the rest of this chapter, you shouldn't be surprised by now with the results in Table 2.5.

It's the same story as before: those with ADHD looked at porn more often than those without, but this was much truer for the women than the men. However, the gender effect was much bigger with men looking at much more porn than women do. Putting this together then, in the couples where the man has ADHD, there is a bigger difference in porn use frequency between the two partners compared with the couples where the woman has ADHD—bigger differences potentially give couples more to disagree about and may require more empathy to understand the other person's position.

It was also interesting to see that respondents masturbate more often than they use porn, meaning that they don't use porn every time they masturbate. This difference is even greater when you consider that the porn use frequency potentially includes times when the respondents looked at porn but didn't masturbate and when they used porn as part of a sexual encounter with their partner. This runs contrary to anti-porn advocates' claims that porn use invariably runs out of control—if so, then one would think that porn use would have taken over all of the respondents' masturbatory sessions

Table 2.5 Porn Use Frequency

ADHD women: 24x/yr every 15.2 days	>>	Non-ADHD women: 12x/yr every 30.4 days
ADHD men: 108x/yr every 3.4 days	>>	Non-ADHD men: 86x/yr every 4.2 days
ADHD women: 24x/yr every 15.2 days	<<<	Non-ADHD men: 86x/yr every 4.2 days
ADHD men: 108x/yr every 3.4 days	>>>>	Non-ADHD women: 12x/yr every 30.4 days

and they just haven't. I talk more about porn addiction in *Chapter 11: What about Porn?* (spoiler: porn isn't addictive).

Partner's Porn Use Frequency

In addition to asking respondents to report how much they look at porn, I also asked them how they felt about their own and their partner's porn use. I will cover those feelings shortly in the section *Porn Use Feelings*, but when I asked how they felt about their partner's porn use, they had an option to respond that, to their knowledge, their partner doesn't look at porn. Perhaps it was an evil moment, but I thought it would be interesting to compare how many respondents said that they don't look at porn versus how many said their partners don't look at porn. Since there is such a massive effect of gender on porn use, I had to compare men's self-reports with women's reports of their partner's porn use, and vice versa. Take a look at the data in Table 2.6. In the interest of simplicity (and because in this case they weren't much different), I lumped ADHD and non-ADHD folks together.

It seems that both men and women underestimate the likelihood of their partner watching porn, at least sometimes. Women especially tend to underestimate the likelihood of their male partner watching porn—a quarter of them watched it at least sometimes, unbeknownst to their female partners. Meanwhile, one in six guys didn't think their female partner watches porn but she did at least sometimes. These are not insignificant numbers for either gender.

My goal here is not to out anyone or to force some uncomfortable discussions. However, as a general rule, secrets can be problematic, regardless of what is being hidden, because it removes the other person's ability to have some input on the topic—and runs the risk of unhappy discoveries. Some make the argument that solo sexual

Table 2.6 Percent of Respondents Who Don't Watch Porn

	Self-Report	Partner's Report
Men	11	38
Women	47	63

experiences don't require a partner's approval, but I think there is a difference between having a preemptive discussion as a courtesy versus seeking permission.

If the porn use (or whatever) is being intentionally withheld because you are worried that your partner would be upset about it, then you have a dilemma on your hands. You can either stop doing the secret activity (which you may not want to do) or break the secret by talking it through with your partner (which you may also not want to do). Discussions about porn often wind up getting into other bigger topics that have nothing to do with porn, like the acceptability of masturbation and sexual fantasies, sexual attractiveness, intimacy and honesty, autonomy versus dependence, etc. I talk more about all of this in *Chapter 11: What about Porn?*

Sexual Barriers and Porn Use

As I did with masturbation, I also looked to see if there was a relationship between respondents' frequency of porn use and a long list of potential barriers to a more satisfying sex life. I will talk more about those barriers later, in the section *Barriers to a More Satisfying Sex Life*, but for now, it was extremely interesting to see that there were no clear patterns where particular barriers were found to drive more (or less) porn use. Perhaps most surprising, the following were *not* found to have any effect on whether someone looked at no porn, a little porn, or a lot of porn:

- I don't feel that the sex will be satisfying, so I don't even bother
- I am no longer sexually attracted to my partner
- Sex has become kind of predictable and boring
- My partner does not understand my sexual needs or can't please me sexually
- I feel uncomfortable sharing my sexual desires with my partner

I looked at the data by lumping everyone in together as well as by separating people out by gender and ADHD status. I could not find any clear patterns. What this tells us is that how much porn people choose to look at is a personal decision based on factors specific to them and their situation. This means we can't make sweeping generalizations (or at least not any related to the barriers in the survey)—e.g., we can't say that people look at porn because they are no longer sexually attracted to their partner. This may be true for some individuals, but it isn't true for enough of them to change the group averages. Sometimes a lack of results is just as interesting as clear results.

Where this leaves any one person or couple then is to think about and perhaps discuss what causes each of you to look at more or less porn, as well as how you each feel about that. While simple theories may make strong (but probably questionable) predictions about what drives porn use frequency, it's more helpful to figure out exactly what drives porn use frequency for you and your partner.

Porn Use Feelings

In addition to wanting to know how often respondents looked at porn, perhaps more importantly, I also wanted to know how they felt about it—their own porn use and also their partner's. Regardless of gender or ADHD status, on average most people felt that their own porn use had not much of an effect on their relationship and/or sex life, either positive or negative. I will break these data out some more in *Chapter 11: What about Porn?*, but overall people are not that concerned about their own porn use. The number who feel it has a negative effect are counterbalanced by those who feel that it has a positive effect.

But what about how people feel about their partner's porn use? That might be a more interesting question. As it turns out, what is most interesting about the answer has more to do with gender than ADHD. Overall, men felt that their female partners watching porn had somewhere between no effect and a small positive effect on their relationship and/or sex life. By contrast, the ADHD women felt that their male partner's porn use had somewhere between no effect and a small negative effect, whereas the non-ADHD women felt it had a small negative effect. It's also interesting to note that all these averages are pretty close to no effect, but because men tended to rate their partner's porn use a little positively and women rated it a little negatively, there is more distance between them.

As before, these are group averages so if you and/or your partner have some strong feelings about your own or your partner's porn use, then check out *Chapter 11: What about Porn?* and have some good conversations about it.

Huh? Distracted Sex

Perhaps not surprisingly, those with ADHD got distracted during sex more than those without ADHD and women got distracted more than men. Those with ADHD say they get distracted sometimes whereas those without ADHD get distracted infrequently (which was one step below sometimes). Women get distracted sometimes whereas men get distracted infrequently. Once again, we see that both ADHD and gender have an influence.

It's interesting that people can get distracted during something as (presumably) exciting as sex—if so, it's no wonder that people also get distracted during boring meetings. Since everyone has some moments when get they distracted, even during sex, it's important to not make a big thing of it. It happens. Re-focus and move on. Most important, do not make the occasional mind-wandering out to mean something that it doesn't mean—e.g., maybe I don't love my partner, maybe s/he isn't good enough at sex, maybe I'm not good enough at sex, etc. And definitely don't jump to any of these conclusions if you sense your partner getting distracted.

If you find that you or your partner tend to get distracted during sex, then my advice is the same as it is when I talk to clients about staying focused on anything else—identify your most common distractions and try to address them before you start. This might include getting that load of laundry going, locking the door so no one wanders in in the middle, or scribbling out those thoughts rolling around inside your head. Maybe even think about the things that you can do to get more into sex mode—hot shower, music, back rub, etc. This might be more relevant for women than for men—in the survey, women found it harder to switch gears mentally and get into sex mode. This additional time up front may require more planning and also dedicating more time to your sex life, but the reward will hopefully be worth it. Besides, connecting with your partner probably shouldn't be the last thing that gets rushed through at the very end, if there is time.

What would make your sex life better for you?
I have an amazing sex life . . . when I am not surrounded by distractions like clutter and my mind unable to focus on one thing.
ADHD woman, 36, engaged and living together, been together 6–10 years

If you still find yourself or your partner getting distracted during sex (which, again, is normal), then just let that distracting thought go and re-focus on the matter at hand. The more you focus on the distraction or have thoughts or feelings about it (what does it mean that I am so distracted?), the more distracting it becomes. You may find it helpful to focus back in on your body and what you are feeling physically in that moment and let that fill your thoughts. Or maybe talk a little dirty to get you both back on track and synchronized—offer a compliment, say what feels good right then, ask for something, tell your partner what you are going to do next, share a steamy fantasy, etc.

If you find that you get way too distracted during sex, then that may indicate that something else is going on, especially if it feels like you are more distracted than you "should be" (however you define that). It may indicate sexual boredom and you need to mix it up a bit. It may indicate that you have way too much else going on in your life and you need to address that. It may also indicate that you don't feel fully comfortable letting yourself go sexually with this partner or in general. Or you may have trouble allowing yourself to prioritize some fun when there is still (always) work to do. If any of these ring true, then it may be worth spending some time really thinking about this and also discussing it with your partner. You may even find it helpful to talk to a general therapist or sex therapist.

Sexual Effort is Imbalanced, Too

Just as I found that respondents rated themselves as putting in more effort on managing ADHD than their partner does, so too do people feel that they put in more effort in bed. In the area of sex, I asked respondents to answer four related questions:

- When it's time to focus on *your* sexual pleasure, to what extent do you feel that your partner makes that a priority and puts in the necessary effort?
- When it's time to focus on *your partner's* sexual pleasure, to what extent do you make that a priority and put in the necessary effort?
- To what extent are *you* willing to be sexually generous and give your partner sexual pleasure when you are not feeling sexually interested?
- To what extent is *your partner* willing to be sexually generous and give you sexual pleasure when s/he is not feeling sexually interested?

Generally speaking, everyone felt that they put in more effort and were more generous than their partners. This was especially true for the men who felt that their effort and generosity was quite a bit more than their female partner's. The women also rated their effort and generosity as being greater than their male partner's, but the difference between the women's two ratings was about half the difference between the men's two ratings.

But wait, there's more! A cool side benefit of asking respondents to rate both their own and their partner's effort, is that we can then cross-compare the couple's answers (e.g., how much effort do ADHD men feel they put in versus how much effort do non-ADHD women feel their ADHD male partners put in?). When you look at the data this way, you get the same story which increases our confidence in the results: everyone rates themselves higher than their partners rate them and the difference between the self-rating and partner rating is bigger for the men.

Does this mean that objectively men put in more effort and are more generous about their female partner's sexual pleasure, than the women? Not necessarily. Could be, but not necessarily. Also, how would we actually measure it? However, perhaps equally important, is that they believe that they do—and that perception of inequity is potentially problematic. There are many people who enjoy being sexually generous and get turned on by creating and watching their partner's pleasure, so that effort is a win/win. For many men, pleasing their partner sexually is their biggest turn-on, so they are happy to be generous about it—which is an excellent way to entice your partner into getting naked with you again.

However, if you feel like there is an unhappy imbalance in the effort and generosity that you each put in, then there should probably be a discussion about it. Keep in mind that you may each be putting in effort that the other person does not notice and therefore aren't getting credit for. So start the conversation by acknowledging what you appreciate that your partner is doing and then asking what your partner is contributing that you forgot to mention. It may be that some of those efforts aren't being noticed because they aren't something that matters that much to you, but if your partner enjoys doing them, then they should probably continue to do so. Then flip the conversation and ask your partner what they would appreciate more of. Not that your sex life overall has to be perfectly 50/50, and certainly not every sexual encounter, but feelings of unfairness tend to put a damper on things. At a minimum, it's worth checking in on, especially if you would like more sex; if necessary, it's probably worth putting in more effort or perhaps some different effort. As with many other relationship problems, some of the solution may involve getting better at noticing what is already happening and some of it may involve doing some things differently.

Sexual Variety

I asked respondents about their desires for variety and novelty in their sexual experiences:

- In general, to what extent do you prefer to engage in the same sexual activities during all or most sexual encounters versus prefer to have a larger repertoire of sexual activities to choose from for each sexual encounter?
- In general, to what extent do you have a desire for engaging in familiar sexual activities versus a desire for experimenting with new sexual activities?

I predicted (rather confidently) that those with ADHD would want more of both, since folks with ADHD tend to get bored of the same old thing. Apparently, sex isn't one of those same old things—sort of. Much to my surprise, the results were mixed, leaning towards not much difference between those with and without ADHD.

The one thing that did turn out to be true was that ADHD men had a somewhat higher desire for a larger repertoire of sexual activities than the non-ADHD men, but there was no difference for the women. However, the bigger difference was between the men and the women, with the men leaning towards a little more variety and the women leaning towards a little less.

When it comes to a desire to stick with familiar sexual activities versus try new ones, there was no difference between those with and without ADHD. Again, the difference was between the men and the women, with the women leaning towards slightly preferring to stick with familiar activities and the men evenly split between familiarity and variety.

Putting all these results together, you and your partner need to figure out and negotiate what you want your sexual repertoire to look like. Some people may be satisfied with their existing repertoire (whether it involves the same two sexual activities or fifty) whereas others may have an inherent desire to mix it up more or try new things. There can be a complementarity to couples with some difference between their desires for variety and novelty. The person with the higher desire for one or both of these can be the sexual innovator who keeps the couple's sex life interesting, especially over the decades. This is counterbalanced by the person with a lower desire for variety and novelty who keeps the couple's sexual repertoire where things work well.

There are no right or wrong answers on how much variety or novelty a couple should have. As with so many other things, it's a matter of personal preference and comes down to how well the couple negotiates their differences. Generally speaking, the closer a couple is in their preferences, the easier time they will probably have in coming to a mutually satisfying agreement. As we saw elsewhere, the men and women in the couples where the woman has ADHD tend to be more similar in their desires for variety, whereas there was a bigger difference between the non-ADHD women and the ADHD men which potentially makes for a more difficult negotiation.

If you and your partner have a large difference between your preferences in either of these regards (or otherwise), then you will need to work harder to understand each other's position and to come to a mutually satisfying arrangement. However, your sex life and relationship may benefit from this tension if it pushes you both to work hard to find that great solution. By contrast, if you and your partner are quite similar on these dimensions (or others), then you will have an easier time finding agreement, but may need to work a little harder to ensure that things don't gradually get stale. As with so much else, how helpful some particular advice is depends on the couple's situation. Therefore, only some of you will benefit from reading all those articles about *The 37 Mind Blowing Sex Positions That You Have to Try Tonight!*. (It's gonna be a long night. Hydrate well.) Unfortunately, nobody writes articles on *Just Do the Same Old Thing; It Works Well*, so not everyone will benefit from the cover stories in the magazines at the grocery checkout.

Kinkiness

Without getting into specific sexual acts, I asked respondents to rate how adventurous/kinky they are. On average, people rated themselves somewhat adventurous/kinky, although there was obviously the full range of answers given. Generally speaking, the men saw themselves as a little kinkier than the women. This could reflect that the men are indeed kinkier or just that they feel more comfortable endorsing being kinkier—or maybe some social pressure to come across as kinkier, whereas women may have the opposite social pressure, even if they actually feel kinkier. Regarding ADHD status, ADHD women saw themselves as kinkier than the non-ADHD women, but the difference for the men was pretty minimal.

These are self-perceptions of how kinky respondents feel they are, relative to others. Unless I provided a long list of activities for respondents to check off the things that they do and then I somehow rank ordered all those activities from least to most kinky, it's impossible to get an objective measure of something as subjective as kinkiness. But that's OK, since what matters most is how people feel about their kinkiness. Some people get off on seeing themselves as more kinky than others and rule breaking is part of the thrill, whereas others find comfort in knowing that what they are doing is pretty standard stuff.

As with all matters of preference, there's no way to win the argument. My hope is that everyone feels good about however kinky they are, whether that means sometimes having sex with the lights on or tying up the neighbors. As the internet teaches us every day, there is a gigantic range of human interest and there's at least a few people into anything that you could possibly imagine (and lots that you couldn't).

It was interesting to see that those who rated themselves as kinkier also tended to prefer having a larger repertoire of sexual activities and enjoyed trying new sexual activities. So there is something about desiring variety and novelty that overlaps with kinkiness. Probably not surprising. On the one hand, those who add kinky stuff to their repertoire probably by definition tend to prefer move variety. However, those who felt comfortable enough to explore their kinkier desires are probably also more comfortable adding other variety and novelty to their sex life, so this effect probably goes both directions.

Physical and Emotional Infidelity

Most relationships involve implicit and explicit expectations about fidelity. Even in consensually nonmonogamous relationships, there is still an expectation of fidelity, even if fidelity is defined differently. Infidelity can have a significant effect on a relationship, especially if that infidelity is discovered, but even if it isn't. Given this large potential for trouble, I included two questions about infidelity:

- Have you ever engaged in sexual activities of a primarily physical nature without emotional involvement with someone other than your partner without your partner's prior knowledge or consent? This may have been during your current relationship or a prior one.

- Have you ever engaged in an emotional relationship (possibly physical, but definitely involved an emotional connection that would have made your partner uncomfortable) with someone other than your partner without your partner's prior knowledge or consent? This may have been during your current relationship or a prior one.

I purposely separated out physical and emotional infidelity because they are such different experiences and people can feel very differently about their partner's actions depending on which it was. I also asked fairly broad questions (e.g., sexual activities could include kissing as well as intercourse) and asked people to include experiences from prior relationships, so this is going to result in more people endorsing some form of infidelity. The results ranged from a low of 22% of non-ADHD women having engaged in some form of physical infidelity to a high of 49% of ADHD women having engaged in some form of emotional infidelity. Generally speaking, these are roughly in line with the prevalence rates in other research on infidelity. Of course, the rates are significantly affected by how narrowly or broadly you ask the question or define terms, as well as respondents' age and other demographics, so there can be a wide range of reported results.

For both men and women, those with ADHD had more physical as well as emotional infidelity over the course of their lives. Men with ADHD were almost twice as likely as non-ADHD women to have engaged in some form of physical infidelity (39% vs 22%), whereas ADHD women were almost twice as likely as non-ADHD men to have engaged in some form of emotional infidelity (49% vs 25%). These are some pretty big differences.

Looking at gender, men were a little more likely than women to have engaged in physical infidelity, whereas women were a little more likely than men to have engaged in emotional infidelity. However, the differences weren't that big which also kind of makes sense—those men and women in heterosexual relationships need people of the opposite gender to have hookups and affairs with.

As with all the prior results, the goal here is not to out anyone or to force an undesired conversation, but rather to help you reduce the likelihood of any infidelity. Because this is such a common and important topic, I speak at length about infidelity in *Chapter 15:*

Secret Stuff With Other People: Hook-Ups and Affairs, including both how to prevent it as well as how to come out of infidelity with a stronger relationship if it does happen.

Consensual Nonmonogamy

While most couples are monogamous (or at least have a stated expectation of monogamy), some people have an agreement that allows romantic and/or sexual activity beyond their primary romantic partner. I cover this in more detail in *Chapter 16: Consensual Sex With Other People: Other Arrangements*.

In the survey, I asked two questions related to consensual nonmonogamy. First, whether they had ever engaged in consensually nonmonogamous sexual activities (current relationship or previous). Second, if their partner were OK with it, how interested would they themselves be in some sort of consensual nonmonogamy. This question also had an answer option of having engaged in these activities with the current partner.

The responses followed the trends in other parts of the survey in that men tended to be more interested than women and those with ADHD tended to be more interested than those without. Women with ADHD were the most likely to have engaged in this sort of things in the past (about 30%) and the guys with ADHD came in second with 25% and the non-ADHD folks with 18–19%. The survey didn't ask them detailed questions about what they defined as consensually nonmonogamous so it might include dating more than one person at a time or mostly dating one person, but it wasn't sexually exclusive. This may inflate the numbers versus what it might be if I asked about specific types of nonmonogamy, such as polyamory or swinging.

Barriers to a More Satisfying Sex Life

After many questions about all aspects of the respondents' relationships and sex lives, I asked them to rate how much they thought that ADHD adds barriers to sexual activity in addition to what most couples face. On average, those with ADHD rated it as a small effect, whereas the non-ADHD partners rated it closer to a moderate effect.

This probably isn't very surprising and fits with other data from the survey. The non-ADHD partners tend to view the effects of ADHD as being more significant and negative.

This could involve a combination of reasons. It may be that the non-ADHD partners are more aware of the effects of ADHD, in the way that all romantic partners may have some greater awareness of certain behaviors than the person themselves. But in fairness, we all also project our own issues onto our partners so that outside perspective isn't necessarily always more accurate or objective. This difference in ratings may also reflect some differences in personal preferences. For example, the ADHD partners may be less bothered by lateness, just as there are other couples without ADHD who have a difference of opinion about the importance of being on time. Therefore, this wouldn't be a clinical matter, so much as one of opinion. Plus, someone who tends to be very late (or whatever) will be noticed much more every time it happens.

Since the goal of the survey and book is to help couples have more satisfying sex lives and relationships, I got more specific about those barriers by listing twenty-five possible barriers to more

There are challenges being in an intimate relationship with an ADHD person, but there are also many wonderful experiences including an enhanced sex life! I am very blessed with my partner!

Non-ADHD woman, 72, living together,
been together 6–10 years

Whether a couple realizes it or not, the parent-child dynamic that can be present in an ADHD marriage is a real sex killer.

Non-ADHD woman, 35, married,
been together 6–10 years

frequent and/or enjoyable sexual activity and asked respondents to rate how much each of them applied over the last month. By identifying the most common barriers, we can focus on what most needs to be addressed to make improvements for most couples. My hope is that clinicians will also read this book and apply it to their work with couples.

Incidentally, for the people taking the survey (and you if you would like to look at this question in the survey on p. 358), my hope was that looking at the list would help respondents think about their own relationship and their particular barriers. The more specifically you understand a problem, the better position you are in to address it.

I think we can all be heartened about the barriers that were rated the least problematic:

• I don't feel that the sex will be satisfying, so I don't even bother
• I am disinterested in sex in general, not just with this partner
• I am no longer sexually attracted to my partner
• My partner asks too much of me sexually
• I don't understand my partner's sexual needs or can't please him/her sexually

So, the basics of a good sex life are still there for most of our couples. Now we just need to work on the specifics. As we would expect, the four types of respondents had quite different barriers, but with some similarities. However, it was quite notable that non-ADHD women rated more barriers as being significant impediments to their sex life and also rated those barriers as being greater. Kind of a double whammy. The other three types of respondents had about the same number of significant barriers and rated them as being similarly large. This is consistent with other findings from the survey.

I list the top five barriers for each type of respondent in Table 2.7, in rank order from biggest barrier to smallest. In order to make it easier to compare, I placed the couples next to each other, since ADHD women are having sex with non-ADHD men and non-ADHD women are having sex with ADHD men, so the interaction

Table 2.7 Sexual barriers.

ADHD Women	Non-ADHD Men
1. One or both of us are too busy with other things to have time for sex 2. It can be difficult to switch gears from other demands and be sexual 3. I am too tired to have sex 4. There would be more time for sex if time was used more efficiently 5. I'm too angry with my partner to want sex	1. There would be more time for sex if time was used more efficiently 2. One or both of us are too busy with other things to have time for sex 3. My partner acts disinterested in having sex with me, even when I ask 4. My partner is too angry with me for us to have sex 5. I'm too angry with my partner to want sex
Non-ADHD Women	ADHD Men
1. I'm too angry with my partner to want sex 2. My partner seems like another child, lessening his or her appeal 3. I resent that my partner doesn't pay enough attention to me unless he/she wants sex 4. It can be difficult to switch gears from other demands and be sexual 5. I am too tired to have sex	1. My partner is too angry with me for us to have sex 2. One or both of us are too busy with other things to have time for sex 3. My partner acts disinterested in having sex with me, even when I ask 4. There would be more time for sex if time was used more efficiently 5. I feel uncomfortable sharing my sexual desires with my partner

of each of their barriers will probably be important. I didn't include same-sex couples in the data analysis for the survey because I didn't get enough of them to analyze well. You may also find it interesting to compare women to women and men to men.

Do any of these barriers look familiar? How do they match up with your own and your partner's experience?

Comparing these barriers, both by gender and ADHD status, several interesting findings came out. ADHD women feel too busy and too tired and that there would be more time for sex if time was used more efficiently, and have trouble switching gears for sex. Meanwhile, their male partners agree that there would be more time for sex if time was used more efficiently and that they are too busy. Perhaps because of all this and their female partner's difficulties switching gears for sex, they feel like their partner isn't interested in sex. Perhaps because they both feel overwhelmed and disappointed, they both rate anger as a barrier.

Non-ADHD women's top barrier is feeling too angry with their partner to have sex and their male partners' biggest barrier is feeling that their partner is too angry with them to have sex. On the plus side, the non-ADHD women are communicating their anger clearly and their guys are picking it up. This creates an obvious priority for what they can each work on in order to improve their sex life, since it's hard to feel open or generous when either person is angry. Less well matched, non-ADHD women's second biggest barrier is feeling that their partner is like another child, yet ADHD men didn't especially rate feeling bossed around as a large barrier, so either they don't feel bossed around or they don't feel that that interferes with their sex life. This is probably a huge mistake, since there is a ton of genetics designed to reduce in-breeding that kills sexual attraction for those that we see as children—if you or your partner feel like your partner is another child, then addressing that needs to be a top priority. As with the couples where the woman has ADHD,

---

What would make your sex life better for you?
My sex life would be better if I could get my act together before 10 PM and have the time and energy to put the moves on him before we get up for work at 5:30.
ADHD woman, 50, dating, living separately,
been together 0–2 years

the couples where the guy has ADHD also struggle with being busy, tired, and using time efficiently.

Overall, everyone feels they are too busy, but only the women feel that being too tired is a major barrier. This could partially reflect the fact that men's desire for sex is less dampened by fatigue, but probably also reflects that women still do more at home and use up more of their energy (and time) that could be available for sex. Related to this, women have more trouble switching gears from other tasks to feeling sexual. Therefore, simply creating some time for sex doesn't mean that most women will want to jump right into bed—although other research supports the idea that men who help out more with housework tend to get laid more. Some of this is probably related to simply making more time for sex, but it undoubtedly also helps the women to feel cared for and like there is more fairness in the division of labor. In addition to helping with anger, this probably counteracts one of the other barriers that women rated higher than men did: feeling like their partner doesn't pay enough attention to them outside of sex. Noticing the mountain of laundry and pitching in, especially without being asked, for example, is a great way to help your partner feel not only less stressed, but also more appreciative.

The men felt like their partner was disinterested in sex, which is probably often an accurate assessment and fits with what we just said about the women's experience. Therefore, one of the ways to improve your sex life is to find ways to work more effectively together on all the other various demands in your lives. It will probably also involve some discussions about priorities and where making time for your relationship and sex fit in—hopefully somewhere above looking at pictures on Facebook of people that you have never met in person. That's probably the easy part—the hard part is to keep these agreements going, perhaps more for some than others. Therefore, part of your discussion should probably involve what might pull you off track and how to get back on.

At the end of the day, though, you probably won't be able to create the perfect circumstances to make more time, energy, and good will for sex (or anything, for that matter). Life is messy and imperfect and sometimes you need to make a point of using the opportunities that do arise. Or sort of arise. Or that you can kind of do something with. Sometimes just spending some time together and starting to fool around will light the spark of desire, even when you're not really in the mood and your phone is bursting with emails, alerts, and notifications. You may find the mood if you allow yourself to start. And if the mood doesn't come, then you can perhaps do something to help your partner have a good time, even if it isn't what they were initially hoping for. (Word to the wise: if your partner doesn't get into the mood and things change course along the way, handle your disappointment well, so that they will be more likely to take a chance on you next time.)

Sometimes good (enough) sex helps overcome other relationship barriers—or fuels the good will to work on them. I talk more in *Chapter 7: It's All Foreplay* and *Chapter 8: Make It a Priority* about how to overcome barriers and ensure that your sex life doesn't fade away.

The Sexual Eagerness Cluster

After noticing some general trends, I thought it would be interesting to look at all of the survey questions that dealt with how generally sexually interested someone was or, as I call it, the sexual eagerness cluster. (Incidentally, this would be a great name for an aphrodisiac candy bar.) I broke it out by ADHD status and also gender since each plays a separate role. Take a look at Table 2.8.

Some of these differences were stronger than others, but when you put it all together, those with ADHD tend to have higher ratings on most of the questions I assembled into the ADHD sexual eagerness cluster—and the non-ADHD folks had higher ratings on none of them. At best, the non-ADHD folks tied the folks with ADHD on some of the questions, or at least one of the genders did.

As I talk about in *Chapter 9: Sex 101 (and 201, and 301 . . .)* in the section on *Exciters and Inhibitors: The Sexual Gas and Brake*, this could mean that those with ADHD have a stronger desire for sex (more sensitive gas pedal), but it could also mean that they have fewer sexual inhibitors that slow down converting those desires into action (less sensitive brakes). (See Emily Nagoski's (2015) work on sexual gas and brake, although it isn't specific to ADHD.) According to Russell Barkley's response inhibition theory of ADHD (Barkley, 2005), the symptoms and executive function deficits associated

Table 2.8 The ADHD Sexual Eagerness Cluster. The more greater-than signs, the bigger the difference.

	ADHD vs Non-ADHD	Gender
Desired sexual frequency	ADHD women > non-ADHD women	Men > women
Masturbation frequency	ADHD > non-ADHD	Men >> women
Porn frequency	ADHD > non-ADHD	Men >>> women
Feelings about partner's porn use (more positive/less negative)	ADHD > non-ADHD	Men >> women
History of physical hookups	ADHD > non-ADHD	Men > women
History of emotional affairs	ADHD > non-ADHD	Women > men
Self-ratings of kinkiness	ADHD women > non-ADHD women	Men > women
History of consensually nonmonogamous activities	ADHD men > non-ADHD men ADHD women >> non-ADHD women	ADHD women > ADHD men
Desire for consensually nonmonogamous activities	ADHD > non-ADHD	Men > women
Desire for a larger repertoire of sexual activities	ADHD men > non-ADHD men	Men > women
Desire to experiment with new sexual activities		Men > women
Ease of switching gears to be sexual		Men > women

with ADHD are caused by difficulties with inhibiting responses to both new and existing stimuli. There's a lot to this theory and it does explain a lot about ADHD, but for the sake of this specific discussion, it seems like it supports the idea that folks with ADHD may be more sensitive to and therefore more influenced by sexual stimuli, whether inside their own head or in the world around them. In other words, less brakes. This is speculation on my part, but it could be empirically tested by showing folks with and without ADHD sexual stimuli and seeing if one group responds more.

There is another thread of research that may also connect into all this. Genetic studies have found that some differences in the gene known as DRD4 affect the functioning of a certain dopamine receptor and that this may have some influence over the presence of ADHD symptoms (among a bunch of other genes that also each have a small effect). There is other research into DRD4 that shows that some other differences have some effect on people's sense of adventurousness, thrill-seeking, and risk-taking, including number of sexual partners and likelihood of sexual infidelity. First of all, this is extremely complex stuff we're talking about and there is a lot going on here, so there is no such thing as the daredevil gene or the cheating gene, unless you're a fruit fly. It's tempting to oversimplify it, but it isn't that easy. Nonetheless, there does appear to be some converging data here related to DRD4's effects on ADHD and thrill-seeking and my findings related to the sexual eagerness cluster which seem to lean in that direction, too. At an intellectual level, this is all really interesting, but from a practical perspective, you still can't blame any differences between you and your partner on these genes. (It's your parents' fault for giving you those genes. Better yet, blame your in-laws.)

In addition to the effect that ADHD has, gender seems to have a bigger effect. Men rated higher on almost all of the sexual eagerness items, with the exception of emotional affairs; and ADHD women had the most experiences with consensually nonmonogamous activities. So one of the implications of this greater difference from gender than ADHD status is that when you're fed up with your romantic partner and feel like you don't understand each other, you should blame their gender, not whether or not they have ADHD. Is there a pill for that?

Of course, if you talk to your neighbors where neither romantic partner has ADHD and then talk to your gay and lesbian friends, you will quickly find out that there are plenty of other reasons why romantic partners disagree, misunderstand each other, want different things, and don't get along. Whatever their similarities and differences, every couple needs to find a way to use their similarities as a common ground and their differences as an interesting addition.

The Big Three: Sexual Frequency, Sexual Satisfaction, and Relationship Satisfaction

Doing some deeper statistical analysis, we found that sexual frequency and sexual satisfaction are strongly correlated. This isn't surprising because (to a point) more sex tends to make people more sexually satisfied but also, we will tend to do more of something that we enjoy. There was also a strong correlation between relationship and sexual satisfaction, and this undoubtedly goes both ways—we enjoy sex more when we feel generally happier with our partner, but we also feel better about our partner when we're connecting well sexually.

However, sexual frequency and relationship satisfaction are somewhat less correlated—other factors must also be at work. So having more sex will improve your relationship's satisfaction, but only up to a point—it's more important that you be happy with the sex that you're having. And working on your relationship will result in more sex, but only up to a point—there may be some other factors specific to your sex life that are also affecting your sexual frequency.

Despite the fact that most people in the survey said that they would like to have a fair bit more sex than they are actually having, quantity is probably less important than quality. Frequency matters, but it's the overall satisfaction with your sex life and relationship that matter the most. Having more sex is a worthy goal, but focusing on ways to make your sex better will likely lead to not only some more sex but also a generally better relationship.

Bridge the Divide

The survey found many differences between those with ADHD and those without ADHD, but also a lot of differences between men and women. Sometimes the ADHD difference was greater, sometimes the gender difference was greater. Some of these results were expected and some of them were not, but they are all interesting (at least to me). Despite the fact that every person is their own individual, it can be helpful to understand the group averages. It can help us take some things less personally or get a broader perspective when we see that others have some similar struggles.

My hope is that seeing the data helps you to understand your relationship a little better. The rest of the book will take these results and be focused on what you can do to improve your relationship. This begins with the basic idea that understanding yourself and your partner better and perhaps coming to some acceptance of the similarities and differences will make it easier to work well together. Regardless of whether one of you has ADHD (or both, or neither), there will always be other differences between you and your partner. The trick is to continue to find ways to enjoy, appreciate, and benefit from those differences.

Take Away Lessons

Based on the data, a few key points jump out:

- ADHD meds don't seem to have much of a benefit during sex—I did not predict that.
- Most couples are happy with their relationship and sex life in the first year, but that satisfaction tends to drop as responsibilities creep in.
- There is a wide range of sexual frequency, but most people want a fair bit more sex than they are having.
- Men use masturbation to make up the difference between desired and actual sex much more than women do. Masturbation frequency did not have any relationship to respondents' feelings about their partner or sex life.
- Men looked at much more porn than women, and folks with ADHD looked at more porn than those without. There is probably some more porn watching going on than some

partners realize. Most people felt their own porn use had little effect on their relationship and/or sex life. Women on average felt their male partner's porn use had a small negative effect.

- Those with ADHD got distracted during sex more than those without ADHD and women got distracted more than men.

- Most respondents felt that they put in more sexual effort and were more generous than their partners.

- ADHD didn't have much of an impact on desired sexual variety.

- There has been quite a bit of infidelity going on and those with ADHD were more likely to have strayed.

- Both ADHD status and gender had specific effects on what respondents rated as their biggest barriers to a better sex life.

- Those with ADHD tended to have higher ratings on most of the survey questions related to sexual eagerness. (The non-ADHD folks were higher on none.)

- Sexual frequency, sexual satisfaction, and relationship satisfaction are highly correlated, so progress (or setbacks) in one will likely affect how you feel about the others.

3

Make the Most of Treatment

In the survey, I had a section that asked about the types of treatments that respondents had tried, how much effort they had put into it, and how effective they felt the treatment has been. There has certainly been a lot of research already looking at this, although mostly about medication, so we know what works, but there hadn't been any research connecting this to couples' relationships and sexual satisfaction. It was important to include it because untreated or ineffectively managed ADHD will have a different effect on the relationship than when it is well managed. I would even go so far as to say that the couples with completely untreated (and probably undiagnosed) ADHD will have an entirely different experience from the ones who understand ADHD well, put in the necessary effort to work with it, and have found a treatment regimen that works well for them. This is why diagnosis and treatment are so important—and why it can be so gratifying to work with these individuals and couples. Life often gets quite a bit better once you know what you're dealing with.

In addition to seeing how ADHD status and gender impacted respondents' impressions of their own and their partner's efforts and treatment effectiveness, I thought it would be interesting to do some deeper analysis. I compared those who put in the most effort with those who put in the least effort, and those who felt treatment was the most effective with those who found it the least effective. In other words, let's see what the best are doing and how it's working out for them. There should be some worthy lessons in there.

How Hard Are You Working At it?

In the survey, I asked people to rate how much effort they were putting into managing their own or their partner's ADHD. This could involve taking medication, working with a therapist, coach, or organizer, educating oneself about ADHD, using a reminder system, finding apps, and all that other good stuff that is recommended. The non-ADHD men rated themselves as working pretty hard, but lower than the rest of the folks rated their own effort. Those with ADHD are working hard, but so are the non-ADHD women. This fits what I tend to see in my office. There are certainly exceptions, but I get way more calls from women inquiring about services for their male partners with ADHD than I get from men for their female partners (like, almost none) and way more women join their boyfriend's or husband's sessions than vice versa.

My interpretation of the gender difference is that women are socialized to be caretakers of their partners and the relationship in general, so if their boyfriend or husband has ADHD that is negatively affecting the relationship, then non-ADHD women are going to swing into action to fix it, including sometimes working harder at it than he is. If the woman is the one with ADHD, she is going to work on it, too. This isn't to say that men don't care about the relationship, but that guys are less likely to seek help or get involved when their girlfriend or wife has ADHD. They will get involved in other matters, but not as much on this one.

Since we all seek fairness and balance (at least when we feel like we're getting the short end of the stick), this difference in perceived self-effort between the two partners can obviously be a set up for arguments and resentment. But wait, it gets worse!

I'm Working Harder Than You Are

I also asked survey respondents to rate how much effort they felt that their partners were putting into managing their or their partner's ADHD. Perhaps not surprisingly, most respondents rated themselves as working much harder than they rated their partners as working, which doesn't actually add up if you think about it. The only exception here is that the non-ADHD men rated their ADHD women partners as working just as hard as they themselves were. One possible interpretation of this is that non-ADHD men are more magnanimous in their ratings of their partner's efforts and that they don't give themselves more credit than they deserve. While this would be great if it was true, their partners rated these guys as putting in quite a bit less work than everyone else rated their partners. Meanwhile, non-ADHD men rated their partners as putting in more effort than anyone else rated their partners. So basically ADHD women are working much more than their non-ADHD men which can be a set-up for arguments about fairness. By contrast, ADHD men and non-ADHD women rated their partners as putting in about the same effort and there was less of a difference between self-effort and partner's effort, possibly making for less to feel resentful over.

This rating of one's own effort as higher than someone else's is hardly unique to couples with ADHD or getting treatment. We all tend to give ourselves more credit than we give other people, whether they are our romantic partners, coworkers, or neighbors. Part of this is just about information imbalance—we know everything we do but not everything our partner does, since tasks that go unseen may not be counted in the mental tally of who's done what. So when we think back on what we have each done, we remember more of our tasks and fewer of the other person's.

The fact that it is a universal process probably comes as small consolation when you and your partner are in the heat of arguing about workload and you're both totally convinced that you're right. On the plus side, you agree that you each have a romantic partner who is delusional. Also, despite the fact that self-effort was always rated higher than partner effort, the two were correlated—those who worked the hardest tended to think that their partners also worked hard. So there is some justice. If you are aware of this perceptual bias, you can counterbalance it and give some benefit of the doubt or at least round up your partner's effort a bit so you feel less resentful, which is probably more beneficial to you than it is to your partner.

Another wrinkle on this is that the respondents who felt that ADHD had the most negative effect on sex rated themselves as putting in much more effort and their partners as putting in much less effort. This large imbalance creates the obvious problem that when one partner is (presumably) putting in much less effort at managing ADHD, it's less likely that the ADHD will be managed well and will therefore cause more problems for the relationship. However, the perception of such imbalanced effort is also itself a cause of strife, especially when there is a belief that that lack of effort is making things worse. That's a double whammy you're going to want to avoid.

Treatment Effort Matters More Than You Think

Sex is motivating.

OK, probably nobody will debate me on that statement, but I have the data to back it up, at least when it comes to putting in good effort on managing ADHD. Those respondents who put in more effort on managing ADHD felt somewhat more strongly that ADHD added barriers to a more satisfying sex life, compared to those who put in less effort on managing ADHD. Does that negative effect on their sex life create additional motivation to work on their or their partner's ADHD? Seems like it does.

Creating a better sex life is unlikely to be the only reason for someone to put in more work on their or their partner's ADHD, but as a therapist, I look for every motivation I can find to help individuals and couples do better. And since we know that sexual satisfaction tends to correlate with broader relationship satisfaction, there can be ripple effects from every bit of progress.

So, what would be most motivating to get you to put in more effort on managing your or your partner's ADHD? What would be most motivating for your partner?

I also asked respondents to rate how much effort their partners put in on managing ADHD. I then looked to see how that perceived effort correlated with the answers to other questions. Some of the interesting, and not at all surprising, results show that those who feel that their partner puts in more effort on managing ADHD:

- Are more comfortable making sexual requests of their partner
- Are more comfortable fulfilling their partner's sexual requests
- Are more comfortable sharing sexual fantasies and turn-ons with their partner
- Feel their partner makes their sexual pleasure more of a priority
- Are somewhat more willing to make their partner's sexual pleasure a priority (most people already rate themselves pretty high on this one so there is less of a difference)
- Are more sexually generous when not in the mood
- Feel their partner is more sexually generous when not in the mood
- Feel that their partner reads them better sexually
- Feel more positive or less negative about partner's porn use

First of all, those all seem worth aspiring to and would certainly contribute to a better sex life and relationship overall. Perhaps they are returning the favor of good effort elsewhere? Generosity tends to beget generosity. It seems like good effort in and out of bed is rewarded in and out of bed. If so, then we can say that putting in effort on managing ADHD is an aphrodisiac, something that may be worth reminding your partner of if they are slacking.

The lessons here then are clear. First, be a good partner and work hard, in and out of bed. Second, be sure that your partner knows about the work that you're doing and the effort that you're putting in, because we tend to underestimate what our partners do. On the flipside, give your partner a little benefit of the doubt, knowing that they may be doing more than you realize. On the other hand, if you really have doubts about their efforts and it is affecting your sexual feelings towards them (and more), then explain that to them, especially if this is something that is important to them and thereby motivating.

Maximizing Treatment Effectiveness

While generally respondents found that treatment was helpful, those with ADHD rated treatment as more effective than their non-ADHD partners did. I can think of two reasons for this. First, it may be that the person with ADHD is more attuned to what treatment is doing and sees more of the benefits, since they're primarily the one on the receiving end (except for couples therapy). By contrast, the non-ADHD partner needs to infer what the treatment is doing based on what can be observed—e.g., you seem less distracted because you leave fewer half-empty glasses lying around.

The other possibility is that the two partners have different priorities for treatment and in general. For example, I had a couple where it was really important to the non-ADHD wife that all the beds be made every morning because it gave her a sense of order in the world. Unfortunately, there is no amount of medication, therapy, or coaching that will give her husband the same feeling of primal bliss from tightly tucked duvets. Treatment did allow him to help more with breakfast and making the kids' lunches though and maybe sometimes pitch in on the beds, even if only to please his wife. So treatment helped in some ways and perhaps enabled them to better negotiate their difference of opinion about the merits of made beds—just as every couple needs to negotiate their differences.

Which Treatments Work Best?

Because the effect that ADHD has on someone's life and relationship depends on how effectively it's managed, I did a bunch of analysis looking at what treatments respondents tried and how well they worked. Let's start by looking at how much various treatments were used. I asked respondents to indicate all of the treatments for ADHD they or their partner used within the last year. The results are summarized in Table 3.1.

Educating themselves about ADHD and medication were by far the most commonly used treatments, with about two thirds of respondents using each of them. About one third had used lifestyle management and psychological therapy. The other treatments were quite a bit less frequently used.

I then asked respondents to rate to what extent they felt that treatment overall has been effective in managing their or their partner's ADHD symptoms. Most people had used more than one treatment (more on that shortly) and I didn't ask them to rate each treatment individually. This would be good data to have, but the survey was

Table 3.1 Treatments Used in the Last Year.

Treatment	Used	Didn't Use
Educating ourselves about ADHD through books, magazines, websites, webinars, meetings, etc.	2463	817
Medication (stimulants or non-stimulants)	2207	1073
Psychological therapy	1156	2124
Coaching	288	2992
Professional organizer	99	3181
Lifestyle management: exercise, sleep, diet, stress management, etc.	1314	1966
Other	267	3013

already too long. Fortunately, my stats consultant was able to do some crazy number crunching and extract out the effect that each treatment had. Here are those results in rank order, from most to least effective:

1. Medication
2. Lifestyle management
3. Coaching
4. ADHD education
5. Psychological therapy (no effect)
6. Professional organizer (no effect)
7. Other (negative effect)

Most of these results are not surprising and the ones that are do actually make sense when you think about it. In the survey, I asked a very specific question—how effective treatment has been at managing ADHD symptoms. I didn't ask the broader question about how effective it has been at improving the relationship or overall happiness. ADHD symptoms can affect both of those, but so do lots and lots of other things that have nothing to do with ADHD. So while relationship satisfaction and overall happiness are probably what people care most about, the narrower question of symptoms gives a cleaner result.

Let's run through each of the treatments individually. It is well established that medications do a great job of managing ADHD symptoms and for that reason I tend to be a fan of them, for the folks who need them. It also helps that stimulants are pretty easy to get right for most patients, so primary care docs who aren't ADHD experts can do a good job with them, meaning that many Americans have access to a competent local prescriber to manage their meds. However, there is a well-known saying that pills don't teach skills which is absolutely true. All of life's problems aren't solved at the pill bottle, but it is a great place to start because it makes all the other efforts, strategies, and treatments for ADHD work better. Therefore, if you or your partner have not yet tried ADHD medication and have been frustrated with the lack of progress, then it may be worth considering how this piece of the treatment puzzle could benefit the rest. Remember that trying medication is not like getting a tattoo where you are forever changed and you therefore need to make the absolutely best decision. If the medication isn't helping, then you just don't take it again tomorrow. Done.

It was gratifying to see that lifestyle management was second on the list, since I spend so much time bugging clients about it. This involves all that New Year's resolution stuff that we should all do better on: exercise, sleep, diet, stress management, etc. Of course, the knowing is easier than the doing, especially for those with insufficiently managed ADHD (or with meds that haven't yet kicked in in

Everything is about to go awry because my partner is not able to get his medication. I'm not sure about the effect this will have on our sex life, but I can guarantee his depression and self-criticism will increase exponentially. I'm very scared for what's to come.

Non-ADHD woman, 36, living together,
been together 6–10 years

the morning or have worn off at night). Fortunately, you don't need to train for an Ironman, get eight hours of sleep, eat vegan, or meditate ten times a day in order to see the benefits of working on your lifestyle. Even partial progress is helpful. For example, if instead of getting six hours of sleep each night, you get seven (or even six and a half) you will probably find that you feel and function better the next day. Don't let perfectionism, and the inevitable falling short, stop you from doing what you can. And if you fall off the wagon, then just get back on. Tomorrow is a new day.

All my ADHD coach friends will be glad to see that they were #3 on the list. Unlike most therapists, ADHD coaches tend to focus more on helping clients meet daily demands and be more effective by dealing more directly with ADHD symptoms and other barriers. If you're considering hiring a coach, be sure that they know ADHD well (which also applies to prescribers, therapists, and organizers) and ask about their training, because it can be quite variable.

I strongly believe that knowledge is power when it comes to ADHD and I now have the data to prove it in case you would like to be more powerful. Educating oneself about ADHD may not top the list, but given that it tends to be inexpensive and easy, it's a worthy investment. After all, there's no sense in re-inventing the wheel if other smart people have figured some things out before you. So soak in those books, webinars, podcasts, websites, support group meetings, conferences, etc.

As a psychologist, I was surprised (and disappointed) to see that psychological therapy was not rated as having any effect—until I remembered that I asked about ADHD symptoms. Unlike coaching which gets more into the practical matters of daily life, I wouldn't expect therapy to directly address those symptoms. Other research tells us that what it does benefit is how the individual and couple deal with those symptoms and get along. It would also be helpful with the anxiety, depression, substance use, and other conditions that are more likely to come along with ADHD, as well as with the relationship dynamics that can develop. This is a good example of how the specific wording of a question can have a large effect on the answers you get. It probably also doesn't help that there aren't enough therapists with sufficient expertise in adult ADHD, whether for individual or couples therapy, so respondents may not have gotten all the benefit they could have. Therefore, if you are going to see a therapist, make sure they have the knowledge you need them to have.

I was also surprised to see that professional organizers were not found to be helpful with ADHD symptoms. It could be that there were too few respondents to pick up the effect or that there are not enough organizers who really know ADHD well, which limits their effectiveness. However, I think that the real reason for this lack of effectiveness has more to do with who tends to seek the services of an organizer, which I will talk about next.

Finally, I asked respondents about their use of other treatments. Granted, this could be a rather mixed bag, including chiropractic interventions, specific dietary changes (not just eating healthy), natural remedies, brain training programs, supplements, mindfulness, etc., so when we look at their effectiveness, it's possible that the benefits of one are being canceled out by the ineffectiveness of the others. However, other research has not found much benefit for any of these alternative treatments, except mindfulness (and besides, is there anyone that you couldn't recommend mindfulness for?). Interestingly, unlike professional organizing which was found to have no effect, these alternative treatments were actually found to have a statistically significant negative effect. I will talk more about this shortly, but it doesn't change my basic opinion about alternative treatments for ADHD: I am willing to be convinced that they are effective, but until we have the research to prove it, I can't recommend any of them so your time and money are probably better spent elsewhere. This is especially true for proposed interventions that are time consuming, expensive, or just a plain hassle (elimination diet, anyone?) because the significant investment overshadows the unlikely return.

Because finding knowledgeable treatment providers is so important, check out the provider directories list in Appendix B for where to find the professionals who know what you need them to know.

Are More Treatments Better?

The typical advice for managing ADHD is to use a multimodal treatment program that involves using several interventions, and this is what most people tend to do. The average number of treatments used was 2.4. Overall, the biggest improvement came from the first treatment that respondents tried. Adding a second and then third made things even better, whereas a fourth treatment added less and a fifth treatment even less. So far so good, but this is where things get weird—using five treatment methods was more helpful than using four, but using six was actually less effective than using four and using seven was less effective than using two. Huh?

Look at Figure 3.1 below.

This is one of those places where group averages can be deceptive. The reason why the response to treatment seems to get worse after five is that people who have the most severe ADHD and/or co-occurring conditions and/or don't respond well to initial treatments are obviously more likely continue to try more treatments,

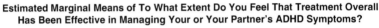

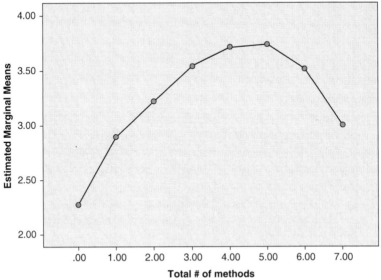

Figure 3.1 Relationship Between Number of Treatments and Effectiveness.

with the hope that they find something that works. Therefore, what we are seeing here is more about initial severity or poor treatment response than it is about treatment making things worse. Those with simpler situations and/or great responses to the first one or two treatments tend to stop there. Mission accomplished.

Since only 3% of respondents used a professional organizer, it could be that they were mostly those who weren't getting a good response to other treatments and therefore the benefits of working with an organizer weren't captured here because of their overall worse treatment response. Something similar may be going on with the alternative treatments, that they were mostly used by people who had not gotten enough benefit elsewhere. It seems unlikely to me that these alternative treatments truly had a negative effect, since mostly it would just be no positive effect, but unlike the professional organizers, they may not have had some positive effect to offset the overall worse treatment response from the folks who used them.

The lesson from this data is that generally more treatments tend to work better than fewer treatments, although with some diminishing returns. Therefore, the recommendation would be to start with the treatments that we know are most likely to be effective (medication and lifestyle management, followed by ADHD coaching). I would also put ADHD education towards the top of the list—given that it tends to be pretty cheap and easy, and it has a good return on investment, even if it doesn't itself make the most dramatic difference. I would also recommend psychological therapy and working with a professional organizer if it seems relevant to your situation. Although I can recommend mindfulness, I can't currently recommend any alternative treatments until we have good data to show their benefit.

Group averages aside, which treatments you ultimately choose will depend on your situation as well as your personal preferences. However, I would encourage you to be kind of greedy about treatment benefits and to not settle for some partial benefit. There is a lot on the line here, so push a bit to maximize what you get from treatment. And probably the non-ADHD partner should also have some input, not only on treatment effectiveness but also on treatment targets.

Take Away Lessons

Based on the data, a few key points jump out:

- Put in good effort on managing your or your partner's ADHD. Your partner is watching what you do and will appreciate it—and possibly base their own effort on what you're doing.
- Without looking for a standing ovation every time you throw a stray sock in the hamper, make sure your partner is aware of the things that you are doing. Perception is reality and you won't get credit for what your partner isn't aware of.
- By the same token, make a point of looking for the effort that your partner is putting in—and not just the obvious stuff. Give some benefit of the doubt when unsure.
- Have a conversation now and then about how you're each contributing so that you each get the credit that you deserve.
- If you feel like your partner isn't putting in enough effort, or effort in the ways that matter most to you, then ask for more (nicely). Explain why it's important to you and ask for a favor if it isn't important to your partner. There will be much more on this in later chapters in the book.
- Discuss not only what treatment is doing (benefits and side effects), but also what you are each hoping for from treatment. If necessary, talk to your treatment providers as well, preferably together.
- Respondents who felt that ADHD added barriers to a more satisfying sex life were somewhat more likely to put in more effort on managing ADHD.
- Managing ADHD is an aphrodisiac. Those who felt that their partner put in more effort on managing ADHD were more comfortable and generous sexually. Seriously.

- Educating themselves about ADHD and medication were by far the most commonly used treatments.
- Medication, lifestyle management, and coaching were found to be the most effective treatments.
- Using more treatments tends to be more effective than using fewer.

4

Role Models: What Can We Learn From the Happiest Couples?

Surveys offer correlations: e.g., people who answered question 10 this way also tended to answer question 17 that way. Correlation doesn't imply causality. We don't know what is causing what (e.g., do happier couples have more sex or are couples who have more sex happier? Or both?). Plus, with topics as complex as relationships and sex, there are undoubtedly many factors at work. However, surveys are a great way to gather a lot of information from a lot of people that we can use to identify effective points of intervention and use aspirationally as goals that could be worth working towards. Having said that, do not feel pressured to do anything you don't feel comfortable doing (e.g. having more sex when you don't want to or when there are issues that need to be resolved first).

What are the happiest couples doing differently from the least happy couples? What lessons can we learn here?

I compared the survey responses given by those respondents who rated themselves highest and lowest on current relationship satisfaction, current sexual satisfaction, and current sexual frequency. I looked at each of these three questions separately, since I didn't want to assume that being more satisfied on one necessarily meant being more satisfied on the others. As one would expect and as other research shows, these three were indeed quite correlated: the respondents who were happier in their relationship were also more satisfied with their sex life and (perhaps because the sex was more satisfying) had more of it. Good sex requires good relationship behavior and good sex promotes good relationship behavior.

This mutually reinforcing process is what drives my agenda behind the survey and this book: help couples do better on both so that they can be happier with both. Sex is too important to ignore and not just because it is itself enjoyable, but because it can be such a big contributor to overall relationship satisfaction. As a therapist who has seen how hard relationships can be, I firmly believe that we can't afford to ignore the potential benefits of a good sex life when helping couples find greater happiness.

Beware of Negative Momentum

There were clear differences between the answers given by the happiest respondents compared to those given by the least happy, across all parts of the survey, from treatment to relationship and sexual matters. This isn't really surprising, since those who are least (and most) happy probably have a lot of reasons for it. However, it's important to keep in mind that our mood and perceptions tend to have a momentum effect. I don't doubt their reasons for being unhappy and I certainly wouldn't suggest that they just need to think happy thoughts, but it is important to remember that our mood colors our interpretation of events, so we tend to see things in a way that supports our original mood. For couples, this means that when we are frustrated with our partner, for example, we tend to notice more of their frustrating actions than their helpful ones, thereby reinforcing that original frustration.

This is not to say that that partner isn't indeed doing frustrating things, but they are probably also doing some non-frustrating things, and they have lost the benefit of the doubt. This is especially true when our feelings towards our partner are more longstanding and intense, making it harder to break out of that negative mindset and maybe give them some credit for their positive actions. When we feel negative, we focus on the negative.

And when we feel negative, we tend to be less generous, so our partner is more likely to feel negatively about us and thereby less likely to act in positive ways. So the struggling couple struggles more.

The Power of Positive Attending

In order to break out of these negative and self-reinforcing cycles, both partners need to work on changing what they each contribute to keeping things stuck. However, there is also a lot to be gained from simply changing our mindset and what we pay attention to. Couples therapists call this positive attending—making a conscious effort to look for and notice the positive things that our partner is doing, rather than just going with the flow of our mood that makes their negative actions stand out more. Our partner still isn't perfect, but they are probably doing more good things than we realize, and they may not be getting enough credit for them. This is especially true when we round down anything that isn't clearly positive—for example, it's possible that they cleaned up the kitchen a bit, but since we didn't actually see them do it, we don't give them the benefit of the doubt.

If you find yourself really stuck with your partner and somewhat pessimistic about change, you may be surprised by how much more good stuff they do than you realize. While it does risk future disappointment to get your hopes up, make an effort to notice the small things that you still like about them and those positive little gestures that they make. This is not to imply that you should ignore the stuff that bothers you, but rather to create some balance and to find reasons to work on what needs to be worked on. And hopefully to work on them in a less aggravated way—which will make your partner more likely to respond well to your requests.

Use the rest of this chapter to perhaps get some ideas about what the happiest couples are doing and to thereby target your efforts. Then approach your partner with what would be most meaningful to you.

The Big Drivers of Satisfaction

Going into the survey, I had lots of theories about what variables would be associated with relationship and sexual satisfaction. This was based on previous research, clinical experience, and common sense. (And some self-serving pet theories.) These are (mostly) great places to start, but it's still worth taking the time to see if they're actually true. To do this, I had my stats guy run an analysis to see what best predicted respondents' satisfactions, at least among the questions that I asked. Doing wide-ranging statistical analyses (a.k.a. fishing expeditions) can find some significant correlations that are just random occurrences, but none them were surprising, so hopefully we're on the right track, especially because most of these results were extremely significant, making it even less likely that it is just random variation.

The biggest predictors of current relationship and sexual satisfaction were:

- Partner had put in good effort on managing their or their partner's ADHD (most people rate their own effort as high, so that doesn't separate the satisfied from the dissatisfied)
- Treatment has been effective in managing their or their partner's ADHD symptoms
- More comfortable making specific sexual requests of their partner, fulfilling their partner's specific sexual requests, and sharing sexual fantasies and turn-ons with their partner
- Partner is more sexually generous and willing to put in the necessary effort, including when they themselves are not in the mood
- Partner reads them well and knows how to please them sexually

Or, to put it another way: a collaborative effort on managing ADHD is noticed and appreciated and also makes the treatment more effective, thereby minimizing the effect that ADHD is having on the relationship, and thereby on their sex life. These happier couples also connect better sexually, partially because they each seem to put in the effort to be generous, accepting, and attuned to each other in bed. All of this is based on many behaviors, attitudes, and bidirectional interactions and there is undoubtedly a lot going on here, but the big take-away lesson boils down to this one general statement:

- Put in the effort to be a good partner

I talked in previous sections about the disconnect between how people see their own efforts and their partner's efforts. Basically, we tend to give ourselves more credit than we do our partners. Partly this is because we know everything that we do, but may not see everything our partner does or may not realize when they are trying to be generous. This leads to two related bits of advice:

- Make sure your partner is aware of your good deeds
- Make a point of noticing your partner's good deeds

I think that this comes down to fairness—if we feel like we are both putting in the necessary effort, it's easier to feel like we're on the same team and that we're working together. If so, the plentiful sexual and relationship rewards follow. So, what would it take for you and your partner to feel like you're on the same team?]

Follow the Leaders

In addition to using hardcore statistical methods to figure out the biggest drivers of sexual and relationship satisfaction, I also compared how the most and least happy couples answered individual questions in the survey to see what separated the two groups. As you might expect, there were quite a few differences, which I will discuss in the rest of this chapter. Take a look and see what you and your partner do well—and what are some areas to work on. We all have areas where we can improve, but it's helpful to learn from the best.

It's likely that the happiest couples are doing a lot of things well, including all sorts of things that I didn't ask about in the survey. It's also likely that some of those other things make it easier for them to do the things well that I did ask about. This is called a third factor where something else is influencing both of the variables that you are looking at. As I said earlier, relationships are complex and multidetermined, so there is always a lot going on. I don't want to give the impression that any of this will be simple or magically transformative. But these happiest couples give the rest of us something to aspire to, even if it will take some other work in order to emulate them on the elements that were included in the survey. As you read the sections that follow, look for some helpful lessons and worthy goals to work toward for your relationship. What is within your power to influence? How do you want your sex life and relationship to improve? What are you willing to do to get there?

Work Hard at Treatment

As I discussed elsewhere, we all have a bias when it comes to assessing how much effort we are putting in compared to how much effort others are putting in. This holds true when it comes to how much effort respondents felt that they and their partner were each putting into managing ADHD. Most people felt that they themselves were putting in good effort, but the happiest couples also felt that their partner was putting in good effort. It's understandable why this matters, since perceptions of fairness and balance in the relationship are important.

This then leaves us with two complementary ideas. First, look for and ask about what your partner is doing. They may be working harder than you realize. If not, then talk about what might help them to work harder—especially in the ways that matter most to you. What can you do to facilitate their doing more of the stuff that matters most to you? If they are doing some things that you don't care that much about, then perhaps their efforts could be better spent elsewhere.

Second, make sure that your partner is aware of what you are doing, so that you get the appropriate credit (while keeping in mind that tooting your own horn too often makes it seem like you're actually doing less). This greater awareness benefits your partner in that they will likely be appreciative of those efforts and feel better as a result—resentment rarely benefits anyone. If you could be working harder, especially if your partner is doing quite a bit more, then think about what it would take to do so in the ways that matter most to your partner. It's tempting to cut corners or coast from time to time, but it's extremely unlikely that that isn't being noticed, so don't talk yourself into believing that it isn't.

There's also a third option here. While more is often better, sometimes greater happiness comes from being more satisfied with less. It's possible that one or both of you has expectations for how much effort will be put in that go beyond what can be accomplished, given your other demands or given each of your levels of interest. This doesn't necessarily mean lower expectations, but rather the right expectations. Holding too tight to expectations that aren't working only prolongs the dissatisfaction. It's a judgment call as to whether you should keep pushing for more/different from your partner versus accepting that it isn't going to happen. If you stubbornly cling to your demands, you are going to be disappointed and frustrated. If you give in too easily, you aren't going to get much. Where exactly that best place is between the two is a judgment call that involves considering what your partner is willing and capable of, what the general circumstances are, and how important this is relative to your other priorities. Damn, relationships are hard sometimes. . . .

Find Effective Treatments

Since we know how unmanaged ADHD can affect relationship happiness for both partners, it isn't surprising that the happiest couples felt that treatment was more effective. Although I asked specifically about how effective the treatments were at managing ADHD symptoms, obviously a relationship is about much more than ADHD. Nonetheless, if you feel like ADHD is still causing more trouble in your relationship than you would want, then you may want to re-consider what treatment approaches you are using. If something doesn't seem to be working as well as it should be (and you both get a vote on this one), then talk to the provider about it. Maybe some changes are in order.

Whether you change the treatment or not, monitor what happens. Most treatment providers are only as good as the information that you give them. Help them do their job better by giving them plenty of the right kinds of information. For this reason, I often suggest that the romantic partner be involved in at least some of those meetings, in order to provide their perspective. Not only may they notice some different things, but they may also have some different priorities for what treatment should accomplish that are worth including in the discussion.

If you still don't feel like you are getting the results that you want, you may need to switch providers and seek out clinicians who really know what they're doing with ADHD. Sometimes generalists can do a good job, but sometimes you need someone who is a bit more of an expert. Depending on where you live, this may not always be easy to find. And you may need to go out of your insurance network. I can very much appreciate the logistics of traveling farther and paying more for a specific clinician, but it's a judgment call as to whether it's worth it. Depending on what your closer and cheaper options are, and how motivated you are to improve things, it may be. Remember, something cheap but of little benefit doesn't really have great value, especially if you consider additional suffering that could have been prevented or reduced earlier. I list some provider directories in Appendix B where you can perhaps find those better clinicians.

Throughout the process, keep your eye on the bigger picture—this is not just about managing ADHD symptoms. This is about creating a better relationship and sex life. There are probably multiple ways to get there and happiness shouldn't require the complete banishing of all traces of ADHD. Focus on whatever is most important to your happiness and try to let the smaller things go.

Finally, if your motivation starts to slide, and if having more or better sex is important to you, remember that managing ADHD well can be an aphrodisiac.

Have More Sex

The couples who have more sex tend to be more satisfied with their sex life. On the one hand, this isn't surprising, but it probably also reflects that those who enjoy it more are also more likely to do it more (more on that later). Although greater sexual frequency is more correlated with higher sexual satisfaction, it is also correlated with greater relationship satisfaction. Again, this influence undoubtedly goes both directions—having more sex helps couples feel happier with each other overall, but also being happier overall helps people want more sex (with their partner, that is).

It's important to note that just having more sex isn't likely to increase positive feelings if the sex isn't very good. And feeling pressured to have sex when you don't want to is a great way to guarantee that the sex will be bad—and that you will be less likely to want it next time. More sex only helps if it's good sex and both people want it. So if there is something going on that is making the sex less desirable for either of you, then it's worth working on that. There can be many, many possible reasons why someone feels dissatisfied with their sex life and I will discuss many of them, and ways to improve things, in the second half of the book.

The good news in all this is that most people actually want more sex than they are currently having, sometimes much more. Interestingly and ironically, the folks who are having sex daily would actually prefer, on average, to have slightly less sex. So more is better, but only to a point. The goal is not actually to have more sex, but rather to have the right amount, whatever that is for you and your partner. This probably means more sex, but might also mean less sex, particularly if it feels like the greater quantity is interfering with quality.

Overall, the average desired sexual frequency was two to four times per week, which is quite a bit more than what most respondents are doing now. How much happier would many of these couples be if they got to a point where they were indeed having sex that often? Wow. There is clearly a lot of pent-up desire here. However, if everything in your relationship stayed exactly the same except that you had sex more often, you and your partner would probably feel somewhat better about the relationship overall, but this ignores the bigger goal here which is to work on whatever is getting in the way of having sex more often. Addressing these barriers will probably have a bigger impact on your overall happiness. If having more sex is a motivator to do that work, then go for it.

In order to have sex, someone needs to initiate. In many couples, one person tends to do more of the initiating than the other. While this can bring up feelings of resentment, pressure, and self-doubt, it doesn't necessarily need to be a problem as long as both partners handle it well. In the happiest couples though, both partners tended to initiate just about as often. This makes sense because it kind of doubles the odds of them having sex if there are two people to initiate. While this may reflect that these couples have more similar sex drives which will tend to make things run more smoothly, it also reflects that both partners are taking responsibility for their own sexual satisfaction and are therefore more likely to be happy with how things work out. So if you tend to initiate less, you may want to think about initiating a little more, at least if you feel like that would improve things. There is a lot more to say about initiation since it can be a rather complex topic, so check out *Chapter 8: Make it a Priority*.

Have Better Sex

Having more sex is good, but only if it's sex that you want to have, so let's talk about what made sex better for the happier couples. First, they are more comfortable making specific sexual requests of their partner. Since sexual desires can involve some vulnerability to judgment or criticism from others (or even ourselves), feeling safe disclosing them to a partner is really important, since if you can't ask for what you really want, then you're less likely to be satisfied. If there is something holding you back from being more open with your partner, then you may want to address that, within yourself and/or with your partner.

On the flipside, the happiest couples are more comfortable fulfilling their partner's specific sexual requests. This willingness undoubtedly makes the partner more likely to ask and thereby get what they want. This probably then makes them more willing to agree to their partner's requests, making both people happier. What goes around, comes around. I talk at length about the process of identifying each of your sexual desires and coming to a satisfying compromise in *Chapter 7: Respectful Communication and Negotiation*.

In addition to making more requests for desired activities, the happiest couples also felt more comfortable sharing their sexual fantasies. While the physical sensations of sex can be great, the mental and emotional part can be even more powerful. Playing with fantasies can send your excitement through the roof and sharing those fantasies with your partner can sweep them away, too. Of course, enjoying a particular fantasy doesn't necessarily mean that we would actually want to act on it, something I remind myself of every cold, dark, dreary winter when I warm my spirits with thoughts of moving to some rum-infused, bikini-intensive island in the Caribbean. I talk more about the fun and important topic of fantasies in *Chapter 9: Sex 101 (and 201, and 301 . . .)*. Hopefully actually reading it turns out to be as great as you were hoping it would be. . . .

Perhaps because they are more comfortable communicating about sex in general, the happiest couples also felt that their partner reads them well and knows how to please them sexually. All that earlier communication about what works sexually and what doesn't has trained both partners well, so they know how to get the job done. If you don't feel like your partner reads you well, either in general or in some specific ways, then tell them what would work better. As sex advice podcaster Dan Savage says, use your words. If necessary, get into the nitty-gritty details about what works for you, when, why, and how. Then ask the same about your partner. Most people want to feel sexually competent, so you are doing your partner a favor by helping them understand how to please you. Make your requests sensitively and respectfully and take feedback resiliently, leaving ego out of both sides of that conversation.

The happiest couples also make each other's pleasure a priority and put in the necessary effort to ensure their partner has a good time. However, as discussed earlier, since everyone tends to rate their own effort higher than others', it's important to give some benefit of the doubt and notice what your partner is doing. On the flipside, without asking for credit for every little thing, make sure your partner is aware of what you're doing. Your sex life (or relationship overall) doesn't need to be exactly fair at every moment, but there should be a general sense of balance.

This idea of each partner putting in their share of effort also implies that both are responsible for making the sex satisfying for both. Put in the necessary effort, look for what your partner is doing, and ask for more from your partner if you feel like you're getting a bad deal—and remind them that it's making you less sexually interested. You owe it to both of you to make your sex life better. After all, it's hard to get repeat customers with unsatisfying sex.

Speaking of putting in good effort, I also found that the happiest couples tended to be more sexually generous even when not in the mood. This is important because, even in the best couples, there are times when one person is in the mood and the other isn't. This sexual generosity undoubtedly reflects perceptions of their partner's generosity, both in bed and out, and then prompts future generosity, in bed and out. Good deeds (of whatever kind) tend to be rewarded. This generosity, as well as perceptions of fairness, is especially important in couples who have large differences in their desired sexual frequency. While the lower desire partner may not be interested in a full production sexual experience, they may be willing to pitch in for a smaller number. I talk about this in the section on *Negotiate the Differences* in *Chapter 7: Respectful Communication and Negotiation.*

The happiest couples also rated themselves as kinkier, although I didn't ask them to define exactly what it is that kinky means to them (nor to submit pictures for a panel of judges). I would venture to say that this is related to everything that we have just talked about that makes these couples' relationship and sex life better, so they feel more comfortable expressing and enacting their kinkier desires. The lesson learned here is to make some effort to keep sex interesting and be willing to try new things—and then to not try them again if you didn't enjoy it. An easy exit makes an entry more likely. Sex should evolve over the years and decades—because everything else in the relationship does.

Finally, the happiest couples rated ADHD as less of an additional barrier to a satisfying sex life. If you find that it's having more of an effect than you would want it to, then put in the necessary effort to address it. (See the previous sections on treatment effort and effectiveness, as well as *Chapter 3: Make the Most of Treatment.*) While the happiest couples may have been better able to find ways to reduce the symptoms of ADHD, it is also equally likely that they have found ways to work around them as well as to minimize how much they let those remaining symptoms impact their happiness.

Generally speaking, happier couples tend to focus more on what they appreciate about each other, rather than getting stuck on the annoyances or the things that won't change.

If you find that you're having trouble seeing beyond the ways that ADHD is affecting your relationship or sex life, it may be helpful to consider whether that frustration or disappointment is blinding you to other positive qualities or good deeds. If you're willing to do some really deep self-analysis, you may want to ask yourself whether ADHD has become the easy target in the relationship and that blaming so much of your unhappiness on ADHD is really a cover-up for other issues (e.g., discomfort with your own flaws; need for external control in order to cope with internal anxiety; need to be needed; need to be taken care of, etc.). You may not be happy with what you discover, but if there is something else going on here, then just focusing on ADHD is unlikely to resolve these other issues and you will still be unhappy. A therapist may be able to help you sort this all out, either individually or with your partner.

Masturbation and Porn Are OK

When we talk about someone's sex life, we are usually referring to their partnered activities, but for most people, this also includes solo activities. Interestingly, when I looked at respondents' overall sexual satisfaction and how often they masturbated, I found that there wasn't that much of a relationship between the two. Some of the more frequent masturbators were very satisfied with their overall sex life and therefore used it as a complement to something that was already good, whereas others used masturbation as a substitute when their overall sexual satisfaction was low. On the plus side for these unhappy folks, relying more on masturbation than on partnered activities can reduce the number of fights about improving the couple's sex life and can also help someone resist the temptation of seeking sexual satisfaction outside of the relationship. Less good, masturbation can also become the path of least resistance—for both partners, if someone turns a blind eye to their partner's avoidance of joint activities that is easier than working through what is interfering with better sexual connection.

I also asked respondents several questions about porn (not including their usernames and passwords). Interestingly, frequency of porn use isn't correlated with relationship satisfaction or sexual frequency, so overall porn isn't the last refuge for unhappy partners who aren't getting laid enough—nor the cause of those things. Perhaps more interestingly, there was a U-shaped curve for sexual satisfaction: the most and least sexually satisfied watch the same amount, whereas those who are neither satisfied nor dissatisfied watch the least. The most sexually satisfied may feel confident in their partnered sex life and thereby feel less guilty about being sexually attracted to others and use porn more or may even watch with their partner, whereas the most sexually dissatisfied seem to use porn (and masturbation) as a substitute for partnered sex.

When I asked respondents how they felt about their own porn use, the happiest couples feel more positive about it, perhaps because they don't see it as detracting from their relationship and sex life, since things are good. Therefore, if you feel bad about your porn use or that it's detracting from your sex life or relationship, then address it within yourself and/or within the relationship. This may involve watching less/none, watching different porn, and/or working out an acceptable arrangement with your partner.

On the flipside, the happiest couples also felt quite a bit less negative about their partner's porn use, perhaps because they don't see it as taking away from their sex life and relationship. If you feel like your partner's porn use is having a negative effect, then address it, but perhaps don't make a thing of it if you are otherwise satisfied.

Porn (and sometimes masturbation) can be a highly contentious and even politicized topic that deserves much more discussion. If this is a concern for you or your partner, then definitely check out *Chapter 10: Taking Some Personal Time: Masturbation* and *Chapter 11: What About Porn?* for more on this and how to work on it if it's a problem.

Take Away Lessons

Based on the data, a few key points jump out:

- There were many clear differences between the answers given by the happiest respondents compared to those given by the least happy. There is momentum to how we feel, as well as what we pay attention to, so making an effort to notice your partner's good qualities and deeds may have a positive effect on how you feel about them.

- A collaborative effort on managing ADHD is noticed and appreciated and also makes the treatment more effective, thereby minimizing the effect that ADHD is having on your relationship and sex life. And if your current treatments aren't getting the job done, then try something new.

- The happiest couples had more sex, but it's important to ensure that that sex is good for both partners. This involves valuing your partner's pleasure, being generous and accepting of your partner's turn-ons, communicating directly about your own desires, and perhaps exploring some kinkier options if that will keep sex hot.

- The happiest couples didn't feel that their own or their partner's masturbation or porn use were a problem. It was seen as an add-on to partnered activities, not a comment or threat.

- Bottom line: be a good partner, in and out of bed, to get more of your partner's best.

Section II
Principles of Great Sex Lives

Introduction: Your Sex Life is Worth Working On

Given that this is about a quarter of the way through a book on sex, I am probably preaching to the choir here, but I firmly believe that your sex life is worth working on. Whether it's good but you want it to be great, whether it ain't what it used to be and you want to bring back its former glory, or whether it was always pretty flat-lined and you want to breathe new life into it, sex lives can almost always be improved.

It's definitely possible to have a happy romantic relationship without any sex at all—it isn't an absolute requirement. It's also possible to have a happy romantic relationship with only occasional and/or so-so sex. However, sex therapist and researcher Barry McCarthy, PhD found that a good sex life adds about 20% to the happiness of a relationship (McCarthy & McCarthy, 2013). Adding that 20% won't make it worth staying in an otherwise terrible relationship and taking it away probably won't tip the scales on an otherwise great relationship. At the extremes, that 20% might be a rounding error. But for most of us, that 20% might make the difference between passing and failing, or at least between taping our report card to the fridge versus forging a parent's signature.

Missing out on all or most of that 20% may also mean that we need to work a lot harder in the other parts of the relationship, since we're starting the semester with an 80 before anything else has even happened. Whether your sex life adds 5%, 10%, or the full 20% to your and your partner's relationship happiness, I want it to add as much as is reasonably possible.

Fortunately, sex involves individual and relationship skills that can be developed like any others. The chapters in this section will help you and your partner create that mutually desirable sex life. There won't be any pictures or lists of the top ten positions for multi-orgasmic meltdowns, but it will teach you most of what you need to know to work with your partner to make the bedroom a much more exciting place. Or to turn some other place into your bedroom. This will involve some basic facts on the mechanics of sex (e.g., why lube can be a great addition), but mostly will involve improving your relationship generally and also specifically as it impacts your sex life. Most of this will benefit you way beyond the bedroom.

What would make your sex life better for your partner?

My partner likes to stay in his comfort zone, so never having to accommodate my sensation-seeking would be better for him. I think our sex life would be better if he would care enough to read a book about sex.

ADHD woman, 27, dating, living separately,
been together 6–10 years

5

Sex Makes You a Better Person

Really? Sex makes you a better person?

Absolutely. Keeping sex great over the years and decades with the same person will indeed involve the kind of personal and relationship growth that can't help but make both of you better people overall.

To have a consistently good sex life, you need to behave well before, during, and after sex and you need to work well with your partner on all sorts of things that have nothing to do with sex. This process has great rewards, but can be a lot of work, especially as the relationship deepens, gets more complicated, and stretches over the decades. The couples who are the happiest through this process are the ones who hold themselves and their partners to high but reasonable standards and strive for self-growth. They take personal responsibility and challenge themselves to work on their issues. This makes them better partners, but also indirectly pushes their partner to also bring their best and become a better person and partner. This might mean working on their own or their partner's ADHD, but it also involves everything else that the couple might be struggling with.

What would make your sex life better for you?
  If we had good communication and a deep, intimate relationship, sex would be much more enjoyable for me and less of a chore. If I felt truly seen . . . truly understood . . . and truly prioritized, I would feel more free to let go and enjoy sex, and see it as an important part of our relationship.
Non-ADHD woman, 42, married, 6–10 years

This process of individual and shared growth enables them to keep their sex life vibrant. For most people, a better sex life isn't the only, or even primary, motivator for this difficult work, but it's hard to keep your sex life humming along without doing this work. This is why I say that sex makes you a better person—it's yet another motivator to do that other personal and relationship work that is a prerequisite for a great sex life. And because sexuality can feel like such a sensitive and vulnerable topic, it takes some great communication and relationship skills to find ways to negotiate the two partners' differences and create a great sex life that meets both of their needs. So, sexuality is both a powerful motivator and also a great testing ground for those important skills that will benefit all other parts of the relationship. Even if we just want to get laid, there is so much more going on there when it happens in committed relationships.

What would make your sex life better for you?
  Sex would better for me if I could relax enough to allow myself to enjoy what my partner does. If it's not the perfect touch, at the perfect time, in the perfect way. . . . I tend to dwell on the negative versus enjoying the positive. Maybe that's not an ADHD thing, but I can't help thinking that "normal people" would be able to do it better. Essentially, I'm so aware of being different, that the way I respond to anything my hubby does MUST be abnormal.
ADHD woman, 44, married, been together 21+ years

Peace Sometimes Requires War

Early in most relationships, everyone is polite, interested, and focused on what they like about each other, so there are few fights. Nobody is making excessive demands and both partners try to be considerate of each other. In the survey, the vast majority of respondents were quite happy with their relationship and sex life in the first year. These are fun and usually easy times. Unfortunately, this peace is partially maintained by avoiding too much honesty and disclosure, as partners feel each other out and see what the other can handle.

As the partners' differences begin to emerge and become more noticeable, a more complete picture of the other person is revealed and we don't like everything that we see. Of course, we all have things about ourselves that we wish were different, so we shouldn't expect our partner to be more perfect than we ourselves are. Not only do we begin to see more of the differences between us, warts and all, but it also matters a lot more now that the relationship has become more important. Acquaintances don't bother us as much because what they do and who they are doesn't have as much of a direct impact on our life and happiness. With a committed partner, we're caught between being bothered by their shortcomings and therefore want to push them to work on them, but we also don't want to lose this important person from our lives so we may be inclined to try to ignore the problems. Damn, that's a tough dilemma.

Sometimes these increasingly obvious differences between partners feel insurmountable and the relationship ends, which may be for the best—hopefully both partners learned some good lessons about themselves and relationships and go on to find a better match next time.

Even when the couple stays together, this process of disillusionment is normal, inevitable, and ultimately a good thing if the couple is able to hold onto each other's positive qualities while tolerating the less desirable ones as they work through the struggles that evolving relationships bring. Even when partners are really similar in all the important ways, they won't want all the same things at all the same times. This is probably the time that ADHD symptoms become more obvious or when they are no longer written off as interesting quirks. This is also the time when the non-ADHD partner's less productive attempts to deal with those symptoms become more noticeable (i.e., annoying). So the tug of war begins: "stop telling me what to do!" versus "stop doing those things that make me angry!".

The big three argument topics for most couples are sex, money, and parenting, all of which can be impacted by ADHD. These topics are hardest because we tend to care much more about the outcome of a disagreement when one of these is center stage, unlike discussions about what to have for dinner. In addition, these big three tend to have mutually exclusive options—sex usually requires a personal involvement from both partners, a dollar can't be spent twice, and partners need to make at least generally compatible parenting decisions. It's easier to take one for the team on other topics or to come up with an easy compromise that everyone can be happy enough about ("OK, we can watch my movie next time.").

It's these less obviously solvable impasses that require more nuanced discussions and sophisticated negotiations to come to a sustainable agreement. This requires reflection to figure out what you want and why, empathy to understand your partner's position, and probably some good self-soothing for when things get heated. The best solutions are probably not simply a 50/50 split down the middle where each partner is half unhappy; rather, find those deeper solutions that both people can feel even better about. This isn't kid stuff and isn't for the faint of heart. It requires solid self-awareness and negotiation skills and a genuine desire to create a solution that you can both be happy with.

It can be even harder to work on the big three when too much of your time, energy, and good will toward each other are constantly

> The non-ADHD person really needs to move beyond taking anything personally and really just go with the flow. (However, don't compromise your self-respect and values. Don't put your self-esteem into the hands of your partner.)
> *Non-ADHD woman, 35, married, been together 6–10 years*

chewed away by the little million—all those mundane matters of daily life, like cleaning up leaked toothpaste from the bathroom counter (and arguing about who left the cap off). Even if you lived by yourself, you would still have to deal with all these boring details of life, but when you live with someone else it adds an extra element of disagreement about which options are higher or lower priority: is organic milk worth the extra cost? Is it more important to load the dishwasher or wipe off the counters? Does it matter if shoes are left in the living room? Few of these are questions with factual answers, but rather are about personal preference (and possible value judgments, such as that only degenerates don't understand why doilies are what separates society from chaos).

It's probably safe to say that couples where one partner has ADHD are more likely than the neighbors to have more of these sorts of disagreements. Sometimes the person with ADHD genuinely has a different opinion than their partner, but sometimes they may agree (e.g., "of course it's a good idea to pay bills on time") but have trouble executing consistently. If these slips evoke strong reactions from their partner, then they may dig in as a means of self-defense ("it's only a twenty-dollar late fee, chill out!"). Hopefully no one is such a fragile flower that one of these arguments breaks the relationship bank, but constant skirmishes can trickle away positive feelings and put both partners on guard against the next disappointment. This becomes even more complicated when deeper psychological meaning is read into these events ("if you loved me more, you would just pay them on time" and "if you loved me more, you wouldn't constantly criticize me"). It's death by a thousand cuts—forget about getting around to addressing those bigger, existential, relationship issues.

Fortunately, the process of hashing through disagreements with our partner is the best education in these important life skills, even if it can often feel like trial by fire. When we first start dating as a teen or young adult, we're all pretty clueless, but the lessons begin the very first time there is a whiff of disagreement. Yay, learning! As with most learning curves, there are a bunch of failed tests and missing homework, but little by little we figure out how to do relationships better. Some people are quick studies, perhaps because they had skilled role models, whereas others really struggle to make progress or get stuck in old behaviors that perhaps never worked that well even in the beginning.

As much as a committed relationship can feel like a windowless prison in those dark moments, it can also be the pressure chamber where a lump of coal becomes a diamond. Committed relationships are harder to walk away from, so we are forced to address disagreements or remain unhappy. Doing that hard work of addressing the disagreement in a new and more productive way can feel almost impossible, but remaining stuck feels totally unacceptable, so we're really caught in between. As empowering as it can feel to stubbornly dig in and hold our ground, eventually most people decide that there has to be a better way. They realize that there may be more happiness to be found in changing what they themselves do, rather than holding out hope that their partner will finally make all the necessary changes. As much as these impasses can bring out the worst in each of us (and they do), they can also bring out our best—usually after we finally get sick enough of the worst.

If ADHD is part of the mix in your relationship, then getting that figured out and addressed probably makes it easier to work on the rest of your relationship. It's probably reasonable for the non-ADHD partner to expect that their partner with ADHD will take it seriously and actively work on it, especially on the ways that impact the relationship. Meanwhile, it is probably also reasonable for the ADHD partner to expect their partner to also educate themselves about ADHD, give credit for good effort, and not expect perfection (defined as the non-ADHD partner's way of doing things). There is plenty more to relationship bliss than managing ADHD, but it is definitely a good step in the right direction—relationships are hard enough without adding that fuel to the fire.

Sometimes ADHD becomes the convenient excuse to not deal with these other personal or relationship problems—e.g., "How can we work on these other issues when your ADHD/your constant criticism of my ADHD is causing so many other problems?" There may be some truth to this in that ADHD is at least a partial cause of lots of fights, but it isn't the only thing going on there. No relationship is so simple that a disagreement is about just one thing, so what else isn't being addressed there? What's the history that is coloring how you each respond to the situation of the moment?

Of course, this avoidance move isn't unique to ADHD. Couples can also get stuck in other topics, like money, and therefore not have to deal with what else is also going on in the relationship or in the deeper issues that underlie that topic. Or we can justify avoiding difficult conversations by being too busy to have the necessary time and energy. It can feel easy to justify this when work and parenting obligations really don't leave much time for anything else. It's easy to just keep chugging along, day after day, without really working on the relationship. Quality time together, sexual or otherwise, just seems to not happen often enough, even if no one has an outright agenda to avoid it.

Whether subconsciously or intentionally, all of this makes it easier to avoid having these difficult conversations. This then is the challenge: to push ourselves to carve out the time and energy to have difficult conversations about messy topics. That's a tough sales pitch, except that it's the only way that things really get better and it's worth it if you can get there. As much as I can look back over the twenty years of my relationship and wish that both of us had done a lot of things differently (as in, way better), I also know that things wouldn't be better now in our sex life and relationship overall if we hadn't slogged through some of those bad times.

Happy Couples Fight Better

Disagreements are inevitable in relationships, whether romantic, friends, coworkers, roommates, etc. Two people won't always want the same things at the same times. Happy couples don't necessarily have fewer disagreements, they're just better at handling the disagreements that do arise. To do this, they use the three rules of fighting better.

First, they fight respectfully. This means no low blows, saying things that they later regret, or winning at too high a cost. They remember that how this disagreement gets resolved will influence lots of other interactions, including some that have nothing to do with the topic at hand. For example, you may win the discussion about where to go for Thanksgiving, but then lose out for the next few days when your partner is more distant. Or maybe you give in on Thanksgiving but handled the discussion so badly that your partner is angry about it, even though they got what they wanted. It's not just about how the disagreement ends, but also about how you got there. Being able to manage your emotions well and to take the other person's perspective are key skills for fighting respectfully—easier said than done, but definitely worth working on. ADHD, anxiety, depression, and substance abuse can all make emotional regulation much harder, so therapy and/or medication may be an important part of improving the relationship. For ADHD specifically, stimulant medication and/or one of the alpha-2 agonists like guanfacine or clonidine can help slow down emotional reactions and help the person have some more perspective.

Fortunately, the better one person behaves, probably the easier it is for the other to behave well—and the inverse is definitely true in that bad behavior tends to evoke bad behavior. If someone struggles to behave well in these discussions (arguments), then it's worth some serious reflection on what else is getting triggered there and some major efforts to respond differently. This may require some help with a therapist who can help you find different ways of responding. It may also help to identify what the interaction pattern between the two of you is and how you each evoke certain responses from each other, with the goal of responding differently.

Second, happy couples resolve problems productively. This requires sticking through to the end to create a solution that can actually be employed and is sustainable. Rushing too quickly to resolution, or just pulling the ripcord on an argument to get out of it, can create solutions that seem OK at the time, but don't really

> Sex would be better for my partner if I could be able to be more focused on him and not blurt out totally unrelated comments during sex. Some of these have become jokes now, and sometimes he jokingly says things I've said during sex back to me, and then we both laugh. So even though it would be better if I didn't blurt things out, we've been able to use it to build our relationship.
>
> *ADHD man, 31, married, been together 3–5 years*

resolve the bigger issues or take the complexities into account. Then it's just a matter of time before the same problem comes up. Or perhaps it's a reasonable solution that could work, but one person decides later that they aren't happy about it and goes against what was decided without bringing it up for another discussion.

If you find that you keep having the same arguments on the same topics, then it probably means that you haven't yet figured out how to resolve it and that both of you need to try to understand the problem more deeply, clarify your own perspective on it, understand the barriers for your partner, and then come up with a new solution that takes enough of it all into account. Then you need to commit to that solution, even when it's hard to do and you don't feel like it. This can be a real process, but you will both understand yourselves and each other better for it—which may make it easier to know how to handle whatever else comes up later.

Finally, happy couples are better able to move on after a disagreement. Of course, this is easier to do if you both behaved respectfully (mostly), even in the heat of the moment, and have faith that you came to a positive resolution. There will be new disagreements, so you want to build some good feelings between you to be able to better handle what comes next. And to enjoy each other meanwhile.

It's probably easier to move on from a disagreement if you can be flexible about what the solution is or how it is carried out. This is especially true if you and your partner have different ways of handling things—while we all prefer our way, it may be that neither one is inherently better than the other, as long as both work. And when things occasionally don't work out as we initially hoped, some picking of battles or being flexible about process or outcomes can avoid a lot of fights. There is a balance to be struck of knowing what is most important to you and pushing for that, while also recognizing which battles are best left unfought. There are no rules for which way to lean, so much as that the happier couples tend to find that right balance.

Couples who are able to handle anger well are then better able to share passion. It's hard to lose yourself to the vulnerability of passion if unresolved anger is lingering. The couples who are able to keep sex hot over the decades are the ones who are able to deal with conflicts in a friendly (or friendly-ish) way and come to resolutions that neither sell themselves short nor trample their partner's desires.

Good partners push each other to be better people—and lead by example.

The Double-Edged Sword of Desire

Wanting drives us to pursue what we desire. This can be a good thing if we are able to (eventually) get what we want. If we have sharpened some skills or grown in some way for that effort, then all the better. For example, wanting more peace in your relationship can push you to work on how you and your partner solve disagreements. Progress here will likely come from some personal growth on both of your parts. If you really want more peace, then you will be more willing to overcome some significant discomfort to achieve it, meaning really working at controlling your part of those angry interactions, holding your partner to that same high standard, and maybe even investing time and money to see a therapist.

How motivated we are to work at something depends on how much we want it, how much effort and discomfort it will take, and how likely we think it is to be successful. This gives us three points of intervention to work on if we want to increase our own or someone else's motivation.

The survey found that there is a big overlap between respondents' overall relationship satisfaction and their sexual satisfaction. This has been well documented elsewhere. What this tells us is that working on one will benefit the other (but since it isn't a total overlap, there are also other factors that influence people's satisfaction in each of these two areas). I also asked respondents how important their sexual satisfaction is to their overall relationship satisfaction, looking at one direction of that bidirectional relationship. Most people felt that it was indeed pretty important, with the men rating it a little higher than the women but ADHD status having no effect. This runs counter to the cliché that men are a bunch of hornball idiots who can be motivated to do just about anything if it increases their odds of getting laid and that women don't care that much about sex. Awesome—I love research that teaches us something new.

Having a strong desire can be a double-edged sword. On the plus side, if we get what we want, whether we have to work at it or not, we will likely be quite happy about that. Unfortunately, thwarted desire can cause great unhappiness. Having a strong desire for a better relationship or sex life that you have not yet achieved can be a driver to do the work to get there. It may spur a lot of fights and may not always be pretty or graceful or even useful, but it can eventually move mountains. And if there is a general sense that things are in motion, even if it isn't entirely clear what is happening or how long it will take, then we may remain optimistic about eventually getting somewhere that we want to be and hang in there, doing the work. These couples may have occasional fireworks, but that may just be what it takes to come to a better place, if the relationship survives the process. Growth is sometimes born of struggle.

By contrast, those who have a strong but thwarted desire and have stopped fighting for it may be at risk in a quieter way, both for personal unhappiness and other relationship problems. They are at risk for giving up, for settling for something significantly less than they want. They may hang in there, maybe for the kids, maybe because they don't want to be divorced, but they aren't happy about it (and their partner probably isn't either) and that unhappiness is probably spilling into other parts of the relationship. They may resign themselves to their fate and no longer try to improve things. Granted, none of us get everything that we want in life and growing up involves being able to accept that some dreams will remain unfulfilled. (I'm still waiting for that call that Iron Maiden needs me

I've grown resentful that by the time he notices, I'm unhappy. I've always wanted more sex than him. But the lack of intimacy, the thing that makes you want that person and hold them in your thoughts and create opportunities to hold each other, that's worse. I feel invisible and am shocked when others notice me. I'm starting to forget I'm sexual at all. I'm at high risk for an affair. I'm not needy or insecure. I'm lonely.
Non-ADHD woman, 47, married, been together 11–20 years

to take over vocals.) This may be a smart judgment call if this really is an irreconcilable issue and they have decided to focus on and enjoy the parts of their relationship and sex life that are working well. However, settling may be less helpful if this dissatisfaction continues to interfere with enjoying the rest of the relationship, but they haven't yet decided to either accept it as unchangeable or do the hard work to change it. Peace is often found in that midway point of knowing that they have changed what they can and accept what they can't, and are focusing on enjoying the parts that they do like.

Those who suffer the most are those who still really want what they know they won't get. The desire remains, but the door is closed. They feel acutely the absence of what they can't have. They can't figure out how to make the right things happen, but they can't imagine forsaking the thwarted desires either. This can feel torturous, as if they are being torn in two. Those who feel that a good sex life is really important to their overall relationship satisfaction and maybe overall life satisfaction and feel really disappointed with their sex life will likely not be suffering silently, or at least invisibly, and their partner will probably be aware of that dissatisfaction—they probably feel a lot of pressure about it, in addition to whatever their own dissatisfactions are. These are the individuals and couples who haven't yet figured out what they want to do. Can they really come to accept that their sex life (or whatever) will not become what they want it to be, but find ways to enjoy the rest of their sex life and relationship? Or is it an untenable situation that eventually breaks the relationship—or possibly leads to infidelity which perhaps then breaks the relationship? The horns of this dilemma can be a really tough place to be.

Life involves hard choices. The Declaration of Independence guarantees Americans the rights of life, liberty, and the pursuit of happiness, but remains wisely silent on what it will take to attain that happiness and the likelihood of success. Happiness can be achieved by doing the work to get what we want, as well as by accepting that something is either unattainable or that it isn't worth what it will take. (Having no singing ability nor any band experience makes that call from Iron Maiden pretty unlikely.) The challenge then for all of us is to decide what to fight for and what to accept.

Maximizing happiness involves ongoing judgment calls about this important balance. Striving risks disappointment, but settling risks less fulfillment. We all have to make our own choice, at this time in our lives, under these circumstances, about what will bring us the most happiness.

Self-Esteem, Self-Acceptance, and Other-Acceptance

ADHD may be a neurological condition, but it drives a lot of psychology, including in the romantic partner. ADHD influences the kinds of experiences that both partners have which then influences how they both feel about themselves and each other. This then influences how they continue to interact with each other. This effect will probably be much greater when ADHD hasn't been diagnosed or treated, making it easier to make incorrect assumptions about what ADHD behaviors mean (e.g., "If I was smarter, then. . . ." or "If you loved me more, then. . . ."). All of this can affect both partners' self-esteem.

We all look to our romantic partners to make us feel better—sometimes in small, practical ways and sometimes in large, existential ways. We want a partner who will make us feel better about ourselves, by loving us despite our flaws and shortcomings. This emotional support is one of the great benefits of romantic relationships.

The price tag for this support and the challenge for all of us is to return the favor and love our partner despite their flaws and shortcomings, including all that really annoying stuff they do. This can feel easy to do in the bliss of new love, but can begin to feel like a bait and switch when their real self comes out ("I can't believe how irresponsible/controlling you really are!"). This is when the real

> After 12 years, our sex is more fulfilling and carefree than ever. It took me a long time to feel confident in what I wanted and be focused in bed. It's like meditation. I have to be present in my body.
>
> *ADHD man, 36, living together, been together 11–20 years*

work of relationships begins—how do you hold on to your sense of integrity by continuing to be supportive while also tolerating those parts of your partner that are different from you? How do you muscle up the courage to disclose your most sensitive thoughts and feelings and also respond well when your partner reveals theirs?

Given that our sexuality can feel like one of our most sensitive areas, it can be tempting to stick with the obvious activities that are least likely to evoke a negative response from our partner. This does tend to avoid fights except that it eventually tends to make sex less interesting. Playing it safe like this can lead to what is called left-over sex: after eliminating all those activities that one of you isn't into, you have the kinds of sex that are left over. This may be all you need, but it may also get repetitive over time and leave you unfulfilled.

The eventual itch for more challenges us to reveal more of ourselves and express some desires that our partner may not be so into—and challenges us to stand true to our desires even if our partner has a bad reaction ("You want to try *what?!*"). Our partner's opinion matters, so it can be tempting to back away from that revealed desire to lessen the conflict and/or judgment ("Umm, just kidding. I don't really want to do that. Never mind."). On the flip-side, it can feel threatening when our partner reveals a desire that we aren't into. What does this mean about them? What does it mean about me? What does it mean if we do it, or if we don't? We then

---

What would make your sex life better for you?

Vanilla [sex] is under-stimulating and frustrating to me. I seek out better experiences all the time and don't want to suppress my desires. As a submissive ADHD person, I get off on being told what to do and prefer physical intensity. BDSM provides the external reinforcement, structure, and stimulation I crave. I feel stifled and self-conscious with my partner, as he doesn't understand why anyone would need this.

ADHD woman, 27, dating, living separately,
been together 6–10 years

need to be the one to manage our response and strive to understand why our partner might be interested in this.

In these sensitive moments, we watch each other closely for signs about how this is all going over—is it OK? Can I reveal more? Should I backtrack? Do I want you to share more or to recant? Some of this communication is verbal, but a lot can be nonverbal and happen really quickly based on very small signs—and therefore be easily misread. If we ourselves are kind of uncertain about something, it's easy to read judgment into our partner's expression or response, even if they don't necessarily feel what we are assuming they do. And yet, if we believe that they do, then we may go with that and not try again later. This may put a limit on how fulfilling our sex life will become, especially if there are too many of these roadblocks and dead ends. If we rely too much on our partner's approval of our sexual desires, we won't want to risk revealing more than we know they will accept—nor challenge them to understand why something turns us on.

This desire for a better sex life is then one of the drivers that pushes us to figure out what we really want, sexually and otherwise, and to find a way to tell our partner directly and honestly—and to tolerate their disagreeing, wanting something different, and maybe even responding badly. Meanwhile, we need to do the same for them—find a way to tolerate what they reveal to us without getting judgmental or overwhelmed by it. We need to stand by what is true for us without getting offensive and we need to be able to hear what is true for them without getting defensive. Neither of these is an easy task, especially when bigger differences arise or even when small differences arise on really important topics. But this ability to keep our heads on is crucial if we are to have a productive discussion and negotiation about what we are actually going to do.

This is especially true when that discussion requires some deeper exploration of what is behind each person's preferences—why is that interesting to you? Why is it important to you that we add that to our sex life? What if we didn't? And on the other side, some exploration of why this new activity feels threatening or isn't of interest. What would it mean about you, your partner, or your relationship if you did add this to your repertoire? How would you feel about yourself if you agreed to your partner's request versus if you didn't?

There's nothing like disclosing a secret desire to a partner to challenge us to really think about what we want and why—except for maybe hearing our partner's disclosures. It can feel scary to risk judgment or even rejection but it can feel incredibly empowering to realize that we can survive that judgment—as individuals and as a couple. Being able to be OK with, and maybe even appreciative of, the differences between you allows a lot more honesty between you which gives you a lot more options about what you do together. This tends to keep passion alive over the long term.

If we tie our feelings of desirability or attractiveness to our partner's level of interest in us, it puts a lot of pressure on them to always show that interest. This may be easy to do in the early days of the relationship, but what about when real life starts to intrude on that white-hot passion? And what about when aging or busy schedules change our bodies and we don't look the same naked as we used to? All of this is a set-up for resentment from the partner who gets tired of needing to give all those reassurances and therefore a set-up for disappointment in the receiver when the partner eventually falls short. It also puts a lot of performance pressure on both partners to really look like they are all fired up, even when sometimes they are tired or preoccupied with other things. Being able to feel good about yourself, warts and all, is an important life skill that makes for much less relationship drama.

In a similar vein, tying your sexual self-esteem to your partner's response to what you're doing to them (e.g., how hard or wet they get, how quickly they orgasm, etc.) will tend to make sex into work. Rather than a shared and relaxing experience with the goal of enjoyment, it becomes a stressful performance test, probably for both of you. How much pleasure your partner is getting from having sex with you depends not only on what you are doing, but also on what they are doing for themselves (e.g., allowing themselves to get lost in the sensations of the moment, asking for what they want, etc.). Sometimes the magic happens more reliably than others. Being confident enough in one's sexual abilities makes it easier to enjoy spending the time together, regardless of speed or number of orgasms or other metrics. This also makes it easier to take suggestions and feedback. All of this ironically makes sexual experiences more likely to meet those performance standards, even if those standards are actually less important. The more pressure, the easier it is to get psyched out, which makes various performance problems (like erectile disorder) more likely. Being confident in your sexual abilities makes sex much more about the pleasure than the performance.

Between the Hammer and the Anvil

Creating and then maintaining a great sex life is no easy task. Same goes for relationships overall. The good news and bad news of committed relationships is that they are hard to get out of. This can increase the suffering when we feel trapped, but it also motivates us to do the hard work to make things better. For many people, a crummy or nonexistent sex life is too hard to tolerate, so they feel pushed to address what is getting in the way because they want to keep the relationship. Crappy sex with this partner is unacceptable, but so is ending the relationship to seek out better sex with someone new. The only option that is left is to find a way to have a good sex life and relationship with this partner. This is how sex makes us into better people—that unfulfilled desire pushes us to be a better partner and person which then also pushes our partner to do the same. Both partners benefit. And so do the kids, if you've got them.

Sex may seem like it's just a good time and hopefully it mostly is. The dirty little secret of sex is that playful sex requires work before, during, and after to keep it fun.

I love my husband. It can be difficult to balance my need for space with his hyperfocus on intimacy. In the end though his ability to hyperfocus and enthusiasm for everything in life is what I am most attracted to. The balance is something I struggle with, but having him in my life is worth every moment!
ADHD woman, 41, married, been together 11–20 years

Take Away Lessons

- Great sex and a great relationship require individual and relationship work that will make both of you better people in lots of other ways. It isn't fun, but it is worth it.

- Disagreements, and even arguments, are normal and to be expected. The challenge is to handle those disagreements respectfully and to (eventually) get to a resolution that both partners can feel OK about.

- Sex can be a double-edged sword. It can make us miserable when our sex life and relationship are tanking, but can be a powerful motivator to do that hard work to do what it takes to keep sex passionate and the relationship exciting.

- Keeping sex hot may mean finding a way to be OK with what turns us on—and our partner. Passion isn't always PC.

- All the emotional, legal, and financial entanglements of committed relationships make them harder to get out of and thereby motivate us to find ways to make it worth staying. This may cause us to be miserable at times, but hopefully it also pushes us to work on what we would rather not.

6

Respectful Communication and Productive Negotiation

Even if you got together with a sexual partner by swiping them on a dating app, there is still a lot of communication that happens before, during, and after sex. Well, for good sex. Or if you want to have sex with this person again, whether they are a one-night stand or a long-term partner.

Great technical skills don't automatically translate into great sex if they aren't applied at the right times to the right places in the right ways. This is where good communication factors in. While there is plenty of nonverbal communication going on in sex, there is a lot to be said for talking directly about what you each want, both before anything happens as well as in the midst of the action. And possibly as a debrief after. This is especially true in long-term relationships where the couple has to find a way to create a shared sexual repertoire that continues to keep both partners happy as their lives and relationship evolve over time. No easy task.

This chapter will talk about that talking. There is a lot to be said here, and probably also between you and your partner, but if you are able to keep those discussions respectful, then you can probably work through whatever differences exist. This may not be an easy process at all times, but as I described in *Chapter 5: Sex Makes You a Better Person*, it is these sometimes difficult negotiations that drive personal and relationship growth.

Be Accepting

Sex is one of those topics that people can have very strong opinions about, yet there are few right or wrong answers, so it comes down to finding a way to accept our own and our partner's turn-ons. Even if we don't understand them and even if some of those turn-ons turn us off or make us uncomfortable, we can still find a way to be OK with the idea that our partner likes it.

As a nonsexual example, my cousin absolutely loves the way that aquavit complements the flavor of liver pate. To me, it tastes like washing down cat food with turpentine. I'm certainly not going to order it for myself, but I can understand that tastes vary and am happy for him that he has found something that he enjoys so much. Fortunately, I don't need to eat half of it in order for him to have some, so it is easier to be OK with his enjoying it when I am an uninvolved observer. If for some reason, the restaurant did require me to choke down my share, then I would choose to eat somewhere else, but I wouldn't judge him for wanting it now and then. Similarly, accepting your partner's sexual interests doesn't obligate you to participate in them—whether or not to do anything about a desire is a separate discussion.

It's probably safe to say that most conversations, regardless of the topic, go better when the participants make an effort to understand each other's positions, as well as be honest about their own positions. This may be extra difficult, and therefore important, if ADHD gives the two partners very different perspectives and preferences. This requires making the sometimes (really) significant effort to not fall into judgment because it shuts down conversation and makes a productive agreement less likely. Acceptance doesn't require agreement or even understanding—I will never understand why my cousin likes that stuff but I can be OK that he does. Sometimes, though, we can understand why the other person is into something, given what else we know about them. For example, someone may understand why their partner likes to be thrown down and ravished, since it allows their partner to overcome some sexual self-doubt and feel irresistibly desired. This understanding makes for a better conversation in the moment and perhaps relationship overall since it reduces inaccurate and possibly unhelpful assumptions.

If you find that your conversations or negotiations break down, you may want to take a look at what happens and in particular look for where judgment gets in the way. If you find that you (or your partner) gets judgmental, then you may want to step back and ask yourself these questions:

- What, specifically, is it about this topic that makes you uncomfortable?
- What are the feelings behind the judgment: shame, guilt, fear, self-doubt, uncertainty, anger?
- What is your fear of what would happen if you were more OK with this desire (whether or not you act on it)?
- What can you do to calm yourself down in these moments?
- What can your partner do to help you calm yourself down in these moments?

These are hard questions and your first, easy answers are most likely not the whole story. Dig deeper. Go toward what makes you uncomfortable, rather than toward the same old easy answers. If those same old answers didn't resolve the disagreement before, they aren't going to magically do the trick this time. What else is going on here?

The goal is not only to remove obstacles to you and your partner more fully understanding each other and therefore being able to have a better conversation about what you each want your sex life to look like. This honesty and intimacy can also be incredibly exciting as you explore your own and your partner's turn-ons, especially the stuff that is at the edge of your comfort zone. It can be a blurry line between fear and excitement. Vulnerable disclosure within a context of acceptance can be transformational.

But Maybe Not Too Accepting . . .

There's a bit of a contradiction when it comes to sexual excitement. On the one hand, it's important to feel comfortable with our own sexual desires, with disclosing those desires to our partner, and with hearing our partner's disclosures. This gives us more freedom or options within a particular encounter. Within this safety, disclosure feels possible.

On the other hand, safe and comfortable can also feel boring. Where's the risky edge that makes sex feel exciting? Perhaps more for some people than others, there is something extra exciting about knowing that they are doing something transgressive, taboo, or uncommon or that they are letting themselves get swept away in the excitement of the moment and reveal something that they themselves or their partner aren't totally comfortable with (at least after the fires have burned out). This involves some risk, but adds the adrenaline that can be missing from staying well within the bounds of one's typical repertoire.

There is definitely a place in the world for easy, reliable maintenance sex. It may not rattle the plaster off the ceiling, but it keeps the couple connected. It's kind of like dinner—sometimes you go out somewhere spectacular, but mostly we have quiet dinners at home. Since not every sexual encounter can be a peak experience, being good at having (and appreciating) steady maintenance sex is important. However, the couples who are able to really keep things interesting over the decades are probably the ones who can, at least sometimes, add a little more risk and try some things. Related to this, the happiest couples from the survey were the ones who felt more comfortable asking for what they want, giving their partner what they want, sharing their sexual fantasies, and generally being more sexually generous.

The Rich Tapestry of Sexuality

Although biologically sex all boils down to getting a sperm and an egg together, the ways that humans have found to accomplish that task vary greatly. Not to mention that the vast majority of sex is recreational rather than procreational—even when a couple is trying to get pregnant, it usually takes a bunch of tries before a sperm finds an egg and an egg develops into a fully formed baby. This very low hit rate has led some to theorize that the purpose of sex is far more often about creating social or emotional connections than about creating babies—which then benefits the babies. Women can only get pregnant during a small part of each month, yet they gladly have sex all those other days. And most of the time the guys aren't complaining either about the lack of fertility. Not to mention all the folks who have a great time with same-sex encounters where there is no possibility of conception. And all the sexual activities that people enjoy that could never lead to pregnancy (e.g. oral sex).

This wide range of desires isn't limited to sex. As a species, we're pretty omnivorous. We're adapted to be able to survive and even thrive on a wide range of food options, making use of what is available in our particular environment. And I'm not even talking about scrounging for something decent at the rest stop on the turnpike. Different cultures find some items delicacies (monkey brains, anyone?) but others repulsive (gas station hot dog, anyone?). Some people are vegan by choice and others are gluten free by unfortunate circumstance. High tech gastronomy uses organic chemistry labs to fashion creations that, well, at least started out as food.

The meaning and perhaps value of a particular sexual activity depends upon the culture within which it takes place, as well as the specific subculture (e.g., a particular neighborhood), as well as the family culture. Therefore, as societies change in other ways, sex also changes. Surveys that look at the frequencies of various sexual acts find that some activities become more common whereas others less, with a general trend in the US and elsewhere of a broader range of sexual activities becoming generally acceptable. The fact that sexual trends evolve over the years seems pretty strong evidence to me that sexuality is influenced not only by biology, but also by environment and that therefore there are no sexual acts that are inherently superior to others. In addition, an individual's sexual interests probably evolve over the years—most thirty-year-olds have some different sexual interests than they did when they were teens.

All of this is to say that there are many ways to be sexual and although we all have our preferences, there is no one way that is inherently superior to others. This may be worth remembering if you find that one of your own or your partner's fantasies or desires make you uncomfortable. You don't necessarily need to like it, enjoy it in the same way, or choose to try it, but conversations without judgment tend to go over better.

What Do You Want to Do and Who Do You Want to Do it With?

When we talk about sex in general or even about specific sexual acts, we sometimes think about sex as if it was one thing, but there can be a lot of variability in not only what happens, but also in how each person feels about what is happening and what they are getting out of it. Since conversations do better with specificity so that both partners can talk about the same things at the same times, you may find it helpful to think and speak more specifically when you and your partner talk about sex.

There are many elements that contribute to how someone experiences a sexual encounter and how appealing they find it, such as:

- *Other participant(s)* Who is involved (e.g., current partner, sexy coworker, movie star, imaginary person, etc.)? What makes them appealing?

- *Activities* What is happening in that sexual encounter (e.g., oral sex, sex in the shower, getting tied up, using sex toys, etc.)? Who's doing what (e.g., active participant, observer, giver/receiver, etc.)?

- *Dynamics or mood* What is the emotional tone of the encounter (e.g., playful, hungry, romantic, "forced," etc.)? How much is each participant present in their body versus absorbed in fantasy?

- *Specific interests* Are there specific elements that are particularly arousing (e.g., large breasts, hairless, feet, being observed, etc.)?

Given everything that goes into a sexual encounter, even something as straightforward as missionary position with one's partner in the bedroom can have a lot of variability, depending on who initiated, what gets said, what each person is fantasizing about, the energy between the participants, and the overall mood. This also means that each partner can have a different experience of the same situation. Similarly, two people can love the same restaurant, but for one it's mostly about the food and for the other it's about the vibe (a.k.a. hot waiters).

What really gets you going? How well does your partner know that? What really gets your partner going? How well do you know that?

I don't believe that we are obligated to share our every sexual (or nonsexual) desire, fantasy, or thought with our partner. Having said that, the better a couple knows each other, the more likely they are to find mutually satisfying options in their sexual encounters. The rest of this chapter will help you and your partner integrate each of your individual sexual desires into a shared repertoire.

From Thought to Action

When a couple first gets together, they need to figure out how to mesh each of their individual desires into a joint endeavor. This includes relatively simple things like how hot or cold they like the car, all the way up to big questions like how many kids they want and how they handle money. Just as they need to make sure that they are compatible in all these other ways, they need to make sure that they have enough overlap and no deal breakers sexually. Some people may have these discussions right up front, but it's usually a process of gradual discovery. As they begin to be sexual together, they probably start with "standard" stuff (whatever they think that is) then gradually suggest more specific interests that they may have. No one likes to be shot down, so we usually look for signs that this new partner will be OK with our new requests. A partner who shows that they are open and even eager will tend to hear more requests, more quickly.

As these new desires get brought up, each partner needs to decide if they want to add it to their shared repertoire and, if so, how. Because many of us feel sensitive about our sexual interests, it's easy to feel judged—and unfortunately, also easy to feel judgmental about our partner's interests if they differ too much from our own. This sensitivity makes it easy for discussions to break down, leading to a lot of hurt feelings and perhaps avoidance of subsequent discussions. This places predictable limits on at least one partner's sexual satisfaction within the relationship, but probably both. Not that partners are morally obligated to disclose their every dark little secret, but one or both of them may be happier if they were able to share a little more. The following steps can help you and your partner communicate better about each of your sexual desires and negotiate if and how they get integrated into your shared sex life.

Step 1: Identify Your Sexual Desires

Before we can have a productive discussion with anyone else, we need to put in the work to be clear about our own desires. It's easier to wait for our partner to present an idea and then decide whether or not we like it. And it's definitely easier to just expect our partner to know how to please us, sexually and otherwise, even if we haven't yet figured it out—which is really quite a trick when you think about it. This is part of that new relationship glow—"this person is so amazing they definitely just know!" Unfortunately, even the most perceptive partner eventually missteps enough times that we are faced with the reality of needing to actually talk through what we each like and don't like.

Whether you are in a new relationship or have been together forever, it's still worth spending some time thinking about your sexual desires, since they very well may have evolved since the beginning of the relationship. It's good to check in with ourselves every now and then.

How well do you feel you know yourself sexually? To what extent have you explored various sexual options, at least mentally, to see how you felt about them? Sexuality is a big topic with all sorts of influences on how we think and feel about it. Consider the following questions:

- Where did you learn about sex—first and along the way?
- What influence did your family have on how you feel about sex?

- What influence did your friends have on how you feel about sex?
- What influence did society at large have on how you feel about sex?
- What influence did media, including porn, have on how you feel about sex?
- What influence did each of your relationships/sexual partners have on your sexuality?
- In what ways do these various influences agree and conflict?
- Do the lessons learned from these past influences still fit your life now?
- What parts of your current sex life do you really love? Why?
- What parts of your current sex life feel unsatisfying or even problematic? Why?
- What sexual activities from your past do you miss now?
- What do you wish you could try sexually?
- What sexual experiences make great fantasies, even though you don't necessarily want to act on them? What is it about those fantasies that turns you on?

There is no speed bonus for answering these questions as quickly as possible. Instead, linger over them. You may also find it helpful to talk them through with your partner, a therapist if you have one, or possibly a close friend, in order to get their perspective on you.

As you reflect upon each of these questions, you will almost certainly find both parallels and contradictions. Sexuality is complicated and multifaceted and we receive all sorts of messages about it, so it takes a willingness to tolerate ambiguity and contradictions in order to really sort through it all. For example, you may wonder, "How can I be this kind of a person at work or with my kids, but also sometimes want to be this kind of a person during sex?" People are multifaceted and bring different parts of themselves to different situations. Or we need to reconcile what we actually want and who we are with the messages we have received about what we should want or be. The answers to all of these questions can help you sort through it all and then form a foundation of self-understanding to help you better answer this last question:

• What does your ideal, but realistic, sex life look like now?

You may be able to identify where some of your preferences, turn-ons, and turn-offs came from but others may remain a mystery. You may find that you have an easier time feeling comfortable with your desires if you understand where they came from or why they get you going. Also, the more comfortable you are in your preferences, the easier it is to share it with your partner, if you choose to. This intimacy of knowing and being known is part of what makes relationships special, but sharing these desires with your partner also means that you can choose to enact some of them or just have fun together with the fantasies. It makes sex hotter.

Feeling secure in your preferences also enables you to better weather an initial bad, weird, judgmental, or awkward response from your partner if you disclose it, without getting angry or defensive or immediately retracting it. Those moments of disclosure can be scary because we value our partner's opinion and there is a risk in sharing something new. Unfortunately, if we play it too safe and only request what we already know will get a positive response, then our sexual repertoire will likely remain rather small and sex may get repetitively boring. This reminds me of an old Robin Williams line, where he says, "I don't understand all the hoopla about same sex marriage. After all, anyone who has been married for a while knows that it's all the same sex anyway." If we are too hesitant to admit to ourselves and our partner what we want, then our sex life will get stale.

In addition, if we are uncomfortable about something about ourselves, we may be extra sensitive about our partner's response and assume that they are being critical, even at times when they aren't directly commenting on it. Or we may assume that they will respond badly to it because we ourselves aren't at peace with it, but because we never actually say it out loud, we never have the opportunity to find out that they may actually respond better than we feared. We may even blame their disapproval (real or assumed) for our own negative or ambivalent feelings about our desires. This is one of the ways that couples get all tangled up—they blame each other for what they feel rather than stepping back and really sorting out how they themselves feel.

For example, if a guy occasionally looks at porn but feels kind of guilty about it and hasn't reconciled within himself whether it's OK to be sexually attracted to other women, he may assume that his wife is too uptight to understand why he enjoys it and then use that as a justification for not bringing up the topic. Because he hasn't discussed with her where porn fits into their relationship, he feels guilty for hiding it from her which gets blurred together with the question of whether he feels that it is OK to be attracted to others. He may then get weird and awkward any time porn or even masturbation gets brought up, however obliquely, which causes his wife to also get a little weird because she senses his tension. He picks up on that and takes it as proof of her disapproval and therefore all the more reason to avoid that conversation. All this mental machination is going on and we don't even know how his wife actually feels about it! The better he can figure out where he stands on all this, including the related issue of hiding it from his wife, the better able he will be to talk to her directly about it. She may not be happy about his being turned on by porn, but it will almost certainly be a better conversation if he brings it up in a direct and confident way than if he waits to get caught.

It's also worth noting here that sex is one of those topics where there can be a big difference between what people say and what they do. It can be really hard to get an accurate reading of others' sexual practices based on what they bring up in conversation or acknowledge. There have been countless examples of politicians getting in trouble for saying one thing but doing another, but the only difference with politicians is that the rest of us don't wind up on the news when we get caught. Ultimately, it doesn't matter whether your turn-ons are really common or rather unique, but it is likely that there are quite a few people out there who are at least turned on by, if not acting on, the same things that you find arousing.

Because sexuality is such a personal and core aspect of who we are, feeling at peace with your turn-ons and sexually confident can help you feel more confident in other parts of your life. Doing the work to figure yourself out and feel OK about what you find can benefit you in nonsexual ways as well.

Step 2: Understand Each Other's Sexual Desires

Since sex is (at least sometimes) a shared experience, we need to share our preferences with our partner so that we can each know what our options are. Otherwise sex would just be a bunch of awkward, silent staring at each other where neither person knows what to do. Whereas most people feel completely comfortable disclosing their favorite color, sharing sexual preferences can feel like the most personal or revealing disclosures, so it is easy to hold back in order to avoid any feared judgment. It's also easy to feel threatened by our partner's interests (or what we worry their interests might be) if they push us past our comfort zone.

This may all be especially true when a couple has struggled in other ways and bears too many scars from those unproductive battles. If undiagnosed and/or insufficiently unmanaged ADHD has brought out the worst in both of you and has had a negative effect on your relationship overall, it can make it harder to feel comfortable sharing on sensitive subjects like sexuality. This is yet another reason why it's so important for both partners to work at getting that ADHD under control. If this is true for you, then perhaps check out *Chapter 3: Make the Most of Treatment*. And if there are other issues between you, then work on those, too. It's not just about ADHD.

Intimacy, the process of knowing our partner and being known by them, isn't always easy and we can't request to only disclose the parts of ourselves that will be received well. And yet, intimate relationships challenge us to accept not only ourselves, but also our partner, to face our hesitations and perhaps choose to disclose anyway and to tolerate the discomfort that our partner's disclosure evokes in us and respond well anyway. The more secure we are in ourselves, the easier it is to put something out there for possible judgment and to observe our partner with less of our own judgment. This ability to be confident and present, even in the face of disagreement, enables us to be more honest and foster greater intimacy with our partner. This is definitely easier said than done, but is perhaps the most important of all relationship skills. Because sexuality involves more vulnerability than many other topics, it becomes especially relevant here.

Exploring each other's turn-ons can also be a lot of fun. The vulnerability and risk of these disclosures can add to the excitement of it all. Some of these conversations will happen in the heat of the sweaty moment, whereas others will happen fully dressed in front of the TV—"Hmm, what do you think about that?" There's something to be said for a certain amount of openness to new experiences, while also stopping short of joining a cult.

Exploring each other's turn-ons can also drive personal and relationship growth by getting into sensitive areas. Approach these conversations with curiosity as you seek to better understand your partner's sexuality. And perhaps curiosity about your reactions to those disclosures—what do they evoke in you and why? Does it tell you anything interesting and possibly new about your partner? If it makes you uncomfortable, step back and ask yourself how else you could understand this new information. Ask for clarification if you need more information and ask for a break if you need some space. Don't assume that expressing a sexual desire equates to a request—we will talk next about how to negotiate what actually happens with these disclosures. Try to avoid judgment or deciding too quickly what you approve of or not. If something weirds you out, then ask your partner more about why it fires them up. You may still not get it, but you know them a little better at least, which is usually a good thing. And sometimes we can enjoy our partner's enjoyment, even if we don't enjoy the act itself.

Some of these conversations may go south if a disclosure evokes a response along the lines of, "I can't believe you're into *that.*" These are those million-dollar moments where at least one of you needs to find a way to hold onto yourself, keep your head on, and not take your partner's words or feelings personally. If you're on the receiving end of one of those comments, give your overwhelmed partner some time to calm down and wrap their head around this new disclosure and what its implications might be. Remind yourself of the bigger picture of this relationship, the other parts of it that are good, the ways that you have resolved disagreements in the past, etc. Most importantly, focus more on breathing that reacting. In these emotional moments, our first reactions usually aren't our best ones. Don't add any fuel to the fire of your partner's emotions. Give them some space to get their head back on, then continue the conversation: explain why this disclosure was important for you to do and then explain what it does and doesn't mean, as well as what your intentions are about acting on it.

If you are the partner who is on the receiving end of a disclosure that makes you uncomfortable, try to stay in the moment without letting your mind run away with possibilities. If you need some time alone or in silence to think about this and perhaps calm down, then ask for it. Once you are able, come back to your partner and try to focus more on asking questions than on making statements or setting boundaries—your first job is to really understand what your partner is saying, rather than running away with assumptions. Use curiosity to gain understanding, with no expectation of any decisions to be made yet. (That comes in the next step.)

New couples need to have more of these conversations as they each learn more about their new partner, but even couples that have been together a long time may need to occasionally have a conversation to talk about sexual desires. Sometimes it can take a while to get comfortable enough within oneself about a turn-on to feel comfortable sharing it with someone else, even a long-term partner—or especially with a long-term partner whose opinions matter the most. Sometimes our desires evolve and new interests appear. So this ability to have deep conversations continues to be important.

All this discussion of disclosure brings up a related topic which is the difference between secret and private—or, are we required to reveal our every fantasy, desire, and passing horny thought? It depends. Each couple needs to decide how much disclosure they want. Some may feel that their partner is being unfairly withholding if they don't tell all, or interpret their silence as a lack of trust in them. Others may feel, perhaps accurately, that their partner will not react well to some disclosures and that the relationship would not be improved, at this time, with that disclosure. Or perhaps they want to enjoy some of their fantasies on their own, unaffected by anyone else's impressions.

Unless you find something in your partner's browser history or a mysterious receipt from the hardware store, you can't know what dirty thoughts roll around inside their head. I can respect a Don't Ask, Don't Tell approach for some thoughts, while also appreciating that relationships are often more fulfilling and exciting when there is at least enough that is shared. There is a balance that each couple needs to strike on this that is almost certainly influenced by where they are in their relationship (honeymooners versus old timers, currently on solid versus shaky ground) and what else is going on in their lives. The question I would ask you is, do you feel like your current level of disclosure with your partner is working well for you?

These discussions about sexual disclosure are important ones and therefore deserve good circumstances so they can go well. This means, not last thing at night. Not right before or during sex where one of you won't appreciate a detour if things go poorly. Not when the kids might run in. And although ADHD meds may not have a clear benefit on how the sex goes, they probably do have a benefit on how these types of conversations go. Medication can help not only with paying attention and listening, but also with emotion regulation. If you find that conversations generally go better when the medication is active, then make a point of taking your meds and then talk during those times—and also resist having the conversation when it is less likely to go well. We want a success here.

Step 3: Negotiate the Differences: Create Our Sexual Desires

There are many, many ways that people can get turned on sexually—what is exhilarating for one person may be a total turn-off for another. There are plenty of theories, but we still don't know definitively why people develop the turn-ons and turn-offs that they do—some combination of nature and nurture? It's probably more likely that we can add activities to our turn-on list more so than remove them, at least on purpose, but our sexual desires can evolve over the years and decades. Sometimes this is the influence of our partners and our experiences with them, sometimes it's part of our overall personality development. (For a really interesting deep dive into sexual desires, check out Dr. Justin Lehmiller's *Tell Me What You Want: The Science of Sexual Desire and How It Can Help You Improve Your Sex Life*.) Regardless, some variety over the decades probably keeps couples more interested and engaged over the long haul.

> *What would make your sex life better for you?*
> Anything new, literally anything.
> *ADHD man, 32, dating, living separately,*
> *been together 3–5 years*

Wherever they came from, we can divide our sexual interests into four categories:

1. *What I know I like to do.* These are the activities that we are comfortable with and enjoy doing.
2. *What I am willing to do for you.* Some activities may not be all that inherently interesting, but we are willing to do them because our partner enjoys them. Sometimes our partner's pleasure makes an otherwise uninteresting activity much more exciting. Sometimes it's just about generosity.
3. *What I might be willing to try.* These are the activities that, under the right circumstances, we would consider trying. Sometimes the hesitation has to do with our own comfort about this desire, sometimes we're concerned about how our partner would react to the suggestion. Sometimes there is a recognition that it sounds great in fantasy but that the reality may be a bit messier.
4. *What I am not interested in trying (at least now).* These are the activities that actively turn us off because they feel threatening, discomforting, or just weird. While most of these activities probably won't go from a yuck to a yum, perhaps some of them will. (Never say never.)

You may find it helpful to think about which activities fit where for you, as well as discuss them with your partner. Your current sex life probably consists mostly of the overlap between things that you and your partner both like to do, with perhaps a few things that you are each willing to do for the other. The activities that at least one of you would like to try (and the other is willing) are your areas of potential experimentation and the activities that at least one of you is not interested in trying are your current sexual limits.

Good behavior from our partners, by not being demanding or guilting, will make us more generous and willing—as will general good behavior outside of bed, too. Direct requests, with an ability to handle rejection, tend to get us more of what we want. If there is something that you would like to try but your partner isn't so into it, ask what would make it more interesting or safer for them. Perhaps explain why it turns you on and why you would like to do it with *them*—help them find a way to be turned on by it.

If there is something that you would like to try but your partner is really not into it, then think about and explore if there are other ways to have a similar experience or get that same physical and/or psychological feeling from doing something else that would be acceptable. Happy couples find ways to ensure that both partners are getting enough of what they want without either feeling coerced.

Ultimately, you may need to give up some options, at least for now, but that may be easier to accept if you feel like at least you had a real discussion about it. Pulling off a productive conversation on potentially emotionally loaded topics like sex can sometimes be a real challenge. Most of us probably aren't very good at it when we first start having those serious relationship discussions, but that process of fumbling our way through helps us get better at identifying our needs and desires, expressing them in a helpful way, empathizing with our partner's needs and desires, tolerating sometimes difficult loggerheads, and ultimately coming to a mutual agreement. I wrote about this process in *Chapter 5: Sex Makes You a Better Person*. If you feel stuck in your sexual negotiations, this would definitely be worth checking out, as would *Chapter 12: When the Negotiations Break Down*.

Step 4: Negotiate the Differences: How Often Do We Do it?

It's not uncommon for the two members of a couple to have at least somewhat different desires for the frequency of sex—about a third of the time it's the woman with the higher drive. There's probably a fair amount of biology at work that determines our desired frequency, but there is also a lot of social learning that influences how comfortable we are acting on those sexual desires when they do begin to bubble up. It can also be very situational, based on how happy or stressed we are, comfort and/or novelty of our partner, what else is going on in our life, the physical setting, etc. In addition, Emily Nagoski, PhD has written extensively on responsive desire, wherein some people can get turned on and really enjoy sex once they get going, but don't find themselves desiring sex as often as those with more spontaneous desire tend to (more on this in a few paragraphs).

There is a lot that can influence how often we want to have sex. But even if a couple somehow has exactly the same drive, they won't always want sex at exactly the same times, so there is still a need to negotiate out those differences when one wants it and the other one doesn't.

Whether you're the partner who wants more sex overall (or just wants it more right now) or the one who generally wants it less, it all comes down to generosity—from both partners. For example, the person who is less interested may generously offer to do something to give their partner a good time, even though they're not in the mood themselves. However, what is offered may be different from what their partner was hoping for, so that is where their generosity comes in—to graciously be happy about what is being offered, rather than get stuck on what isn't; to enjoy what they are getting, rather than wishing for more.

At other times when one of the partners is not interested in any sexual activity at that time, then the act of generosity may involve allowing their partner to freely meet their own needs on their own if they choose to. The generosity for their partner involves being good about their disappointment, making a shared sexual experience more likely next time, since nothing kills sexual desire better than guilt and resentment. Basically, it comes down to asking respectfully and answering respectfully. Plus, if you both feel comfortable asking for sex, as well as declining it, confident that you will get a decent response either way, there will probably be more requests and therefore more opportunities to do things together.

Emily Nagoski, PhD has written in *Come As You Are* about how sexual desire can be both spontaneous and responsive. Sometimes desire arises seemingly on its own or quickly from passing sexy thoughts, without much effort. Sometimes though, desire takes longer to build and you may find that you don't start wanting sex until you have already started flirting, kissing, and touching. In other words, sometimes desire follows activity. This should absolutely not be used as a manipulative justification to push someone to do something they don't want to do, but if you know that you tend to get in the mood if you allow yourself to start down that road, then you can try to start things on good faith, with the idea that you may wind up wanting it.

Yet again, generosity here is key. If you feel generous and decide to play along to see if you can kindle some desire, then you still retain the right to change course along the way if the spark never turns into a flame. However, you can increase the odds by educating your partner on what to do to help you find that interest. The generosity on the more interested partner's part is to be good about it if plans change. This good behavior will be rewarded with more opportunities next time to try again. As in so many other ways, good sex is a collaborative process and generosity tends to be a good thing in relationships. Good deeds tend to be rewarded, both in bed and out.

Each couple will need to find its rhythm of how often they are sexual together. Couples who have more similar desired frequencies will probably have an easier time finding a satisfying rhythm, whereas those with much larger discrepancies will have to work harder to negotiate the difference. In the survey, there was a smaller difference in desired frequency when it was the woman who had

---

What would make your sex life better for you?
Groping my breasts while I do my chores and smacking my ass when I walk by is NOT foreplay. Neither is cat calling me when I leave to take the kids to school. A kiss goodbye without honking my breast would be nice too. I feel like I am married to an impulsive teen with raging hormones. Controlling the impulsive groping and constant sex remarks would make my sex life better. I have to be in the mood to have sex . . . and the constant daily badgering and groping is a MAJOR turn-off.
Non-ADHD woman, 43, married,
been together 11–20 years

ADHD, so those couples (on average) may have an easier time of this than the couples where it's the guy who has ADHD. This greater discrepancy may have been influenced by the fact that the women without ADHD also rated more things as a barrier to a better sex life and rated those barriers as being greater, so these couples will likely have to work harder at overcoming those barriers. This will likely involve a combination of actually addressing some of the barriers so they are less of a problem, as well as working on ways to pump up desire and be sexual even when some barriers remain, since if we wait for everything to be resolved, none of us would ever have sex.

The challenge for every couple is to get to a place where both partners feel satisfied with how often they have sex, even if it is a little more or a little less than their ideal amount. Since satisfaction is a function of experiences versus expectations, we can find that happiness both by flexing on how often we have sex and also on how often we feel we can reasonably expect sex. Finding this happy middle ground involves recognizing both partners' desires as valid, accepting other time demands yet still striving for something better, and then finding something that you can both be happy with.

In the survey, the folks who were happiest in their relationships were more comfortable being sexually generous when they weren't in the mood, so there is a lot that the higher desire partner can do to up their numbers that probably have nothing to do with sex. If you are the higher desire partner, think about and also ask your partner about how to make the relationship overall better, particularly in the ways that will make sex more likely. If you are the lower desire partner, perhaps do the same, if you want to want more sex. For more on reconciling differences in desired frequency, see the section *Disagreements About How Often We Do It* in *Chapter 12: When the Negotiations Break Down*.

Step 5: Negotiate the Alternatives: What Can I Do When You're Not in the Mood?

In addition to all this talk of shared sexual experiences, it's probably also worth spending some time talking about what each of your options are if one of you is horny and the other one just isn't. What are the acceptable options here? Is masturbation acceptable? If so, which accoutrements can be added into the mix: porn, written erotica, sex toys, etc.? And do you want to know what your partner is up to, or would you prefer to not know?

And what about sexy activities that don't actually involve masturbation or orgasm—how do you each feel about them? This could involve reading awesomely trashy erotica, listening to sex-related podcasts, visiting celebrity news websites "for the articles," or intensively studying the lingerie catalogs that show up with relentless frequency in your mailbox. These aren't sexual experiences per se, but they are certainly more sexual than most of the mundane stuff that we fill our days with and they can certainly feed the sexual imagination. How do you each feel about these sorts of activities?

There are no right or wrong answers here for any of this, so much as that it is generally helpful for couples to actually talk about this stuff, so there are fewer unhappy discoveries. It's always amazing to me how many clients I've had who have been married for a long time and have no idea about their partner's masturbation habits. Not that we are required to disclose these things to each other, but it can be interesting or even arousing to know this about your partner. Plus, the better you understand your partner's erotic landscape, and vice versa, the more likely you each are to create more fulfilling shared experiences. Having these conversations ahead of time can also prevent sudden arguments when an unexpected discovery forces awareness that both partners are not on the same page on this topic.

Masturbation is a big enough topic that it deserves its own chapter, so you can read much more about it in *Chapter 10: Taking Some Personal Time: Masturbation*, as well as about the possibly equally large topic of porn in *Chapter 11: What about Porn?*. As with everything else related to sex, and relationships more broadly, what you and your partner decide about solo activities is a lot less important than that you put in the work to come to a mutual decision about it.

The Importance of Being Good at Rejection

We don't always get what we want, at least exactly when or how we want it. Yet how we handle the inevitable disappointments affects how likely we are to get what we want next time or get what we want in other ways. It all spills forward. Therefore, being good at both receiving and giving rejection are really important skills in long-term relationships, especially with something that can get as sensitive as sex. Good behavior tends to be rewarded and bad behavior tends to be punished—and we can't expect our partner to behave better than we do.

There can definitely be a momentum effect in couples—how we respond to this current situation is influenced by what came before. Nothing in a relationship happens in a vacuum. When we're feeling generally pretty good about each other, we tend to give a bit more benefit of the doubt and respond well, even when our partner has a bit of an edge. When we're feeling angry, frustrated, or resentful, the momentum goes against us and it can feel like our partner is guilty until proven innocent. Therefore, it's that much more important to be able to maintain that positive momentum and to bounce back from negative feelings. This resiliency is a crucial relationship skill since life (and our partners) will inevitably bring frustrations and disappointments. Couples that had extra struggles from undiagnosed ADHD may have to work even harder now to overcome that negative momentum—and will benefit all the more from doing the work to make things good.

When it comes to sexual negotiations, whether it's about having sex now or what makes it into your shared sexual repertoire, the

---

What would make your sex life better for you?

If my husband did not become hyperfocused on the need for sex. My sex drive comes and goes depending on stress. He uses sex as a coping tool. Being asked to have sex without any foreplay for me is a turn off. The more, however, I say not right now the more hyperfocused he becomes which leads to a vicious circle of neither of our needs being met. What would make it better would be if he would be less hyperfocused and worried that it "will never happen again."

Non-ADHD woman, 41, married, been together 11–20 years

goal is to keep the discussions focused on how to reconcile what you each want sexually, without too much mental math going on in the background about how your partner will respond if there is a difference of opinion. If one or both of you are worried about feeling either guilted or ignored, it's hard to have a direct conversation and less likely that you will both be happy with the outcome. And yet, ADHD (especially if undiagnosed) tends to make both guilting and avoidance more likely, as the partners try to figure out how to handle those seemingly unpreventable frustrations. It totally makes sense, but doesn't actually help.

Both guilting and avoidance tend to drain away desire, not just in that moment, but also into future encounters if resentments remain—and to spill out into lots of nonsexual situations, too. Both guilting and avoidance are unfair emotional manipulations and, not surprisingly, each tends to provoke the other. We all have our less than perfect moments, but couples who can find ways to talk directly about what they each want and what they are each willing to give tend to not have to fall back on these less productive attempts to resolve disagreements.

If you feel that there is too much guilting or avoidance in your sex life (or relationship overall), then it will almost certainly be worth trying to find some better ways to negotiate with your partner. You may wind up talking about sexual matters as well as nonsexual matters, but probably more important is to talk about *how* you talk about these topics. The process, not the content—what do you each do in those conversations, what do you each evoke in the other, how else could you each handle yourselves in those sensitive moments? If you and your partner find that you can't come to some agreement on a particular topic, then you may find it helpful to step back from that content and instead focus on the process by which you discuss it. It's likely that using a different process (e.g., taking a break when someone gets worked up, being more fully honest about what you feel, asking more exploratory questions about what your partner feels, etc.) will move the conversation along better.

Although the responses from the survey were mixed at best when it comes to the effect of stimulant medication on sex, I would venture to say that these potentially difficult conversations will probably go better if they are had when the medication is working well. And not at the end of the night when everyone is tired. The medication can help the person with ADHD to attend better to what their partner is saying as well as perhaps put a bit more of a pause in before reacting to either person's emotions. If you find that these conversations go better when medication is involved, then you each have a responsibility to take advantage of the times when the medication is active, rather than procrastinating and waiting until it gets to be too late. While we can all be tempted to avoid potentially hairy conversations, they tend to go better if we bite the bullet and make them happen under better circumstances—which probably makes them less hairy.

Desire Killer #1: Guilting

I've written elsewhere about the importance of sometimes being generous with our partner. When it comes to sex, this could involve allowing ourselves to be convinced to do something together when we're not initially in the mood. If the consenting partner feels like they have a genuine option to pass, but they decide of their own free will to participate, then this will probably be a positive experience for both. But if the consenting partner feels pressured and like they don't have an easy option to say no, then at least one person, but probably both, won't feel good about it—before, during, or after.

Feeling pressured or guilted makes sex feel like a chore ("Crap, it's Tuesday—gotta take out the recycling. And have sex."). It's hard to get the best out of your partner if they don't really want to be there. So it's technically sex but much less exciting than it could be. It may succeed in giving the initiating partner an orgasm, but it's hard to feel good about sex with someone who is clearly not that interested in being there.

> Due to his immature coping skills, hubby used to call me the frigid midget when I was too tired for sex after working hard all day. This made me feel unloved which made it even more unlikely for us to make love. . . . What a silly thing to do.
> *Non-ADHD woman, 46, married, been together 21+ years*

If you find that there are times when sex feels more about obligation than desire, it's probably really important that you take a look at what is going on. If you find yourself using guilt (at least sometimes) to get your partner to agree, you need to ask yourself what is happening in you, in your partner, in your relationship, and/or in your sex life that makes that feel like a viable option. For example, does your partner's lack of interest in sex feel like a lack of interest in you or a comment on your sexual desirability? Have you really invested yourself in understanding what will help your partner be more interested in sex and then doing those things? Are there unresolved relationship issues that are tanking good feelings for each other? Are there problems with pain, performance, or pleasure when you and your partner do have sex?

If you find yourself giving in to guilt, then you need to ask yourself some similar questions about what is happening in you, in your partner, in your relationship, and/or in your sex life that makes it feel like you can't say no and stand by it. What is it about your partner's reaction that feels so difficult to tolerate? If your partner reacts poorly to a no, then that reaction probably needs to become the topic of conversation. Why is it so hard for them to be respectful about the fact that you aren't interested? Explain the effect that feeling pressured has on your feelings about sex, about your partner, and about the relationship overall. If the goal is a better sex life, then finding better ways to decide when and how to have sex is crucial. You may also need to explore and discuss what are the other issues that perhaps need to be addressed first in order to help you want sex more.

Using guilt, in small or large doses, may work in the short-term but tends to poison the relationship in the long term. It involves unfair manipulation by one partner, but the consenting partner also plays their part by allowing it to happen by not holding appropriate boundaries. This leads to two complementary questions:

- Why can't the initiating partner tolerate not getting what they want and discuss their desires in more productive ways?
- Why can't the consenting partner tolerate their partner's disappointment and discuss their own desires in more productive ways?

These can be really big questions that may go way beyond sex, but if you and your partner can each work on your part of it, you may find that your sex life and relationship overall both improve. This is one of those ways that sex drives personal and relationship growth.

Desire Killer #2: Avoidance

Guilting can be pretty obvious and most people would agree that it isn't a good way to get what you want. By contrast, avoidance can be a little bit harder to spot—after all, it's the absence of something. Avoidance may involve not only finding ways out of having sex with one's partner, but also dodging conversations about the lack of sex—and maybe even denying that there is any avoidance of those conversations. ("Huh? What? I am?")

Someone who is avoiding sex (or whatever) may use semi-plausible but ultimately empty reasons for not wanting to have sex now (e.g., "I'm just kind of tired."), as a way out of getting into the real reasons behind the lack of interest. Or perhaps they are clear about their reason for not wanting to have sex (e.g., "you're just not nice enough to me,"), but then aren't willing to work on overcoming that reason—which may suggest that there are some deeper reasons at work that they aren't acknowledging. Some folks may be so good at avoidance that they keep things from getting anywhere close to sex, so their partner doesn't even have the opportunity to make a move; for example, by being so immersed in the kids or work that they rarely have alone time with their partner. They may even use guilt to push back their partner's sexual requests (e.g., "How could you even ask, knowing how much I have to do?"). Other folks may say that they are potentially open to sex but then require things to

> She wants me to not mention sex generally during the week and on weekend days, as she thinks I'm being passive aggressive, but I'm just really in love and lust for her and want to express it and seem to not be able to do that. . . .
> *ADHD man, 56, married, been together 11–20 years*

be so perfect in the relationship, in the house, and in their life that it never gets there. In this case, the goal is not about having everything just right, it's about finding reasons to not have sex.

Some folks may also be kind of ambivalent about sex and therefore be unclear in their own mind about their level of interest (e.g., "I'm kind of in the mood, but I'm still pretty angry with her."). This then gives their partner mixed signals about whether they should or shouldn't try to move things along. The partner may then vacillate between trying to make a move and backing off—they may just try to push things along or they may give up. Odds are that neither partner will feel great about either outcome, nor enjoy the process. A direct conversation about the ambivalent partner's hesitation may help clarify what is happening and what each of their options are.

While we all absolutely have the right to not be sexual when we don't want to be, stonewalling is rarely an effective problem-solving method, regardless of the topic. While it may avoid an uncomfortable discussion in the moment, it just kicks the problem down the road, but with more confusion and/or resentment added into the mix. Avoiding tends to evoke other problematic behaviors on the other person's part: guilting, begging, demanding, whining, avoiding other parts of the relationship, and/or getting needs met in other (probably less consensual) ways. Let the good times roll. . . .

So it's OK to not have sex, but you should probably then be honest with your partner about why you don't want to, especially if it involves anything significant beyond not being in the mood at that moment. We talked in the earlier section on guilting that it's

---

What would make your sex life better for your partner?
    The only thing I can think of that would make her sex life better would be for me to never ask her for sex and leave her to her sex toys instead.
        Non-ADHD man, 51, engaged and living together,
            been together 6–10 years

important to be good at taking rejection well, but it is also equally important to be good at giving rejection well. In this case, that means being able to say no directly, honestly, and decently. This means resisting the urge to throw in a dash of guilt of your own (e.g., "How could you even ask at a time like this?"). Use your words to express how you feel—get the job done without laying it on too thick.

If you find yourself tempted to avoid sex with your partner, especially if this has been going on for a while, then you should probably ask yourself what is getting in the way. What would help you want sex more? Is it about sex in general or about sex with your partner specifically? Do you need to stand up more for what you want sexually? Does your partner need to step down a bit on what they want sexually? Is it about your sex life specifically or something in your relationship?

And if you're not talking with your partner about all this, especially if they are trying to talk to you about it, then you need to spend some time on that bigger question, too. What is it about that discussion that you are fearful of? What is it about your partner's reaction that you are trying to prevent? What do you worry might happen if you opened up that conversation? You may find it most productive to start by talking about the avoidance, rather than about sex itself. Why are you hesitant to discuss it? How does your partner see what is happening here? What would help the two of you to have a good conversation? What might be a sign that it's time to take a break?

If your partner is avoiding not only sex but also talking about that lack of sex, then you may also want to start by talking about the avoidance. Why does your partner feel uncomfortable about getting into this topic? What can you do to make the conversation easier for them? If you find yourself still stuck, then you may want to tell your partner about how the lack of discussion, as well as perhaps the lack of sex, is affecting you and how it is affecting other parts of the relationship—again, don't lay it on too thick. You can't decide what anyone else will do, but you can be clear about the effect of their actions on you and what you feel like your options are. You may need to broach the topic more than once and you may need to talk about it more than once to cover everything, get into some of the deeper reasons, and come to some sort of mutual resolution.

It Takes Two to Tango

One of the realities of adult relationships is that we can't make our partner do what they don't want to do, unless they agree to it. However, we can be clear about what it is that we feel and want and we can make an effort to try to understand what our partner feels and wants. We can also set some limits on what kinds of behavior we're willing to tolerate and make choices about how we will respond to less productive behaviors.

In relationships, we respond based on what has come before. If you don't like what your partner is doing, then it may be worth thinking about what you can do differently in order to draw out different responses from them. As we just discussed with guilting and avoidance, both partners play their part and both partners have the ability to shift the dynamic. If you feel stuck in a problematic dynamic with your partner, then doing more of the same will likely bring you more of the same. What can you do differently? What are you responding to in your partner's behavior—and what is your partner responding to in yours? The better you understand this back and forth (and can be honest about your own part in it) the better you can see what your options are for more productive responses. And it probably goes without saying that the easy responses are the ones that you're already doing, so the new ones will tend to be those that take more willpower.

It's your choice as to whether the effort of the new responses is worth it, but it's probably unlikely that much will change unless at least one of you tries to do something different. If you're the one reading this, then that probably means you. (Damn!) Take heart, though, in the fact that regardless of which one of you initiates, the other will have to follow suit with some changes of their own. So in the end, there is still justice. (Fine. . . .)

Take Away Lessons

- As a species, humans have found a wide range of ways to get turned on and express their sexuality. As individuals, we probably have some pretty strong preferences about what turns us on or off. As much as we may feel that some are more right than others, ultimately it's just a matter of opinion.

- Every individual and couple needs to figure out what is and isn't of interest and perhaps why. This may involve some serious thinking and deep conversations.

- They then need to negotiate the differences and create a sexual repertoire that keeps both partners satisfied, without excessively pushing either one's discomfort.

- Couples who are able to keep their sex life hot (and relationship great) are able to handle rejection without guilting or avoidance.

7

It's All Foreplay

You can meet someone in a bar or on a hookup app and have sex with them with minimal prior interaction, but when it comes to sex within a committed relationship, sex always occurs within the context of the entirety of the relationship and everything else going on in each person's life, including all sorts of things that have nothing at all to do with sex but still impact it. Therefore, to create and maintain a good sex life, you and your partner need to sometimes address the nonsexual matters that could interfere.

Some people's sex drive is relatively unaffected by these nonsexual matters (or even heightened in response to stress), whereas others find that it takes very little to push their desire for sex onto the back burner—or off the stove and out of the kitchen. There is a wide range of normal on this dimension, so there is nothing right or wrong here, but a couple who wants to have sex with each other needs to find ways to get onto the same page at the same time, at least sometimes.

In the survey, sexual satisfaction and relationship satisfaction were highly correlated, something that totally makes sense and has

> *What would make your sex life better for your partner?*
> My partner tells me he likes to get me in the car and drive because we talk and things don't pull my attention for a while. Making time for him is all it takes.
> *ADHD woman, 36, engaged and living together, been together 6–10 years*

been proven by lots of folks before me. It's also safe to say that the influence goes both directions. If you want to have better sex, you probably need to work on your relationship. If you want a better relationship, you probably need to work on your sex life. However, these two satisfactions aren't 100% correlated which means that each is also influenced by other factors, but the big overlap between them makes it hard to escape the fact that working on either one benefits the other. Therefore, even if one of them is much more important to you than the other, you should probably still work on both if you want to have the biggest impact—including on your partner and their willingness to do their work.

The goal of this chapter is to improve your sex life by helping you work on all those factors that influence how likely you are to have sex, many of which come down to improving your relationship. So, it's really about improving your relationship. So that you can have more sex. . . . Like I said, these two overlap a lot.

Bottom line: it's all foreplay.

It All Spills Forward

Relationships are always the culmination of everything that came before the present moment—the good, the bad, the struggles, the misses, the successes, the failures. If you've been together a while and gotten through that easy first year or two, then you likely have had all sorts of experiences together. Probably more were positive than negative or you wouldn't still be together, but that doesn't mean that some of those old scars don't still linger and ache from time to time. And then there are those little annoyances from twenty minutes ago.

Yet, despite all these negative experiences and feelings, we still have to find ways to feel positive about each other, to give the benefit of the doubt, to move beyond setbacks, to problem-solve effectively, and to collaborate generously to create a happy life together. I have a saying that you can't leave the past in the past if it's still happening in the present—if it's more of the same, it's hard to take the situation of the moment as an isolated event. This is a good reason to work on recurring patterns or problems, since every new occurrence will evoke all those old feelings all over again—as in, reactions that seem over the top for this one little incident. However, the corollary here is that if the past is in the past and not bleeding into the present, then there may come a time to leave it behind and move on. Wipe the slate clean. If you find that you just can't or that you keep getting triggered by reminders of past misdeeds, then you may need to really reflect on what it would take to let it go and to ask yourself what you are getting by holding onto this resentment as well as what it is costing you.

One of the great things about treating adults with ADHD is that those frustrating old patterns that just never seemed to change can finally shift for the better once they understand and begin to get on top of their ADHD. And this applies equally to their partner and their relationship. Not that suddenly everything is perfect and everyone gets everything that they want, but enough aggravations legitimately change for the better that it is possible to accept the rest and be happier with their life, relationship, and sexual connection. There is also some good cause to trust that these positive changes will stick, so it continues to spill forward in a helpful way, rather than adding to the pile of frustrations.

What would make your sex life better for you?
If I could rely on my husband to do what he says he is going to do out of the bedroom.
What would make your sex life better for your partner?
If I wasn't so resigned and angry.
Non-ADHD woman, 60, married, been together 21+ years

The Sex Funnel

Everything in your life potentially impacts your sex life, even if it has nothing to do with sex. This may be less true if we are talking about solo activities because then you only have to get yourself worked out, but when we add a partner into the mix and want to make things happen with them, it becomes kind of exponential. Some things in your life make sex better and more likely to happen, whereas others detract from sexual enjoyment or make it less likely. This is the sex funnel (no, unfortunately, this is not a ride at an adult-oriented theme park). Everything in your life goes into the top of the funnel, mixes around, and then affects your sex life at the bottom. OK, maybe that's a little simplistic, but my point here is that sometimes to address complex matters, we need to look further afield. While the sex itself may begin once the clothes start coming off, there are a million things that happen before that moment that determine whether that moment arrives in the first place.

Everything that happens between you and your partner is foreplay. It's just a question of whether that makes sex more likely or less. Let's take a look at both—how to overcome the barriers as well as how to boost the enhancers.

What would make your sex life better for you?
If my husband was able to be present more of the time (outside the sex time!) Effort is sexy!
What would make your sex life better for your partner?
If I didn't ever mind if he was never present. In other words that nothing in the relationship ever affected sex for me.
Is there anything else that you would like us to know?
Is this such a struggle for everyone? I constantly wonder if there is something wrong with me—like why do I care if he feels like a stranger so much of the time?? (but I just do)
Non-ADHD woman, 60, married, been together 21+ years

Overcome Sexual Barriers

If everything that happened since your last sexual encounter is fore-play for the next sexual encounter, there are some couples who unfortunately have so many disagreements and disappointments that they never get past the very beginnings of foreplay to a point where it feels like there is anything building toward sex.

As it turns out, most of the barriers to a better sex life have little to do with sex itself so much as about getting around to being sexual together or preserving positive feelings toward each other so that couples want to have sex (with each other). For the survey respond-ents, the least problematic barriers to a better sex life were the ones that were most directly about sex:

- I don't feel that the sex will be satisfying, so I don't even bother
- I am disinterested in sex in general, not just with this partner
- I am no longer sexually attracted to my partner
- My partner asks too much of me sexually
- I don't understand my partner's sexual needs or can't please him/her sexually

By contrast, the sexual barriers that were rated as the greatest were mostly about life and relationship factors getting in the way of sex. I shared this table earlier, but let's take another look at it (Table 7.1). The barriers are quite different based on gender and ADHD status but it's easy to see how some of them interact between the two members of each couple.

It's probably not that hard to see how ADHD, especially when it's not sufficiently well managed, can contribute to all of these bar-riers, either directly or indirectly. It's also not hard to see how the dynamics that can develop within a couple when one person has ADHD will also have their impact, so this isn't just about the person with ADHD. The cliché is that the non-ADHD partner gets tired of having to do more of the work and be the responsible one because ADHD undermines their partner's consistency, so they become increasingly resentful and angry. Meanwhile, the ADHD partner

Table 7.1 Sexual barriers.

ADHD Women	Non-ADHD Men
1. One or both of us are too busy with other things to have time for sex 2. It can be difficult to switch gears from other demands and be sexual 3. I am too tired to have sex 4. There would be more time for sex if time was used more efficiently 5. I'm too angry with my partner to want sex	1. There would be more time for sex if time was used more efficiently 2. One or both of us are too busy with other things to have time for sex 3. My partner acts disinterested in having sex with me, even when I ask 4. My partner is too angry with me for us to have sex 5. I'm too angry with my partner to want sex
Non-ADHD Women	ADHD Men
1. I'm too angry with my partner to want sex 2. My partner seems like another child, lessening his or her appeal 3. I resent that my partner doesn't pay enough attention to me unless he/she wants sex 4. It can be difficult to switch gears from other demands and be sexual 5. I am too tired to have sex	1. My partner is too angry with me for us to have sex 2. One or both of us are too busy with other things to have time for sex 3. My partner acts disinterested in having sex with me, even when I ask 4. There would be more time for sex if time was used more efficiently 5. I feel uncomfortable sharing my sexual desires with my partner

gets tired of the constant criticism, disrespect, and micromanaging and therefore retreats, minimizes, and covers up. There is a certain reasonableness to each of their behaviors, but each person's attempts at coping with their partner's problematic behaviors only increases them—they're caught in a loop. This dynamic seems to be more common and more intense when it's the guy who has ADHD, but every couple has its own dynamic and generalizations always have their contradictions. If you find it helpful in understanding what is going on in your relationship, then use it, but only if it helps you and your partner move forward.

Regardless of how it plays out for you and your partner, if insufficiently managed ADHD is affecting your relationship and/or sex life, that would probably be a good place to start. It's definitely not the end of the story though because no relationship is so simple (or perfect) that a prescription and a planner will solve all its problems. But it's definitely a good place to start, both for its direct effects on daily life, as well as a show of good faith. I won't get into specific treatment options or strategies here, since that has already been covered in my previous books and lots of other places, too. Suffice to say that if ADHD is still having more of an effect on your life, relationship, and/or sex life, whether it's you or your partner with ADHD, then do what you need to do to remedy that. You may want to start with *Chapter 3: Make the Most of Treatment* to see what the survey respondents found most helpful.

You may find that some of the barriers in Table 7.1 apply in your life. If so, how does it play out for you and/or your partner? What are the nuances that make an important difference? How has this evolved and changed, or not, over the course of your relationship? What else has gotten in the way of a better sex life—and not just the obvious, superficial answers, but the deeper levels? By contrast, what helps you overcome these barriers?

If your goal is to have a better sex life, your biggest barriers may be the obvious place to start since they will likely have the greatest

> I am tired of being physically hurt during sex because my impulsive partner insists that I will one day like certain bedroom tricks. I have lost so much trust with my husband in the bedroom due to his impulsive behavior, therefore we have less sex, and just plain boring sex.
>
> *Non-ADHD woman, 43, married, been together 11–20 years*

impact. However, they may also be the most complicated, most deeply entrenched, and hardest to change. If so, it sometimes works out better to start with some low hanging fruit—it may not create a paradigm shift in your relationship, but it does give a positive bump that fuels subsequent changes. For example, something as simple as loading the dishwasher after dinner and expressing some appreciation for the effort may be an easy change to make that improves the emotional tone before bed. Especially when you really feel stuck, every little bit of positive movement is important. Then make a point of looking for, noticing, and expressing appreciation for all those good deeds your partner does.

Boost Sexual Enhancers

I talked in the last section about how poorly managed ADHD can be a sexual barrier. Fortunately, the inverse is also true: those respondents who were most satisfied with their relationship and sex life felt that their partners put in more effort to manage ADHD (their own or their partner's). Yes, putting in effort on ADHD is an aphrodisiac: write reminder notes, get laid.

Interestingly, most everyone thought they themselves were doing a pretty good job of it, so the happiest folks weren't working that much harder than the unhappiest. We all tend to give ourselves plenty of credit, but tend to be less generous when it comes to assessing others. Therefore, it may be best to start by having a conversation with your partner about what you are each doing, so that you each have equal knowledge and everyone gets their due credit. If changes need to be made, then do it, but it's better to start with a clear picture of what is already being done, correct any misperceptions, and then put your energy into what your partner will appreciate most.

The goal here is to get on the same team and to feel that there is some parity in the relationship, something which is definitely not the case in the cliché dynamic of the angry responsible one and the avoidant irresponsible one. It's hard to feel sexually generous when you feel like you're getting a crappy deal the rest of the time and it's hard to be sexually open if you feel that you're getting criticized all the time. Working well together by day makes it easier to work well together at night. And also sometimes during the day, when you can swing it.

There are plenty of other obvious, non-ADHD things you can do in your relationship that will improve your sex life—e.g., be nice to each other, talk respectively, be supportive, continue to invest in spending enjoyable time together, etc. I wouldn't suggest that getting laid more should be your primary motivation to be nice to each other, but the more motivators for that, the better. Some studies have even found that couples who have a more equitable division of household chores tend to have more sex, so there are lots of ways to be good to each other.

What gets you going? What tends to happen on those days that you do have sex that put you more in the mood? What gets your partner going? How well do you feel that you and your partner have a clear idea of each other's sexual triggers? Not turn-ons once the clothes come off, but those little gestures, moods, tones, and interactions that later lead to less clothes? Have you had direct and honest conversations about it? Lately? Spend some time really thinking about this then talking about it. Even when we know each other well, we evolve over time, so what puts us in the mood may change. You should talk about your sex life at least as often as you do your taxes which, for some people, may require doing your taxes more often.

It's also worth noting that the things that make domestic life smoother and that make us feel emotionally supported may sometimes undermine our erotic desires. Sometimes safe and secure clashes with hot and heavy. Being a productive member of society all day can make it harder to be a crazy hornball when it's sexy time. For many people, living a fully satisfying life means accessing different parts of themselves at different times. This means being responsible and methodical when at work or when figuring out which insurance plan to sign up for; being nurturing and playful when taking care of the kids; being social and a team player when hanging out with your partner or friends; but also being dirty and lusty when having sex. Some people have a harder time reconciling these seemingly mutually exclusive parts of themselves, but sometimes life requires us to live with contradictions like these. Often, truth (as opposed to Truth) is multifaceted.

Quality, Not Just Quantity

While most people aspire to have more sex, or at least like the idea of it, it's important to note that that means more good sex—sex that is worth wanting. It's hard to be motivated to work for more sex that is boring or so-so. Yes, definitely, there are a million good reasons to work on yourself and your relationship. However, if you want that bonus motivation that comes from wanting a better sex life and hoping that this hard work of personal development will lead to it, then the sex you're having has to be worth wanting more of. If you suspect that all you're going to get is more uninspired hokey-pokey, then that may lead to a different kind of personal and relationship development: doing what needs to be done to make the sex worth wanting.

Fortunately, as your relationship evolves, you may find that your sex life does, too, and as your sex life evolves, so does your relationship. This is because the same process of honest and intimate communication and effective negotiation and problem-solving is involved in both. This doesn't mean that just focusing on one will automatically and fully spill into the other, but doing a good job in one makes it easier to do the work in the other. For some likely places to start, you may want to check out *Chapter 4: Role Models: What Can We Learn From the Happiest Couples?*

This process of making your sex life more interesting and inspiring may involve some difficult conversations and some honest disclosures that one of you doesn't really want to say and the other probably doesn't want to hear. These are the moments that test us as individuals, partners, and couples. However, if the unspoken is interfering with a better sex life and causing possibly less dramatic but too frequent discontent, it may be better to just bite the bullet and dive into that difficult conversation. In those heated moments, do your best to keep your head and to focus on the conversation, reminding yourself of the benefits that will come from it. Uncomfortable conversations are OK if they help move things forward and improve the relationship.

Take Away Lessons

- Nothing in a relationship happens in a vacuum—it's influenced by everything that came before that moment and also by what is happening outside of the relationship.

- According to the survey respondents, most of the barriers to a better sex life had little to do with the sex itself. The biggest barriers were more about life and relationship factors getting in the way of sex, so work on whatever is having the biggest impact.

- Perceptions of a partner's effort at managing ADHD (and therefore other matters) had a big effect on how respondents felt about their sex life and relationship. Effort is an aphrodisiac.

8

Make it a Priority

I've said before that my goal in doing the survey and the book is to not only help mixed couples do better in bed, but also to do better in all the rest of their relationship. The data from the survey (and other research) backs this up: there is a strong overlap between sexual satisfaction and overall relationship satisfaction and each benefits the other. For couples who are generally doing pretty well and don't have any major issues, sex and passion in general can dribble away. There is no specific intent to do so, it just kind of gets squeezed out of the day—or week, or month. For these couples, it's way more about benign neglect than malicious

> *What would make your sex life better for you?*
> We lead a very busy and active life. Lots of travel etc. which I organize mostly; and sex has fallen low in the list of priorities, to be honest. Thanks for the reminder!!! I will add it to my to-do list. LOL.
> *Non-ADHD woman, 65, married, been together 21+ years*

intent. So let's talk about how to keep sex a bit more front and center in your life.

Make and Protect Good Feelings for Sex

In order for you and your partner to have sex, you both need to want to. This obviously involves making the sex itself worth wanting, but you also need to make sure that you both want to have sex *with each other*. This means keeping good feelings alive when the clothes are on—doing a good job on all that general relationship stuff that builds positive feelings for each other. While every couple has its own strengths and struggles, in the section, *Barriers to a More Satisfying Sex Life* in *Chapter 2: How ADHD Impacts Sex and Relationships*, I discussed the most common barriers to a more satisfying sex life for the survey respondents. Interestingly, none of the top five barriers for each gender and ADHD status had anything to do with sex itself. They were much more about good feelings in the relationship, or lack thereof.

Maintaining good feelings in the relationship involves everything from addressing big existential issues down to dealing with mundane annoyances, like cleaning up dog barf in the living room that definitely wasn't there when I walked through. We probably all wish we had more control over what happens in our lives and there are a million ways that couples respond to the vicissitudes of life, but probably most of this boils down to feeling like you are on the same team, that you're facing the world together. When a couple isn't dealing well with ADHD, it can make them feel like they are on opposite teams in a zero-sum game where one person's gain is

What would make your sex life better for your partner?
He gets in the mood when I do big chores related to cleaning the house. I hate cleaning. It's like the most meaningless activity. But if I did it more, he'd find me more attractive in the moment.
ADHD man, 36, living together, been together 11–20 years

the other's loss. It's hard to feel sexual, much less sexually generous, with your partner under these circumstances, so working on your sex life begins with topics that aren't at all sexual.

In addition to all the logistical, psychological, and relational elements of living together, good sex lives are often built on a foundation of nonsexual affection and touching. Some people find it hard to go from no touch all week to then ripping their partner's clothes off on Friday night. Every little touch is like a quietly smoldering coal that later heats up into a blazing fire. Some of these touches can be passionate gropes with a hungry promise of what will happen later, but for every gropey touch, you probably need at least a few friendly, heartfelt touches (ask your partner for their desired ratio—and what qualifies as what). Depending on your partner, you may need to be generous with a lot of those nonsexual touches—and to not be too obvious about ticking off the required number before you can get laid.

In the survey, the third biggest barrier to more frequent and/ or enjoyable sex (out of twenty-five) for non-ADHD women was:

What would make your sex life better for your partner?
I'm not sure. I don't think he presently cares for sex. He has low to no sex drive. He's pretty distant, physically and emotionally. We don't spend much time together anymore. We are just touching base regarding the kids and finances if we talk at all.
ADHD woman, 36, married, been together 11–20 years

Lack of sex is ruining our relationship. I do almost everything I can to meet her needs and her requests but I don't get my needs fulfilled in return. So why am I in this relationship?
Non-ADHD man, 51, engaged and living together, been together 6–10 years

"I resent that my partner doesn't pay enough attention to me unless he/she wants sex." If this is part of what is getting in the way for you, then this might be a good place to invest some effort.

Even great couples will have disagreements. What sets them apart from the less happy folks is that they resolve those disagreements well by fighting respectfully. They don't cause too much collateral damage in order to win the battle of the day. They also make a point of creating lots more positive interactions to counterbalance the negative ones. Overall, on average, what is the emotional tone of your relationship? What is your ratio of positive to negative inter-actions? When it's bad, how bad does it get—and how good is the good? There are likely many points of intervention over the course of a week where one or both of you can give that perhaps more difficult response that moves you closer together, rather than further apart. This may mean not only managing your own emotions well, but also pushing your partner (respectfully) to hold themselves to a higher standard.

What is the emotional tone of your relationship that will help you and your partner be most interested in sex? What will it take to create that?

Make and Protect Time for Sex

The busyness of life makes it easy to fall into a rut where sex is the last thing that happens at night, after everything else is done—except when there is still too much to do and then sex is the first thing to go. Related to this, survey respondents felt that two of the biggest sexual barriers were:

- One or both of us are too busy with other things to have time for sex
- There would be more time for sex if time was used more efficiently

This is a combination problem: there's too much to do, but also tasks aren't being completed quickly enough. It may be that med-ication and/or working with a therapist, coach, or organizer can improve the efficiency of certain tasks. However, even if you are able to really streamline things, life still involves the need to make sometimes difficult choices about what we take on and how much time we give it. Most of us have no shortage of things we could do—how many retired people have you heard say that they are busier now than they were when they were working? OK, so maybe they're just trying to make us working stiffs feel better, but we are fortunate to live in a time when we have access to all sorts of activities.

If it is important to you, it really becomes a matter of prioritizing your sex life (and perhaps your relationship overall) above some of these other activities. Therefore, if sex is important, it needs to sometimes take precedence over some of these other activities. You may need to draw the line on checking work email, doing another load of laundry, checking to see what has materialized on the DVR, and all that other stuff that pulls at you. If you have kids at home, especially young ones, you may even need to sometimes prioritize couple time over parent time. I know, it can feel guilty to do that, but remember that kids do better when their parents do better. You may also need to address things like the kids' bedtimes and when homework gets done so it isn't intruding into together time.

One of the ways to prioritize sex is simply to do it first so if something gets squeezed out at the end of the day, then at least it isn't that time together. Depending on schedules and who else lives with you and their bedtimes, you may or may not have great options here, but do what you can. Even if sex needs to be the last thing you do, it may be that it is much less rushed and much more enjoyable if you get into bed even just a half hour earlier. That may double your available time and energy and make all the difference that you need.

It's also worth remembering that anything that gets scheduled is more likely to happen—including sex, which is way more fun than

What would make your sex life better for you?
If I went to bed earlier, it would be more frequent!
ADHD woman, 67, married, been together 21+ years

most of the stuff we put in our calendars. I know, it sounds kind of lame and boring, but it works. Creating a designated time to be together, probably for sex, but perhaps not, tends to make some sort of sexual activity more likely. Sometimes you just won't be in the mood and it may not work out every time, but it's probably more likely to happen than if you just leave it to chance. And even if there isn't any sex, you are probably both better off for having spent that time together relaxing. So, make the commitment and put it on the calendar, unless you use an online schedule that is visible to your coworkers. Unless you want to show off.

Scheduling sex tends to work best for couples who are generally getting along well, there are no significant sexual problems, and both people would like to have sex more regularly. Otherwise, it may just be a set-up for pressure and/or disappointment. Scheduling sex is only the solution to benign neglect, so you may need to address other issues first before you pull out your calendar. → *my concern*

One added benefit of scheduling sex is that it gives you something to look forward to and fantasize about. You can also play with the building excitement by flirting with your partner, whether by hiding loving little notes for them to find, dirty texting, or sending them a link to a video and telling them to start stretching. By playing back and forth, you are both more likely to be in the mood when the time finally comes. And if things just don't work out this time, then try again tomorrow.

Finally, for those of you who say you don't want to schedule sex because it should just be spontaneous, let me ask you this: when you first started having sex with someone, how often did you show up with old, ratty underwear?

> *What would make your sex life better for you?*
> My woman actually taking the time to schedule consistent sex with me. We had good sex like three weeks ago but since it's so rare I typically feel resentful even when we do.
> *Non-ADHD man, 51, engaged and living together, been together 6–10 years*

Make and Protect Energy for Sex

As much as sex is a physical act, it's obviously also very much a mental one that requires the right mindset. Not that every time you jump into bed should you be expected to be ready to run a marathon, but sex is usually better if we have some zip in our step. Related to this, women both with and without ADHD rated being too tired to have sex as a major barrier. What this doesn't tell us is whether women are more tired than men, perhaps from having more responsibilities at home, or whether men's libidos are less likely to be dampened by tiredness. Maybe both?

It's easier said than done, especially with insufficiently managed ADHD, but regular exercise, a generally healthy diet, and manageable workload all tend to have a positive effect on your sex life—and most everything else in your life, too. Probably the biggest driver though of how much energy you have for sex is how much sleep you're getting. Based on the national averages, it's probably not enough. I am all in favor of getting enough sleep and spend quite a bit of time talking with clients about it since sleep deprivation affects not only our cognitive abilities but also mood. So it's an unfortunate dilemma when you feel like you need to choose between sex and sleep because there isn't enough time for both. I spoke in the last section about how to protect time for sex by taking it from something other than sleep.

If you find that you're too tired, too often, then you need to identify what keeps you awake too late: internet, TV/movies, cleaning up, getting through emails, reading, gaming, etc. Some people are just night owls which is fine if the rest of their lives cooperate with a later bedtime and wake-up, but can be a problem if they go to bed with the owls but have to wake up with the morning larks. I can empathize with this disconnect, but it isn't sustainable to be chronically

> My husband has inattentive ADHD and finds it difficult to initiate any kind of activity. He runs his own business which leaves him little reserves for much else. . . .
> *Non-ADHD woman, 50, married, been together 6–10 years*

sleep deprived. If you find that your natural sleep rhythm has you staying up later than your morning schedule allows, then you need to be extra diligent about getting into bed on time, including on weekends. Staying up and sleeping in basically jet lags you and will make it harder to fall asleep at a reasonable time on Sunday.

If you find that you justify staying up late and try to deny the negative effects the next day, then it may be worth making an honest assessment of your real need for sleep. How much sleep makes you feel your best? How do you talk yourself into ignoring this? Some people will rationalize staying up late by saying that it is the only time that they get for themselves. This may very well be true, but you probably won't feel better tomorrow for having done it. It may be that the better solution is to be found by looking earlier in the day at everything that is pulling at your time and trying to protect a bit more time for rejuvenating activities. People whose sleep schedules are really out of whack may not feel any better after a good night's sleep or even a really long night of sleep. It may be that it takes several days or a week or two of getting their sleep back on track before they finally feel rested and thereby realize how much worse they felt and functioned before.

Some couples find that they both get more sleep if they make a point of getting into bed together, particularly if one of them (not naming names) can get caught up in activities and then stay up later than initially intended. At a minimum this should help with the amount of sleep you're each getting. It may also make more opportunities for connecting a bit and then perhaps sex.

Even if it's only an occasional happening, perhaps try to make a point of having sex early, at least sometimes. And if it's at all possible, have sex during the day if/when you can swing it—even if just once in a blue moon. Even sneaking in a frantic quickie can be pretty glorious and the rushing can make it extra hot. These may not be frequent occurrences, but even the occasional indulgence can buoy your sex life all those other times when it needs to be the last thing at night.

Make it Happen

The couples who keep having sex are the couples who keep having sex.

That can sound like circular logic, but there's a deeper truth to it. The couples who keep having sex aren't necessarily those who are always happy with each other or don't have other issues. They are the ones who make a point of continuing to have sex, perhaps because they recognize that the relationship won't always be perfect, but that staying connected sexually is still important.

Although I have said elsewhere in the book that the desire to have a good sex life can be a great motivator to work on your relationship, I will also balance that by reminding you that a good sexual connection can make it easier to work on your relationship. And in real life there is no perfect time.

This willingness to jump in bed anyway may be influenced by gender, at least at the level of group averages. When I asked survey respondents about the barriers to a better sex life, one of the top five for the men was, "My partner acts disinterested in having sex with me, even when I ask." Although there are many other factors at work, perhaps the complement of that for the women was, "It can be difficult to switch gears from other demands and be sexual."

Make That Move

So let's see what the happiest and most sexually satisfied folks from the survey are doing and learn some lessons from the best. Perhaps not surprisingly, both partners in these couples initiated sex about equally often. On the one hand, this may reflect the fact that they had pretty similar sex drives, so they avoided the tug of war when one person tends to want sex more often than the other. However, it may also reflect that both partners take responsibility for making sex happen, rather than waiting for the other to make the move. It's kind of like that old joke that being bisexual makes it twice as likely that you'll have a date on Saturday night—both partners being comfortable initiating makes it twice as likely that something will happen. And it probably also means that they have both addressed whatever might interfere with them initiating.

If you find that there is a big discrepancy between you and your partner when it comes to initiating, it may be worth taking a look at what is happening there. It may simply be that the one who tends to want sex first will tend to be the one who asks for it first, so it may

> *What would make your sex life better for you?*
> If my husband could initiate sex and have the patience for foreplay! I make sure much of our life goes as smoothly as possible—but me taking responsibility for sex is a passion killer for me. Do I have to do that as well?
> *Non-ADHD woman, 50, married, been together 6–10 years*

just reflect different desired frequencies. In these cases, the person with the shorter desired time between sex will do most of the initiating. Incidentally, this also applies to all sorts of other desires, including wanting to go out to eat and wanting to deal with overflowing trash cans. But this may not tell the full story. It may also reflect unresolved relationship issues that are slowing one of you down from pulling the trigger. Or it may reflect old lessons about sex, such as that nice girls don't ask for sex or real men are always the ones to initiate. As I've said before, sex is complicated, so perhaps spend some time reflecting on this if it seems like there may be something deeper going on here.

Of course, there's another level to this whole initiating thing. When we ask who initiates sex, we are usually looking to find out who is the one who first makes some sort of explicit request or suggestion. However, ideally that initiator has watched their partner a bit to try to determine whether there is any shot of the request getting a positive answer. Hopefully that initiator has enough general social skills and knows how to read their specific partner enough to know when to ask—and therefore also when not to. This then raises the possibility that the recipient of those invitations may intentionally tilt the odds one way or the other of being asked. For example, if you spend most of the night sitting by yourself growling at work emails, how likely is your partner to make a move? What if you make a point of sitting right next to your partner with your arm around them? It reminds me of the old joke about the husband who claims that he does all the initiating because whenever his wife wears sexy pajamas, he knows that he should ask—who's really making the first move there?

The take home lesson here is that there is a lot that happens that influences whether you and your partner will have sex. Try to be aware of not only what gets said, but also all those unspoken predecessors that influence what you each do. When you would like to initiate, what do you look for from your partner as go-signs? How do you signal your partner that perhaps you might be interested if they initiated—and how do you make it clear that they should save the effort? Have a direct conversation about this. Not only might it lead to fewer missed opportunities when one of you would have been up for something, it also leads to less disappointment when one of you gets their hopes up when perhaps they shouldn't have.

Roll With it

Assuming someone busted a move, what happens next? Not all initiations will lead to sex, but some couples would benefit from figuring out how to turn more of those invitations into acceptances. Of course, if we're looking for a higher hit rate, then we can work on that by improving the quality of the invitations. This may mean educating your partner about the best ways to make that offer, as well as what else needs to happen beforehand, even hours before. And to also ask your partner what you can do to make your initiations more appealing. So, again, have a direct conversation about it.

Assuming it was a decent request, what do you do if you're not really in the mood? You're not absolutely against it, but you're just need not feeling it. My advice would be to consider going with it and see what happens, at least sometimes. Allow yourself to be convinced. This would be especially relevant if you tend to have more responsive, rather than spontaneous, desire, as I discuss in *Chapter 9: Sex 101 (and 201, and 301 . . .)*. If so, you may have a

> *What would make your sex life better for you?*
> If I could let go of all the thoughts that surround the moment and allow the freedom to enjoy all that it is.
> *ADHD woman, 43, married, been together 11–20 years*

great time once things get going, but you just don't get that initial spark as easily or often. Don't sell out your integrity and do what you genuinely don't want to do, but sometimes be willing to follow your partner's initiating and see what happens. You may find that some easy touching or kissing begins to light that spark and then you realize that you actually would be up for some action.

However, starting is not a commitment to finish, so you should never feel pressured or guilted into doing what you don't want to do. And of course, if you're worried that your partner would be upset if things take an unexpected detour, you will probably be less likely to want to start anything in the first place—which is a loss for both of you. As is usually the case when it comes to relationships, both partners have their part to play—the disappointed partner needs to manage that well, perhaps by reminding themselves that handling today better makes it more likely that something good will happen tomorrow. Meanwhile, the uninterested partner needs to feel more comfortable being assertive when they aren't likely to be convinced into wanting sex and to remind themselves that a no usually goes over better earlier rather than later, for sex and everything else.

This brings up the important difference between generosity and coercion. Being generous means making an active choice to do something that doesn't necessarily turn you on in that moment, but you don't feel diminished by it and you perhaps enjoy your partner's enjoyment. It's like watching a boring TV show—you can be a sport about it. By contrast, feeling coerced means feeling forced to do something where it doesn't feel like you have enough of an option to say no (at least without an unacceptable price). It's being caught between two bad options. You may or may not enjoy your partner's enjoyment, but the feeling of being forced overrides any of that pleasure.

If what is being asked is an activity or dynamic that you're not comfortable with, you may also feel diminished or insulted or like you are going against your values and therefore sacrificing too much. However, if you explore the reasons for that discomfort, you may find that there is another way of seeing this activity and that you can find a way to be OK with it—or perhaps not. So it may be worth some conversation with your partner about what it is about that activity or dynamic that is so appealing, what role they would like you to play, how they see you in it, how it may affect how they see you afterwards both if you do it or don't, and about how it all feels to you. This conversation may need several sittings to really get at all the deeper layers, but the clarity that comes from it will likely benefit your sex life and relationship in other ways.

If you really aren't up for what is being asked but find that it is difficult to set that limit, then you may want to explore why that is—what is it about you, your partner, your sex life, and/or your relationship that it makes it feel so hard to hold that boundary? Giving in at this moment is likely to spill forward negatively into other moments, so it usually isn't worth it, even for the partner who is getting what they want initially.

If you did allow yourself to be convinced into starting things and feel OK about it, then it may take some effort to enjoy it. That may sound strange to say, but we can make a choice to enjoy or not enjoy an experience based on what we actively put our attention onto. (I try to convince my son about this when he's complaining about something or other.) For example, do we mentally give ourselves over to the experience or do we stay mentally focused on other demands or concerns? Do we focus on the enjoyable sensations or the itchy and scratchy ones? Do we focus on positive thoughts about our partner or recent resentments? Do we ask for what we want from the experience or passively allow it to be just OK? We are not passive receptacles that experiences are poured into—we actively (although usually automatically) interpret those experiences and make choices about what parts to give more weight to.

Regardless of how the sexual encounter started, we can get ourselves into the mood to enjoy it. How the encounter starts may be less important than how it ends. Ultimately, we are all responsible for our own happiness and this is one of those places where that happens. We can intentionally and actively find ways to enjoy the experience as it is, as well as to shape it into something that we would enjoy more at that moment. Once the juices really start flowing and we get caught up in the passion of it all, it may run a bit more on autopilot, but we may need to work a bit to get over that tipping point. Yes, even enjoying sex can be work sometimes, but the payoff is hopefully worth it.

All of this involves finding ways to get into the mood for sex for your own benefit, as well as for your partner's. This is different from doing your partner a sexual favor when you aren't otherwise interested—that's mostly a benefit for them and that is OK. There is definitely a place in relationships for generosity and to sometimes just do something for our partner's benefit, but if too much of your sex life feels like a favor, then at least one of you (probably both) will eventually become disenchanted with the whole endeavor. This process of allowing yourself to be convinced only works if you're mostly happy with your sex life and relationship but just aren't feeling it in that specific moment. It is definitely not a way to gloss over significant problems, but rather a way to nudge an unconvinced maybe over the line to a happy yes.

Plan B

If one of you happens to be in the mood and the other can't be convinced, then there are several options that can still keep everyone happy. Obviously, one is to take a rain check for another specific time—this isn't a contractual obligation, but should only be given genuinely. Also, some sort of specificity (e.g., "how about tomorrow night?") will likely go over better than some vague promise that makes it harder for the more interested partner to let go of this current opportunity.

Another option is for the less interested partner to lend a hand in one way or another—they may not be up for a full production, but perhaps in some smaller capacity, like giving a handjob or using a sex toy on their partner. Or maybe they lie there (clothes on or off) while the hornier partner gets themselves off, so it's still a shared

---

What would make your sex life better for your partner?
If I was willing to have sex enthusiastically whenever he wanted to. If I say sure, but am really not in the mood, he does not like it.
ADHD woman, 41, married, been together 11–20 years

experience. As I have said elsewhere, sex should not always have to mean intercourse and there are plenty of other great ways to have a good time together. By having at least a few options in your sexual repertoire, it makes it easier for neither partner to resentfully miss out because the sex rounded down to nothing, nor feel pressured into doing what they didn't want to because the sex got rounded up to intercourse. Flexibility and options make it more likely that both people will be OK with the outcome.

Then there's the possibility of solo activities when the other partner just isn't at all interested. I will talk more about masturbation in the next chapter, but some people don't feel comfortable with their partner masturbating without them. While they have the right to feel however they feel, it really limits their partner's sexual options and is likely to increase how much they push their uninterested partner for sex, thereby potentially decreasing both of their sexual satisfactions.

While it's possible to take the position that you don't want your partner to masturbate, and it's possible that they may agree to it, it's much less likely that your partner will be happy about it, unless they just aren't that interested in sex and/or masturbation. Unfortunately, the survey results, and plenty of other research, don't make this a likely situation. If they are interested though, they may try to avoid the conflict by agreeing but then just doing it in secret which runs the risk of unhappy discoveries, at which point you will need to confront what to do about this issue—and also the lie that kept it secret. It may also be that asking your partner to not masturbate feels to them like a lot to ask and you will thereby give up the negotiating chips to ask for other things in the relationship. If you find yourself wrestling with all this, then definitely check out *Chapter 10: Taking Some Personal Time: Masturbation.*

Take Away Lessons

- Couples with satisfying sex lives show plenty of affection and caring for each other in nonsexual ways and address the frustrations and resentments that drain away sexual desire.

- Busy couples need to make a point of holding sacred time for each other in both sexual and nonsexual ways. Sometimes benign neglect pushes sex out of the schedule, even though both people would like to spend that time together.
- Perhaps especially for women, feeling tired can be a sex killer, so it's important to manage your sleep, health, and other demands so that you have something left for special time with your partner.
- Those perfect moments tend to be rare, so we often need to make the best of what is available. Sometimes a willingness to roll with it will spark that desire that was just a flicker when things first start happening. Or maybe there is something else that can be done that will still be satisfying.

9

Sex 101 (and 201, and 301 . . .)

I won't insult you by starting out with information that you already know (tab A goes into slot B), but there is actually a lot more to know about sex than most people realize. This is especially true since most of us had insufficient sex ed at school—way too many states still lack laws that require that sex ed be scientifically accurate. Really?! Accuracy is too much to ask? Accuracy? But that is a rant for another time. . . .

Anyway, even if you had good sex ed, it was probably much more about the biology of reproduction and how to prevent it than it was about pleasure. Considering that the vast majority of sex is had for recreation, rather than procreation, this would be like teaching math without covering how to add up prices at the grocery store. Really complete sex ed involves knowing how to create a pleasurable experience for you and your partner, negotiating the relational complexities of sexuality, and adapting your sex life over the decades. Did you get any of that stuff from your high school gym teacher?

In addition to this incomplete education, our society still can't make up its mind about sex. Most of us grew up with explicit and implicit messages that sex is problematic, a slippery slope to various terrible outcomes, and that other things should be more important—and we still get a lot of those messages. Meanwhile, endless amounts of porn are instantly available and we should all be having crazy sex every night or the editors of *Cosmo* and *Men's Health* will be very disappointed in us. So, between crappy sex ed and conflicting messages, it's easy to miss some important details about sex.

In this chapter, I will share some of the things about sex that you may not know, but will benefit from knowing. I know, I know, you're a sex champ, but trust me, there's some good stuff in here, so at least give it a skim before jumping to the next chapter. If nothing else, it will give you some entertaining tidbits for your next cocktail party.

Healthy Body, Horny Mind

Good sex requires a healthy body, and not just for hanging upside-down from the trapeze. For our naughty bits to perform at their best, we need a strong cardiovascular system, balanced hormone levels, responsive neurology, and all the rest. For example, erections are basically pneumatic cylinders that depend on good blood flow in the rest of the body to fill those holding tanks. Most problems with sexual desire and performance can be potentially impacted by physical conditions and the state of our health. Therefore, we can improve our sex life at our doctor's office, at the gym, and in the grocery store.

To the extent that sexual frequency and intensity decline when we age, declining health plays a major role—it isn't a problem of being old; it's a problem of being unhealthy. Whether you are twenty or eighty, staying physically healthy will help your sex life today and preserve your sexual functioning for tomorrow. This may be especially true as we age because we can't rely solely on the unstoppable sexual power of youth. If the desire for more or better sex gets you to address any health issues, work out more, and make better food choices, then that is a fine motivator as far as I am concerned.

There is also the added bonus that working on lifestyle management (e.g., exercise, sleep, diet, stress management, etc.) was rated by survey respondents to be the second most effective intervention for managing ADHD symptoms. The benefits go on and on. . . .

Still Got it!

Bodies come in all sorts of shapes and sizes. Fortunately, so do desires. Most people tend to prefer some body types over others. Hopefully those preferences match up with their partner, but even if our wildest dreams are exceeded when we first get together, our bodies change over the years and decades and our partner's body may no longer fit into that early ideal. Fortunately, changing bodies don't have to take away from hot sex. Amazing sex doesn't require washboard abs (if that's your thing). Most older couples who are still having phenomenal sex will tell you that they continue to be turned on by and enjoy each other's bodies, despite the inevitable slowing down of aging and any health limitations. Since their bodies changed over the decades, what enabled them to continue to be attracted to each other was that they remained flexible about what it took to turn them on and perhaps to make for a good sexual experience.

In the survey, I asked respondents to rate to what extent various factors were a barrier to a better sex life. It seems like I am preaching to the choir here in this section because no longer feeling sexually attracted to their partner was one of the smallest barriers. And in case you're wondering, only 15% were under 30, most were in their thirties and forties, and more than 20% were over 50. Maybe all that anti-cover girl stuff is sinking in.

Reasonable Expectations, Both Ways

I absolutely believe that great sex doesn't require a small, tight body, but most of us want to continue to stay physically attracted to our partner. What's reasonable to ask of our partners in this department? And, by the way, for them to ask of us? As with so many other things in relationships, when it comes to attraction, each person has a certain responsibility to put in some effort to remain attractive to their partner, but each person also has a certain responsibility to put in some effort to remain attracted to that partner by having appropriate expectations for what it will take to turn them on. And, by the way, sexiness is often equally or more influenced by attitude as it is by appearance.

When it comes to staying in shape, there are hard realities of time restrictions, health limitations, genetic predispositions, etc. that influence what is possible, so we need to have some empathy and forgiveness for our partners (and ourselves). However, if we want our partner to continue to remain attracted to us, we can't expect them to do all the work by shifting their expectations. As an extreme example, you can't show up unshowered, stinky, and dirty and expect your partner to be overcome with lust. We both have our part to play.

Given that sexual performance (and indirectly, desire) is affected by our physical health, it is also reasonable to expect our partners to take care of themselves so they can continue to do all that fun naked stuff. And also plenty of fun non-naked stuff. And also all that unfun non-naked stuff that life requires. We (hopefully) want our partner to stick around for a long time and we also want to be there for them. Fortunately, it's easier to maintain a healthy lifestyle if we do it together, so we get double benefit.

If you find that you feel less attracted to your partner and that it's affecting your sex life, then it's probably worth doing something about it. You may find that you are happier by focusing on the parts of your partner's body that you enjoy the most, rather than getting stuck on the parts that don't look as good to you. After all, we have some control over what we choose to focus on. You may also find that some sexual positions show off your partner's best assets more than others do. It may also be that there are other sexual or relationship matters underneath or wrapped in with this dissatisfaction with their appearance. Are there other things going on here that you may have some ability to influence or that you need to address?

If you feel like at least part of the problem is that your partner has been neglecting their appearance and that you might feel more attracted to them if they put in more effort, then it may be time for an important but possibly sensitive conversation. Approach it carefully, but be honest about how it is affecting your sexual connection. Acknowledge the factors that are contributing to your partner's reduced effort. Ask what you can do to be supportive of the changes that you are hoping for. And take a hard look at your own contribution to this situation—have you been not so secretly critical? Have you been inadvertently contributing, for example, by not helping enough with housework which makes it harder for your partner to have the time to work out? It's probably a safe bet to say that your partner is more likely to make and sustain the necessary changes if you offer ways to support that effort.

And what about you? Are you making the efforts to remain attractive to your partner? It's hard to have credibility asking someone else to do something that we ourselves aren't doing. If you find that your efforts have dropped off, either precipitously or gradually, then you may want to take some time to think about what is happening there. Beyond the obvious reasons ("I'm just so busy"), what are the deeper influences? Are you taking care of yourself in the ways that you should? While I think that we have some responsibility to do what we can to remain attractive to our partners, you may find it more motivating to focus instead on your own sense of integrity as someone who takes care of their health and wellbeing, as well as your desire to be a good partner.

There is all sorts of information available on how to live a healthy lifestyle. Despite all the crazy fads, the most effective strategies probably come down to the basics of eating a reasonably healthy diet, exercising regularly and intensively enough, and getting enough sleep. This is easier said than done for everyone, but especially so for folks with insufficiently managed ADHD, as well as their partners if they are over-compensating. So taking better care of your health and getting into better shape may begin with better managing your ADHD. If you feel like this is at least part of the problem, then check out *Chapter 3: Make the Most of Treatment.*

> My sex life would be better if I was in better shape physically and had accompanying better self-esteem about my body. Sometimes I wonder if my ADHD makes diet & exercise more difficult than it should be.
>
> *ADHD woman, 36, married, been together 11–20 years*

Once again, better sex can be yet another reason to manage other things well.

Exciters and Inhibitors: The Sexual Gas and Brake

Most people think about sexual desire as unidimensional, that we go from uninterested to fired up by essentially adding more desire, kind of like turning up the heat in your house. But anyone who has been instantly yanked out of sexual ecstasy by a voice from down the hall yelling, "Mommy, I barfed," knows that there is also a complementary system that dials down desire. This may sound like sex nerd stuff that no ordinary civilian should care about, but it's actually extremely useful if you want to have more and better sex. Seriously.

The official name of this is the dual control model of sexual response. The brilliant Emily Nagoski, PhD has done a phenomenal job of bringing this scholarly theory to the general public through her book *Come As You Are* (2015), presenting, interviews, blog, etc. And she took the time to video chat with me for this book. So definitely check out her stuff. This section is based on her work, including the use of the terms 'sexual gas' and 'brake'.

Our bodies work hard to keep everything balanced, from blood sugar to sleep/wake cycles to sexual desire. Although the survival of the species is dependent on enough of us having enough sex, sex at the wrong times can lead to less life rather than more. During times of famine or great stress, babies are less likely to survive, as are pregnant women. The sudden appearance of a bear, competing tribe, or current sexual partner's other partner could mean a quick death if you keep having sex. Therefore, we are wired to respond with more desire to some situations and to dial that desire down in response to others. Some of this is hardwired, such as the fact that most people get turned off by someone who is visibly sick, whereas some of it is more personal in terms of what turns each of us on or off.

Sexual exciters are the gas pedal, the stuff that increases sexual desire. Sexual suppressors are the brake, the stuff that reduces sexual desire. Just as you want a car that has enough oomph to get you where you want to go and good enough brakes to keep you from going through a wall, you need enough sexual desire to get the juices flowing but enough restraint to not get arrested. By thinking about sexual desire in terms of both exciters and suppressors, we can work it from both sides to get you more where you want to be. Or perhaps we can put our energy where it's actually going to be most helpful.

For example, if a guy is uninterested in sex, it can look like it's a problem of too little gas. The intervention then may be for his girlfriend to send him some dirty texts beforehand or buy some awesomely slutty underwear. If these are things that he's into, then it should press the gas and he should be more likely to be interested in getting naked with her. But what if the real problem is that he is avoiding sex because he is worried about coming too quickly and disappointing his girlfriend? Is adding more gas going to make things better or worse? What this guy needs is to learn how to apply the brakes better when he finds himself getting close to orgasm before he wants to. He may also benefit from some discussions with his girlfriend about other ways to ensure her good time even if he does come too quickly, so he doesn't feel that performance pressure.

Spend some time thinking about how your sexual desires ebb and flow and how this concept of gas and brake helps you understand that process better. Think about your last successful sexual encounter (however you define success)—what hit the gas to get and then keep things going, for both of you? What feathered the brakes at the right times to keep you on the road? Then think about a missed or unsuccessful sexual encounter and how these concepts of gas and brake may explain why it didn't work out.

Great sex doesn't just fall out of the sky. The better you understand your own and your partner's sexual response, the more you can influence what happens. With knowledge comes power. And fiery orgasms.

Context (Really) Matters

Although sexual desire is an internal experience, it is highly influenced by the context in which we find ourselves, perhaps more so for some than for others. Context has many potential facets, some of which may be more or less relevant at any particular moment, as well as in general to a particular person. Emily Nagoski separates context out into the following facets:

- *Individual mental and physical wellbeing.* Usually the better we feel, both mentally and physically, the more interested we tend to be in sex, but some people find that their interest actually goes up when stressed out.
- *Partner characteristics.* This involves both how attracted we are to them in general, as well as in that specific moment (e.g., little black dress or ratty pajamas?).
- *Relationship characteristics.* It doesn't matter how great our partner looks if we're unhappy with them—or how disheveled if we feel great about them.
- *Setting.* Is this a place that fosters sexuality? Or does the situation demand that you be focused on other things? Is it safe to be sexual?
- *Other life circumstances.* Are other concerns intruding into your mind and competing with sexual thoughts? Or does feeling good about other parts of your life make it easier to access those sexy thoughts?
- *Play factors.* Often sex is at its best when it is playful—which is probably related to most of the previous factors.

Once again, the better you understand what fires up or cools off your (and your partner's) sexual desire, the more you can make sexuality a positive addition to your life. Think about all these contextual factors and how they influence what happens for you. Which have the greatest influence on your sexual desire these days?

> *What would make your sex life better for you?*
> More time to unwind and de-clutter my mind. It's just impossible to relax and pay attention when there's like a gazillion different things demanding your attention.
> *ADHD woman, 27, married, been together 3–5 years*

Which of those can you influence? Some of them may be difficult to change right now, like a newborn who is grinding you into oblivion with sleep deprivation, or perhaps ever. But perhaps some of them can be influenced, such as getting into bed earlier so you are less tired during sex.

Although it may be a stretch to qualify getting more sleep as fore-play, for example, all of these contextual factors can play an impor-tant role in your sex life. If you would like a better sex life, what else do you need to change to get there, including some stuff that otherwise has nothing to do with sex? This is where some creative brainstorming and collaboration with your partner can be really helpful. Go beyond the obvious things that are most closely related to sex (e.g., showering before) and look a little further afield to fig-ure out what affects what, which then affects your sexual desire.

Here's kind of a silly example. Researchers were doing brain scans of women during orgasm. In the process, they observed that their sub-jects were more likely to orgasm in the scanner if they had socks on. While unlikely that this was one of the hypotheses they were testing, a bunch of media outlets nonetheless ran headlines that warm socks lead to more orgasms (gas). Probably more likely is that discomfort in general, and cold feet in particular, interferes with orgasms (brakes). So it's unlikely that socks will make or break your sex life except in cold scanners, but if they help, then add them to the list.

Socks or not, put this greater understanding to work and put in some effort to cultivate the conditions for sex that is worth wanting. What are the ideal conditions (all of them) for hot sex? Where do you and your partner overlap and also differ? When possible, try to create those ideal conditions, while also recognizing that real life usually falls a bit short and that the ability to round up is a good life skill. The more of these small additive affects you can influence, the more likely you are to cross that threshold where sex sounds like fun.

Spontaneous and Responsive Desire

Most people have had the experience of going about their business when perhaps suddenly, perhaps gradually, they find themselves interested in some sex. Most people have also had the experience of not being particularly in the mood for sex, but their partner started moving things in that direction and they found that the desire started building within them. These are examples of spontaneous desire and responsive desire, respectively.

There is a spectrum here between more spontaneous desire and more responsive. People who lean more towards the spontaneous end of things will tend to have sexy thoughts without really trying and will tend to want to act on those thoughts. Meanwhile, people who lean towards the more responsive end may have fewer of those passing sexual thoughts or those thoughts don't necessarily kindle as easily into a desire for action. However, and this is the key part, once they are aroused, they can be just as interested in sex as someone who has more spontaneous tendencies. On average, men tend to be a bit more spontaneous and women tend to be a bit more responsive, but there are also plenty of responsive men and spontaneous women. It can also be influenced by all those contextual factors we talked about previously.

One of the ways of thinking about the difference is that spontaneous desire arises in anticipation of pleasure. The person has a sexy thought or something happens around them that gives them a sexy thought and they think about how enjoyable it would be, so they find themselves desiring it. It's a bit of an automatic association. By contrast, responsive desire is the result of some sort of physical or psychological pleasure—it needs a little more action to get things kickstarted. Some abstract passing thought may not be enough. Similarly, seeing one's partner stepping out the shower, some people may think, "Yes, please!" while others will think, "What should we do for breakfast?" Some people are more sensitive to the potentially sexually relevant stimuli in the environment than others are. Once again, this only refers to what it takes to get someone over that threshold of being interested in sex—once the responsive folks get there, they are happy about it.

Once we are having it and get going, she is multiorgasmic, and we have a beautiful, intimate, and sexy time.
ADHD man, 56, married, been together 11–20 years

Neither tendency is better than the other and both are totally common. Those who are more spontaneous can be really good at getting things going, but if taken too far, can feel driven by their sex drive—and their partners can feel run over by it. Those who are more responsive can be better at picking the right time and place for sex, but if taken too far, too infrequently get over that hump to actually being sexual.

If two partners differ quite a bit on this, they can struggle to understand each other's position, with each wishing the other was a bit more like them. It may help to know that you're both normal. The more spontaneous partner may benefit from finding out their more responsive partner's sexual gas and brake and what contexts fan the flames. The more responsive partner may benefit from reminding themselves that even if they are not interested initially, they may find that interest if they allow things to progress. They may also feel less pressured when they just aren't finding that mood if they allow/ encourage their partner to meet their sexual needs on their own. (See *Chapter 10: Taking Some Personal Time: Masturbation.*)

Two very spontaneous partners will likely have a lot of sex but may not get as much else done, whereas two very responsive folks may find that quite a bit of time passed since the last time they had sex—and then when they do, will wonder why they waited so long. Every couple, no matter their configuration, will have some easy successes and some challenges.

In the section *The Sexual Eagerness Cluster* in *Chapter 2: How ADHD Impacts Sex and Relationships*, I talked about how those with ADHD tended to rate higher on most of the survey questions related to sexual interest. On some questions, those with and without ADHD tied, but the non-ADHD folks didn't score higher on a single one. I suspect that this is because those with ADHD tend to be more affected by sexual stimuli because they don't pause as much to consider the reasons to not let those sexual desires build. Russell Barkley's response inhibition theory proposes that folks with ADHD have a harder time holding back a response to the stimuli around them and therefore don't apply their executive functions as reliably (Barkley, 2005). (This is a really simplified version.) The way that this relates to sexuality then is that perhaps those with ADHD notice and then get stuck on sexually relevant stimuli a bit more while pausing less to consider the other demands or elements of the situation that might discourage them from acting on those desires. Just as someone with ADHD may be more likely to get stuck on their phone instead of doing boring paperwork, they may also get stuck in their sexual thoughts and desires. More research is needed to validate this pet theory of mine, but it's interesting to think about.

The Importance of Foreplay

OK, so this is kind of an obvious one, but it bears repeating. Foreplay is important for a few reasons. Mentally, it helps both partners get into the mood, clear the distractions of the day, and start having fun. Mechanically, it increases arousal which helps men create a firmer and more sustainable erection and, perhaps more importantly, gives women time to lubricate which makes intercourse or any kind of insertion more enjoyable. Relationally, it helps the partners connect and attune with each other before things really get going. All of this makes for a better experience. This may all be more important for folks who are more responsive in their desire, as just discussed.

You can use lube to skip over the need to wait for a woman to get wet (more on lubes in *Everything Is Better With Lube*), but then you lose out on the other benefits of foreplay. And while a quickie can be really exciting or sometimes necessary, good sex doesn't feel rushed. Why miss out on the bigger experience? Try to enjoy the journey as much as the destination. (More on this next in *Enjoy the Process*.)

In the survey, I asked respondents how quickly they became interested in sexual activity. It turns out that that old cliché is true, at least at the level of group averages: yes, men become interested more quickly than women. The men said they need at least some warming up (emotionally, relationally, and/or physically) to get in the mood, whereas women needed a moderate amount of warming up. Surprisingly, there was no difference between those with and without ADHD—not what I would have expected. However, women in the survey reported that switching gears for sex was often harder for them, so spending enough time on foreplay and perhaps starting slowly will help get them in the mood. Whether it takes you a week of good behavior or merely a glance to get in the mood, the

184 Principles of Great Sex Lives

important thing is to know what gets you and your partner going and to then use that knowledge well.

Enjoy the Process

Sex may be a victim of its own success—because orgasms feel so great, it's easy to understand why some people make sex all about the orgasm. I certainly am all in favor of amazing orgasms, but making sex all about that ten seconds can shortchange the much longer minutes that preceded it. It would be like rushing through dinner to get to dessert—this might be a reasonable idea if you don't like your dinner companion (at least at that moment), don't really like what is being served, or only have time for a quick bite. Assuming you have the potential to make more of the experience, try taking your time to savor it all. The orgasm will still be there at the end, so relax and try to enjoy what happens before it. We have enough demands for tasks that need to be completed and boxes to be checked, so don't add sex to that list of performance demands. Use the time to enjoy yourself, to enjoy your partner, and to enjoy your partner enjoying themselves.

If you find that your sex is getting rushed because of time constraints (pretty common), then check out *Chapter 8: Make it a Priority* for ways to create the desired time.

Perhaps not surprisingly, taking the pressure off to get to the orgasm (your own and/or your partner's) can actually make it easier to get there. Performance pressure takes us out of the flow of the experience, disconnecting us from both our own experience and also our partner's. This can increase the likelihood of

---

What would make your sex life better for you?
Engaging better with the nuances before and during the act. I tend to rush to my favorite part and then regret that it's over. When I can reign it in and really be there, in the moment, the connection is better and sex is more satisfying.
ADHD woman, 36, married, been together 11–20 years

premature ejaculation and also erectile difficulties for men and even painful sex for women if things are rushed along before she is ready. By contrast, treatment for these difficulties often involves reducing performance pressure, focusing on enjoyment over outcomes, and increasing mindful awareness of the entire sexual experience.

Ironically, focusing on enjoying the process makes orgasms more likely, but either way, you have had a good time. That good time makes it more likely that you and your partner will both interested in going another round next time because there were no bad feelings associated with this last time. Unless we're talking about one-night stands, the next sexual encounter is always colored by the last one, so keep your eye on the long game.

Most Women Don't Orgasm Just From Intercourse

Even these days, there is still this idea floating out there in the collective consciousness that intercourse is the gold standard for sex—sure, all that other stuff is fun too, I guess, but intercourse is the main event and everything else is just opening acts. While this may be true if your goal is procreation, if you're looking for recreation, then there is no need to be so limited. This may be more true for women than for men (and especially true for some women with ADHD), since although most men reliably orgasm during intercourse, actually most women don't—a fact that shockingly few people know, given that only one third of women actually do orgasm reliably from just intercourse without some additional clitoral stimulation. One third!

Although vaginas are perfectly designed to stimulate a penis to orgasm, clitorises don't necessarily get all the right kinds of stimulation from intercourse. And, no, this is not about penis size, since even enormous penises don't really touch the outer parts of the clitoris during intercourse. It's more about the guy's pubic bone, right above his penis and how that rubs up against the external part of the clitoris. The clitoris also has internal wings that extend downwards around the opening like a wishbone and these may be stimulated by intercourse, but the main head of the clitoris won't necessarily be.

As with everything else in sex, how likely a woman is to orgasm during intercourse is determined by many factors. It also depends how turned on she is in the moment and generally how easily she becomes aroused, as we discussed in the beginning of this chapter. It may also be that some positions hit all the right nerves more effectively than others, as well as that some positions psychologically turn her on more. Plus there are all the relationship factors of how comfortable and excited she is with her partner at that moment.

If you are a woman and find that intercourse doesn't always do it for you, then you are in the majority. This means that you may need some additional stimulation during intercourse or that something else before or after, like oral sex or using a toy, will get you off more reliably. If this is what you need, then don't be shy to ask for what you want and definitely don't think there's anything wrong with you or your partner. This will only make you feel bad and won't actually improve anything. Knowing what it takes to get you off and then feeling comfortable asking for it is going to make your sex life much more satisfying—which will make you much more inclined to want to do it again.

If you're a guy who wants to have more sex, then ensuring that your female partner has a great time, whatever that takes, makes it more likely that she will want to do it again. (Duh.) Do not, under any circumstances, fall into the bullshit trap that a real man should be able to make his woman come just from intercourse and if she doesn't, then it means that you're not a good lover or that your

---

What would make your sex life better for you?

More desire to participate in sex and not feeling so much pressure to have to orgasm to make my partner feel as if he is satisfying me.

What would make your sex life better for your partner?

Not having to use artificial lubrications. He feels he isn't turning me on sometimes due to this.

ADHD woman, 37, engaged and living together,
been together 11–20 years

penis is too small. Unless she actually tells you otherwise, this is not a problem of technique or endowment but of expectations. Also, don't tie your ego to her orgasms. If things don't seem to be working out the way you expected, then ask your partner what does work for her which may be different from what worked yesterday or when you first met. When in doubt, ask—which is pretty good relationship advice in general.

Share Your Toys

Human naughty bits tend to fit very well together in a variety of ways and one can certainly have a fulfilling sex life by going all organic. Having said that, many people also enjoy the variety of sensations offered by sex toys, either alone or with a partner. About half of American women and a third of American men have used a vibrator or dildo at some point and these numbers are only rising. About 30% of women aged 25–39 have used one within the last month (Herbenick, 2017). So that's a lot of nightstands with fun contents. Vibrators have existed for more than a century but they have become much more popular recently as the stigma of owning one (and sexuality in general) has decreased. They're less of a dirty secret and more of a dirty admission. ("Oh, you have that vibrator? How do you like it?")

Perhaps due to this greater demand, the last five or ten years have seen a fundamental shift in the quality of sex toys—which thereby increases the demand. The days of hard plastic dildos and under-powered but over-loud buzzy vibrators are over. The materials now feel much better, are higher quality, and last longer. More body-safe materials are available and more have long-lasting rechargeable batteries. There are also more options for guys as well as some that are used to enhance intercourse or oral sex for both partners. There has also been a renaissance in sex toy stores, making them much more female-friendly rather than female-repulsive. Whereas it used to be that (crappy) sex toys were mostly sold in stores that sold lots of generic porn that mostly catered to guys, the new sex toy boutiques offer an experience that doesn't leave most women feeling like they need to wash their hands. And body. And possibly mind. I'm not sure who the marketing managers were at those old stores, but there seems to have been some turnover.

In fact, the people who work in most of these female-friendly sex stores are extremely nice, knowledgeable, and happy to help—or to leave you alone, if that is what you prefer. I wish every other store had half the customer service that sex stores do. This helpfulness comes in handy when you encounter some of the new concept sex toys that look like they would be used by the aliens in the bar in *Star Wars* (What does this thing do? And where does it go?). I've even seen sex toys for sale in national chain drug stores and department stores, so you can pick up a bunch of boring things like shampoo, dog food, and dryer sheets to hide the real reason why you came in. There are also more websites which offer convenience, anonymity, and possibly a wider selection but I think there is something to be said for being able to see sex toys in real life so you can better judge size and how they feel (in your hands).

Sex toys have really gone high tech these last few years, including some that can be controlled by a phone app over Wi-Fi or Bluetooth. This can make it much easier to access specific vibration programs compared to the little on-board buttons that you need to keep pressing to scroll through the various options, then go through them all again when you over-shoot. You can also create your own patterns and record them for use again. Your partner can even unleash the ecstasy from a thousand miles away if they synch the app on their phone with your specific vibrator. Plus, you benefit from updates that hopefully do more than fix misspellings in the Swahili version of the app. In many ways, app control is a step forward, but it carries some risks which are either embarrassing or hilarious depending on how you feel about them. For example, if you mistakenly answer a video chat call in the middle of changing your vibrator settings, one of your friends may wind up with some unanticipated benefits. You may also want to plan ahead which fingers are going to do what so you don't get a bunch of lube on your phone screen—right where it goes against your face.

Of course, the term sex toy could also encompass other accoutrements like feathers, ticklers, candles, rope, straps, blindfolds, edible creams, massage oils, handcuffs, whips, floggers, clips/clamps, and all sorts of hardware and equipment. Some of this is explicitly designed for sex, but some of it gets co-opted. The human sexual imagination is creative and runs a wide course. Sometimes the creativity comes from the designers at the sex toy company, sometimes it comes from a flash of inspiration by someone at the hardware store or at home who gets a brilliant idea for something they already have.

Despite their relatively common use, there are some who feel threatened by their partner using a sex toy, especially by themselves. This may partially reflect their feelings about masturbation in general. Masturbation can be a pretty big topic all by itself, so it has its own chapter (*Chapter 10: Taking Some Personal Time: Masturbation*). If you or your partner have some strong feelings and a disagreement about solo activities, then you probably want to start there before any hardware gets added.

However, there are also those who feel threatened by sex toys because they offer a size, shape, or experience that they can't compete with. These may be indisputable physical realities, but different doesn't necessarily mean better. Besides, even if a sex toy can rumble the plaster off the ceiling, it doesn't offer the skin to skin human connection that a real person does. So they can be a lot of fun, but they aren't a replacement, nor a comment on a partner's sexual prowess. And if, somehow, using a sex toy actually is an indirect comment on your partner's sexual prowess, then you probably need to have a very direct conversation about that, rather than using the toy as an easy replacement for what you aren't getting from your partner.

If you would like to add a sex toy or two into your solo and/ or shared sexual repertoire, then talk to your partner about it. Be straightforward about your interest/curiosity and answer their questions honestly. Explain how you think this new sex toy will enhance not just your own sexual pleasure, but perhaps also your shared sex life, if relevant. Discuss how this new addition will fit into your sexual repertoire—and reassure them about how it won't. Perhaps offer to use it with them first, so they can see what it does, rather than let their imaginations roam. Perhaps offer to let them use it on you so that it becomes a shared experience. It can be really exciting and empowering to get our partner off, even if there is a mechanical assist.

If you feel uncomfortable about your partner using a sex toy, then explore why that is. What is it about a sex toy that makes you uncomfortable? Would it be the same for any sex toy or do you have some different feelings about the specific sex toy your partner is asking about? What would reassure you that this would be a positive (or at least not negative) addition to your sex life? Would you feel more comfortable if there were certain parameters on how/when/where your partner used it? Do your feelings about sex toys reflect any deeper beliefs about sexuality, your relationship, your partner, or yourself?

As with every other relationship topic, each couple needs to jointly decide what they want to do with this. What exactly they decide matters less than that they both feel OK about it, even if that entails some difficult conversations to get there. And, as with porn and certain other purchases, those conversations probably go a lot better if they are had before a secret purchase is discovered.

Fantasy vs Action

While it is true that sex is a physical act, it is also very much a mental process, at least when it is going well. Assuming that sex is consensual and desired, then letting your imagination roam can enhance the physical sensations and make for a richer overall experience. Fantasies can make sex fun and playful, especially when they aren't bound by the restrictions of reality—we can fantasize about anything we want, including things that we only want in fantasy, not reality. Sex researcher Barry McCarthy, PhD has a great line where he says that no one fantasizes about having sex with their partner in their bedroom in the missionary position (McCarthy & McCarthy, 2014). For most of us, that is easy to get, so we don't need to fantasize about it. Instead, fantasy fills in the blanks on what we want but don't have, at least at that moment.

For example, the vast majority of people have sexual fantasies about someone other than their current partner. Some people may feel threatened by that, but it may be worth considering that the commitment to be faithful only means anything if you have desires for others that you then make a point of not acting upon. If something isn't possible, then it isn't a commitment; it's circumstances.

And, considering that almost everyone has these sexual fantasies, you would be hard pressed to find a different long-term partner who only desires you, so instead focus on keeping things fun and exciting with your partner rather than worrying about what is rolling around inside their head or feeling badly about what is rolling around inside yours.

Some fantasies don't drift far from a person's current sex life, but some fantasies can be a radical departure from anything the person has done recently or ever. For example, many women enjoy so-called rape fantasies, where a man (typically) is so overcome with desire for her that he can't stop himself from having his way with her. There are lots of reasons why a woman (or a man) would find this incredibly arousing, yet almost no one actually wants to be sexually assaulted without their consent. Even when people act out their fantasies by role playing these scenes or engaging in power play/BDSM, it only *looks* non-consensual—both partners understand that they are agreeing to these activities and they can stop at any time. Fantasy gives us all the good parts, without any of the stuff we don't want.

Similarly, when I fantasize about moving to the Caribbean in the winter, I only think about drinking mojitos on the beach, not vacuuming up the sand up afterwards. Or, less pro-socially, when I fantasize about ramming that guy who cut me off in traffic, I only think about sweet vengeance, not prison. So we all have lots of nonsexual fantasies too, most of which make for a pleasant moment but few plans. This allows civilized society to continue on.

Since they occur inside our heads, fantasies are a private experience, but if you keep them all to yourself, you may be missing out on some of the fun. Personally, I don't believe that we have a moral obligation to tell our partners our every dirty thought and, in some cases, sharing too much can result in lots of hurt feelings. Having said that, I think it's worth it to try to create a relationship where you and your partner feel comfortable enough with each other that you can share many, if not all, of your fantasies. In the survey, those who were most satisfied with their relationships and sex lives and had the most frequent sex were also the most comfortable sharing their fantasies with their partner. These folks are doing a lot of things well which made it easier to feel safe with the vulnerable intimacy involved in sharing their most secret desires (and hearing them).

Therefore, I would encourage you to let your imagination roam. You may be surprised where your fantasies take you. Just as your personality and other desires evolve over the years and decades, I would hope that your sexual fantasies evolve, too. You may also find it interesting to explore why certain fantasies turn you on while others don't. Are there patterns or themes across your fantasies? Do they tell you anything about your desires, personality, current life, or fears? Fantasies can be a lot of fun, but they can also be revealing.

You may also find it intriguing to explore your partner's mental playground. Where do your fantasies overlap? Do they turn you on for the same reasons—or different reasons? Where do your fantasies diverge? Even if you totally can't relate to some of your partner's fantasies, can you understand why it might get them going? If not, ask them to explain more about why it turns them on—and maybe also which parts of it they kind of ignore so that the rest of the fantasy works because maybe that is what is getting in the way of you enjoying it, too.

Fantasies can be challenging, whether they are our own or our partner's. Some of them can make us uncomfortable or confuse us. Or they turned us on during sex, but then leave us feeling ashamed afterwards when the passion has burned off. This is OK and totally normal, especially since most fantasies don't comply with the typical rules of society, not to mention the rather narrow definition of acceptable sexual expression that most of us were taught. This is why they are fantasies and not actions—we can play in the possible, and impossible, without getting caught up in the consequences. So you may not like or feel comfortable with all your fantasies, but you probably shouldn't feel bad about them. Same goes for your partner's fantasies.

As you and your partner share fantasies with each other, be clear about what you might want to try out and what you would prefer to just talk about. For example, if your partner admits that they find a coworker sexy, you probably shouldn't immediately look up the company directory to get their phone number. There's a difference between disclosures and to-do lists. Your partner will reveal more fantasies and turn-ons if they have faith in your ability to respect their limits—and vice versa. If you want to hear more of your partner's fantasies, then don't push them to enact what they don't want to. And if you want to have fun sharing more of your own fantasies, then don't push your partner to enact what they aren't yet comfortable with.

Sharing fantasies can be great fun but, like so much else in relationships, it's all about pacing, timing, and reading your audience. When you get it right, it can create sex that burns the room down.

For a really interesting exploration of people's sexual fantasies, check out Dr. Justin Lehmiller's *Tell Me What You Want: The Science of Sexual Desire and How It Can Help You Improve Your Sex Life*.

Sex into the Older Years

I believe that couples should stay as sexual as they want to be, for as long as they want. So, contrary to popular wisdom, plenty of older folks continue to have a robust sex life. Of course, we should probably define terms here—what does "older" mean? When I was in my sex therapy program, one of my classmates announced that a local organization was looking for a presenter to talk about sex for older adults. That's great! My classmate then went on to say that "older adults" meant over forty. Forty! That's crazy! (I was forty-five at the time.) Therefore, from now on, "older" is defined as at least ten years older than my current age, preferably twenty.

There were several interesting findings from the survey respondents when it comes to the effect of aging on sex. Current sexual satisfaction, sexual frequency, masturbation frequency, and desired sexual frequency all decreased gradually over the years. While some young'uns may find that disheartening, it isn't necessarily as bad as it seems. Less frequent sex and masturbation aren't necessarily a

What would make your sex life better for you?
Nothing. My partner is an amazing lover. He pleasures me more than any husband or lover I had.
Non-ADHD woman, 72, living together,
been together 6–10 years

problem, unless one wants more than they are getting. As it turns out, all the age groups wanted more sex than they were having, but the ratio of actual to desired stayed about the same, so the older folks weren't necessarily doing worse than the younger ones. Not getting enough sex isn't related to age.

Younger folks may take some heart from some of the other statistics for the oldest group in the survey, those who are sixty and older. (In hindsight, I should have broken that into at least one more group: 60–69 and 70 and over.) Those who are sixty-plus were having sex on average every ten days, masturbating a little more frequently, and would have preferred to have sex a couple times a week. So the idea that older folks aren't interested in sex just isn't true, an idea that is supported by a number of other stats, as follows.

Almost half of respondents sixty and over were very dissatisfied with their current sex life, whereas one quarter were at least slightly satisfied and one in eight were very satisfied. There is a decent number of folks who are doing well with their sex life, but there are also a lot who are very dissatisfied, so overall averages don't tell the whole story. My hope is that this book will help everyone be more satisfied, but perhaps especially the least satisfied.

When it comes to sexual frequency, there is a similar pattern where there is a sizable group (39%) who had not had sex with their partner within the last six months, but more than one in eight had had sex at least two to three times per week, and 1.5% had had sex daily.

When it comes to how often they would want sex, no one said they wanted it once a month or less. Good news! Most people wanted sex at least two to three times per month, but one in twelve wanted it four to six times per week and one in sixteen wanted it daily. About a third of respondents hadn't masturbated at all in the last month, but another third had masturbated at least once a week and 3% had masturbated daily. As with the other age groups, there is a lot of pent-up demand here, so that can be a good motivator to work on all aspects of the relationship.

The ways that a couple has sex may change over the decades, so it may look different, but the erotic connection remains. Their interests and turn-ons, as well as what they look for from sex, may evolve. In addition, sexual difficulties like erectile problems or

> Sex changes as we age . . . at first it is pure lust. Now in our seventies, it is about satisfying and concern and true caring and love.
> *ADHD woman, 71, married, been together 21+ years*

vaginal discomfort become more common in older age and other nonsexual limitations, like bad knees, may take certain activities or positions off the table. Like having sex on the table. For these reasons, being intentional about making your sex good and being flexible about how you pull that off becomes even more important, although it's a good idea no matter how old you are.

Everything is Better With Lube

Lube is often recommended for women who don't create enough natural lubrication to make intercourse comfortable. This can be affected by hormone levels and is more common among post-menopausal women, but could be relevant for women of any age—including those who are on certain hormonal birth controls. Sometimes the lack of natural lubrication reflects insufficient foreplay which makes for an easy (and fun) solution. There are also medications, such as antihistamines, sedatives, calcium channel blockers, beta blockers, and cancer treatments, as well as breastfeeding, that affect lubrication.

Regardless of the cause, a little lube will probably make things better for almost everybody or at least add some different sensations. There's really no excuse to not have some in the bed stand, so it should always be available if you need a little squirt. Unless you're having spontaneous, crazy sex somewhere other than your bedroom (kudos to you), then there should always be a little lube within easy reach when the clothes start to come off.

Also, let's get this misinformed insecurity out of the way: if your wife or girlfriend isn't naturally getting wet enough, it does not mean that you're not turning her on (well, not necessarily). If she says she's turned on, then she is. Maybe spend a little more time

> *What would make your sex life better for you?*
> Hate that my body does not lubricate as well as it used to so
> we have to use oils. Hate that part of it.
> *ADHD woman, 67, married, been together 21+ years*

on foreplay (always a good idea) to see if that improves things, but
don't get caught up in the head trip that she isn't into you. Her level
of lubrication is neither an endorsement nor an indictment of your
studliness. Instead, ask her what she wants you to do and just grab
the lube.

And if you're a woman who is drier than she used to or would
like to be, don't hang any ego on that ability. Considering how easy,
cheap, and effective (and wonderful) lube is, you would be lucky if
this was your biggest problem in life.

Besides intercourse, there are also all those other non-intercourse
options that involve touching, feeling, rubbing, sucking, and/or
licking that are improved with lube. As I have stated repeatedly,
intercourse is great, but you will probably enjoy your sex life more
if you have more options, rather than fewer. This is especially true
if there are any constraints on your sex life, such as performance
issues like erectile difficulties, pain with intercourse, etc.

Fortunately, there has been an explosion of options when it
comes to lube and even your local drug store will probably have
a surprising array of options on the shelf. Some lubes are thicker,
some are thinner. Some are water-based for easy clean up, some
are silicone-based for use in the shower or to reduce drying out,
and some are a hybrid for the best of both worlds. Which you will
like best depends on individual preferences and what you're doing,
but I encourage you to try a few, since you won't know what you're
missing until you try it.

There are a couple things to keep in mind though. Avoid using
silicone-based lubes with silicone toys or they can break down the
toy's surface. While it can be impressive to be able to say that you
wore out your favorite sex toy and fun to go shopping for something
new, it's sad to see a toy go before its time. If you're using latex

condoms or dental dams, be sure that the lube is appropriate—mineral and baby oils will break down latex, which is yet another reason to not use them. Unless you're a teen sneaking around and improvising, buy some grown-up lube.

Even the premium lubes are a pretty good deal on a per-use basis, especially if they make sex into a much better experience. Given this relatively low price and how much benefit (i.e. pleasure) you can get from it, I think it's well worth it. If you think of it in terms of value (benefit versus cost), then lube can be a great deal. If you go into a sex store, they will probably have samplers that you can try (between your fingers, that is), as well as single-use or small samplers to purchase, so you're not committing to more than you want. I once picked up a bunch of these little packets at a sex ed conference. I wouldn't say that any of them were terrible, but in trying out a bunch of them, my wife and I definitely had our preferences. So find what you like. Then occasionally try some new stuff.

You can also get flavored lubes that can add some variety to oral sex, as well as stimulating lubes that add feelings of heat or cold. However, a relative of mine who shall remain nameless reported that she found one of the warming lubes "too spicy," so you won't know what you like until you try it. You may find that some of these lubes are better for some activities (like a handjob) than others (intercourse). If it turns out to be a dud, then it's no big deal. If it turns out to be terrible, then it's something to laugh about together. If it is irritating, especially to sensitive vaginal tissues, then give it to someone you don't like.

If you have an itch for variety, then trying some new lubes is a cheap and easy way to scratch it. And prevent scratching.

Specific and/or Narrow Sexual Interests

Why do we each have the particular turn-ons and sexual interests that we do? Why do some people like big boobs but others prefer small ones? Why do some people prefer taller partners whereas others prefer shorter ones? Why are some positions hotter than others?

The answer to all of these questions is, who knows. Perhaps we each have some theories, based on past experiences, sexual and otherwise, but it usually isn't that clear what drives our preferences—again, sexual or otherwise. This is also true for folks who have specific sexual interests (e.g., high heels, being seen while having sex, etc.) or narrow sexual interests (e.g., they can only achieve orgasm in a very particular way). Some of these interests may be labeled as paraphilias, such as voyeurism or exhibitionism, in the DSM which is the official psychiatric diagnostic manual. However, it should be noted that paraphilias or other narrow interests are only a problem if someone feels distressed about that interest and/or gets themselves into trouble with it (at which point it is called a paraphilic disorder). It should also be noted that the folks who decided on the categories of paraphilias didn't use any data on how common various sexual interests are—which makes it kind of hard to then assess what is rare, let alone problematic.

Regardless, if someone has a specific or narrow sexual interest, it can make it harder to find a partner with similar or at least overlapping and/or complementary interests. Some people may require this specific sexual interest to be present in order to enjoy themselves, whereas others may feel like it adds to the pleasure, but isn't required. As with everything else in relationships, the more flexible you can be, the easier it is to make it work with your partner, whereas those who are more limited in their desired sexual repertoire will probably have to work harder to find a complementary partner and to then keep things humming along so both partners' needs get met. This would be the same thing if a partner had a very limited food repertoire of what they liked while their partner had a desire for more variety. The difference is that the talk about sexual interests may feel more personal and get more emotional loading than the food topic.

Depending on what the specific sexual interest is, some people may struggle to accept this about themselves, particularly if it feels outside the mainstream of what this person thinks "normal" sexuality should be. And their partner may also have some strong opinions. Paraphilias can really challenge our ability to be accepting and supportive. This may be where the rubber really meets the road when it comes to honest disclosure and intimacy. If you and/or your partner are struggling with this, remember that disclosing and discussing a paraphilia (or any turn-on or any other topic) doesn't automatically require a commitment to action. Just focus on understanding each other: What is it about this paraphilia that turns you on? What else could we do to get some of that sexual juice, if we don't go all the way with it? How important is it to you to act on this? And for the other partner, What does this evoke in you? What are your concerns? What are some ways that you could enact at least parts of the paraphilia without feeling like it's too much?

These may be some challenging conversations, but intimate relationships will always have their share. But if you can hang in there and make your way through these conversations, you will both be better off for it. If you're really getting stuck, check out *Chapter 5: Sex Makes You a Better Person* and *Chapter 6: Respectful Communication and Productive Negotiation*.

Whips and Chains and Floggers, Oh My

BDSM is an umbrella term that covers a huge range of activities—and it's more popular than you might think, both in terms of what people fantasize about as well as what they actually do. After all, all those millions of copies of those infamously poorly written books about monochromatic gradations weren't just bought by sociologists.

But first, let's define terms—keeping in mind that there is some overlap and also some lumping together and that people can sometimes use these terms differently. B and D stand for bondage and discipline. Bondage is some sort of physical restraint, ranging from lightly tying a lover's hands together to some really serious rope play (like, *really* serious). Discipline involves some sort of more psychological control over someone which could involve physical punishment, but also psychological, for example if someone is verbally demeaned. D and S stand for dominance and submission which involve playing with power where one person (the sub) gives control over certain aspects to the dom. This could be just within a sexual situation, such as the dom telling the sub when they can finally allow themselves to orgasm, or it could be applied more broadly in their relationship. Finally, S/M stands for sadism and masochism and involves the inflicting of pain and/or suffering. This could mean some light spanking or much more serious injury.

> *What would make your sex life better for you?*
> I tend not to like vanilla sex very much. It takes a lot of effort to get psyched up for it, and it feels overwhelming and suffocating. The best sex is in a kinky, high-intensity setting removed from a typical daily environment.
> *ADHD woman, 55, married, been together 21+ years*

The key thing to remember in all of this is that it is all consensual—otherwise it would be illegal. Both parties have consented to what they are doing and ultimately both parties have equal control. So even if it looks extreme and like someone is being taken advantage of, it is all a role play and either party could stop it if they choose to. More complex situations are usually discussed and intricately planned out ahead of time, including safe words and other ways to ensure that it is a positive experience for all involved.

Why does all this turn some people on? As with so much else about preferences, sexual and otherwise, we don't really know. Interest in BDSM cuts across genders, ages, sexual orientations, political leanings, socio-economic status, etc. Those who are into BDSM don't have any greater history of abuse or assault, nor other psychological problems. The only exception to this is that being different from the perceived norm can lead to negative feelings about oneself or social repercussions from others, but this isn't really about BDSM so much as it is about real or imagined social disapproval.

Take Away Lessons

- Good sexual function depends on having a healthy enough body to make everything work, which is yet another reason to eat well, go to the gym, and see the doctor. And yet, you don't need to look like a supermodel to have great sex—or turn your partner on.

- Our sexual interest in any moment is determined by the balance between sexual exciters and sexual suppressors. Understanding what hits your sexual gas and brake (and your partner's) can be really helpful, not just to increase desire but potentially also to improve performance.

- Enjoyable sex for most people involves a process that begins with foreplay and perhaps ends in intercourse, but that isn't just about rushing through to the orgasm. Take your time and enjoy the journey.

- Although intercourse may be highly effective at giving men orgasms, most women need at least some additional clitoral stimulation to get over the top. Sex toys can be an excellent way to provide that additional stimulation, either during intercourse or separately.

- Fantasy can be an excellent way to increase the intensity of a sexual experience. Some couples like to share fantasies with each other, whether or not they choose to act on them.

- Older folks continue to be interested in and benefit from regular sex. Some of the activities may change over the decades, but this is just another way that flexibility can be beneficial in relationships.

- Lube can be one of the easiest and cheapest ways to make sex feel even better. Whether you need it or not, consider spending a few bucks and seeing what all the fuss is about.

- Some people have rather specific turn-ons which may require more discussion with partners in order to find a way for both people to be happy in their sex life. As with every other difference of opinion, couples need to find a way to negotiate effectively.

- BDSM and other kinky activities can be used to heighten the intensity or add another dimension to sexual play.

10

Taking Some Personal Time: Masturbation

When most people talk about sex, they are usually referring to sex with someone else, but most of us also have sex with ourselves. Looking at the survey data, about 90% of men and two thirds of women had masturbated at least once in the last month. More than 10% of men and a few percent of women had masturbated daily. So this is not a rare activity, which is good because it can be an important part of one's sexuality. Solo activities can be enjoyable in their own right, but can also be a safer and easier place to explore what feels good physically and what turns us on mentally, which then benefits us when someone else is involved, too.

Sometimes masturbation is used as a substitute when partnered sexual activities aren't available, but masturbation can also be its own experience that doesn't try to take the place of partnered sex. It is certainly easier, less complicated, and possibly quicker (or longer if we prefer) to spend some time on our own without needing to concern ourselves with someone else's sexual needs. It's just a different experience—not better, not worse. As I have said repeatedly, having more options tends to make it more likely that we will be happy with the outcome.

By the way, this chapter doesn't include any mention of porn (that's the next chapter). Porn is a whole big topic unto itself. Discussions about porn tend to go much better if you have first figured out where you each stand on masturbation.

The Ethics of Masturbation

Since most relationships are monogamous, all sexual activity that involves another person needs to be with their romantic partner. Within this context then, is it fair to your partner to use up some of your sexual desire on solo activities since then perhaps you will have less sexual energy for them? On the flipside, is it fair of your partner to expect that all of your sexual energy will be available for them? (I will talk about nonmonogamous relationships in *Chapter 16: Consensual Sex With Other People: Other Arrangements*.)

The survey data has some interesting things to say about these questions in the next section, but let's start with some of the relevant ethical principles that may be involved in how we think about masturbation. As is often the case when we wax philosophical, things get complicated, nuanced, and contradictory. When it comes to masturbation within monogamous relationships, two competing principles apply:

- We own our sexuality and therefore have the right to please ourselves when we want to. We choose when we want to share that sexuality with someone else.

- One of the implicit agreements in monogamous relationships is that by giving up sex with other people, we gain a partner who is generally sexually available.

Taken to extremes, it's unreasonable to assume that someone will choose to stay in a relationship (or at least stay monogamous) if their partner is never or rarely sexually available, but it's also unreasonable to demand that one's partner be sexually available when they aren't interested. Whereas almost everyone would agree that forcing a partner to be sexual when they don't want to be is unfairly coercive, isn't it equally coercive to tell a partner that they can't masturbate on their own? Some will find this to be an extremely controversial assertion and I will address that further in the section on *Is Masturbation Cheating or Criticism?*. Generally speaking, relationships work best when there are mutual agreements rather than forced adherence.

The simple solution to this masturbation dilemma is to limit solo activities to only those times that we have first checked to see if our partner is interested. If they aren't, then masturbation is acceptable. In other words, we give our partner the right of first refusal. This sounds great but isn't always practical—are you supposed to call your partner and ask permission first? ("Honey, can I rub one out? Also, we're out of milk.") How much lead time are you supposed to give them? What if they say that you should just masturbate, but then they change their mind after and decide that they did indeed want sex? Or if they say that they want to have sex later but then change their minds?

Fortunately, since the rest of life and relationships isn't perfect, we shouldn't have to be perfect here either, but instead should focus on acting with good intent. If you will perhaps be less interested in doing sexy things with your partner and if your partner will be disappointed if you were to masturbate now, then perhaps you should hold off or check in first—except when you really want to have some fun on your own. It's kind of like eating the last leftover slice of pizza—sometimes you should generously save it for your partner, sometimes you should check to see if they want it, and sometimes you get to just chow it down and hope they forget it was in the fridge. It all comes down to balancing both of your sexual desires and creating an overall sex life that works for both of you where you each feel like the other is being considerate of your sexual desires.

It should also be noted that there are plenty of ways to help our partner have a good time sexually, even if we aren't interested in the full package, including extras and bonus features. So our partner may not get everything that they were hoping for, but they may still enjoy what they do get, along with a rain check for next time. Someone who masturbated earlier can still be part of their partner's fun, even if they themselves are less interested in coming again.

We should pause for a moment here and acknowledge that, for some people, sex begets sex—and also sex begets masturbation and masturbation begets sex. That is, the more sexually active someone is, the more interested they are in being sexually active. For some people, masturbation kindles their appetite rather than sates it. Therefore, if you are worried that your partner's solo activities are cutting into your own nookie, you may want to check in to see whether that is actually true. Don't shoot yourself in the foot.

It should also be noted here that telling your partner that they can't masturbate may be a set up for more hounding for partnered activities than you would want. This can be one of those scenarios of be careful what you wish for. Telling your partner that they can't masturbate and also telling them that they need to round down their sexual frequency to yours probably won't go over well and will either lead to ongoing hounding for partnered sex, resentful acquiescence, and/or furtive sneaking. No winners there.

Whether you want your partner to check in with you first and whether you want to know when your partner masturbates is a different question. Some people find it extremely hot to hear about their partner's solo activities ("So, um, any videos for me?") whereas others prefer a Don't Ask, Don't Tell policy. As with so much else in relationships, it's all about personal preference. What you and your partner do is probably less important than that you have an agreement that you both feel OK about.

Men Masturbate to Make Up the Difference (But Women Don't as Much)

Let's stiffen up that squishy philosophical stuff by bringing some hard science into this discussion, beginning with someone else's research, then seeing what the survey results have to say. David Ley, PhD wrote on his *Psychology Today* blog about a study looking at how masturbation frequency relates to the frequency of partnered sexual activity (*Masturbation and Marriage*, May 17, 2017). As Dr. Ley writes:

> Two main theories have been promoted about the relationship between masturbation and partnered sex. The complementary theory proposes that people masturbate within a relationship in order to enhance their partnered sex. So, masturbation might increase and improve the partnered sex. In contrast, the

compensatory model suggests that people in relationships masturbate as a means to substitute for sexual desires (whether in quantity, quality or type) that go unmet within the relationship.

What was unique about the study that he writes about is that they added the variable of how content participants were with their sexual frequency, rather than simply how often they had sex. If you're having sex twice a week and are happy about it, you may have less of a desire for masturbation than if you would like to have sex four times a week. Seems like a pretty important variable to add, right? The studies that didn't consider satisfaction with sexual frequency seem to implicitly assume that everyone wants about the same amount of sex which is clearly not the case. Based on respondents to my survey, there were definitely people who would have preferred to have sex with their partner but settled for masturbation because their partner just wasn't interested.

Hopefully not surprisingly, this other study found that it does indeed matter how satisfied you are with your sexual frequency, not just how often you're having sex. However, it was really interesting that they found a big gender difference: men tended to masturbate in a compensatory way, using it to make up for the desired sex that they aren't getting. Meanwhile, women tended to masturbate in more of a complementary way—the more sex they had, the more they masturbated and vice versa; one primed the pump for the other. Obviously, these are group averages, so there are individual differences, but the trends were there. This is yet another example of the old lesson of not assuming that someone else does things in the same ways and for the same reasons that you do. Think about how masturbation relates to partnered activities for yourself, then talk to your partner about how it works for them.

As I wrote about in *Chapter 2: How ADHD Impacts Sex and Relationships*, when you add my survey respondents' frequency of partnered sexual activity and their masturbation frequency, the men's total is almost exactly the same as their desired frequency—like, amazingly almost exactly the same. They are clearly using masturbation in a compensatory way to make up for the partnered sex they aren't getting. By contrast, women desire less frequent sex but are also masturbating much less, so they are falling about 25–30%

below their desired total frequency, so they are not using masturbation as much as a compensation.

I then compared masturbation frequency with sexual satisfaction in order to bring in this key variable from Dr. Ley's blog. As the study predicts, less sexually satisfied men masturbate more while more satisfied masturbate less. In other words, the less satisfied guys are using masturbation in a compensatory way whereas the more satisfied don't need to. The difference for women though was pretty flat—in my data, sexual satisfaction didn't seem to make much difference in how often the women masturbated, so most women are not using masturbation in a compensatory way.

A separate analysis found that the difference between desired and actual sexual frequency was a significant contributor to sexual satisfaction, but there were also other significant variables, so it may be that those other variables play a bigger role for women than for men. Therefore, masturbation may not serve the same purpose for both genders when it comes to its relationship to sexual satisfaction. All of this suggests that it may be worth some conversations with your partner about how masturbation fits into your private and shared sex lives.

Are Sex and Masturbation the Same?

Both partnered sex and masturbation tend to lead to orgasms (but don't have to), so men seem to use masturbation as a way to make up for the orgasms they aren't having with their partner, more so than women do. Regardless of orgasms, we should keep in mind here that partnered sexual activities and solo ones can offer different experiences and may serve different purposes. This may be truer for women than men, but just because men seem to substitute masturbation for partnered activities on a one-to-one basis doesn't mean that they view them as equivalent. After all, I might order pasta if the restaurant is out of chicken, and enjoy it as well, but that doesn't mean that they are the same thing to me.

Another noteworthy finding is that, although there is large individual variability, most people masturbate at least sometimes, regardless of gender, age, or how satisfied or dissatisfied they are with their partnered sex life. While this may simply reflect times when a partner isn't available to scratch that itch, it almost certainly also suggests that partnered and solo activities meet different needs—again, they're both great, just not the same.

So, if you are happy with your sex life, then perhaps your partner's masturbation (or your own) isn't something to make an issue of. This is especially true if you're a straight guy who wants more sex with your female partner—the study in Dr. Ley's blog tells us that you should be happy about her masturbating since it probably increases, rather than drains away, her desire to do things with you.

It may be worth spending some time thinking about how masturbation fits into your overall sex life and relationship, then talking with your partner about it. Some questions to consider:

- What have you been taught about masturbation—by family, friends, and society?
- How does being single versus in a relationship change how you feel about masturbation?
- How do you each feel about masturbation—your own and each other's?
- Does your partner know about your solo activities—how often, where, when, why, and what you do? If not, why not? And would it be better if they did?
- What do you know about your partner's solo activities? How do you feel about it? Would you like to know more?
- How is masturbation similar or different from partnered activities for each of you?
- What can you and your partner do in relation to masturbation to improve both of your overall sexual satisfactions?

Perhaps more so than even other sexuality topics, masturbation often isn't talked about because it can feel so personal and revealing. There's also that fat dose of masturbation-shaming that so many have grown up with. And yet, many people do it with some regularity which is just yet another example that what people say publicly and what they do privately can be very different. The goal here is not to say that you should, nor that you shouldn't, but rather you should feel good about the choice that you do make and that you and your partner have found a way to be on the same page about it. To do this requires some honest and open discussion.

Is Masturbation Cheating or Criticism?

Some people feel like masturbation is cheating, that they are using their sexual energy without their partner. This is presumably based in the belief that when a couple gets together, that part of the agreement is that all of their sexual energy will be exclusively directed towards their partner. This may be placed under the broader umbrella of the sanctity of marriage. There are many people who believe this and feel totally at peace with it (and are therefore probably not reading this chapter). If both partners feel the same way and also have similar sex drives, then it may mostly be a nonissue, since they will get their sexual needs met together rather easily. But what about when one partner doesn't feel this way and also they have a big difference in their desired sexual frequency?

This is one of those places where strict social lessons about how a person "should" be might work for some but not for others. These couples will find themselves smack in the middle of a really difficult dilemma: either the higher desire partner forgoes a lot of the sex that they would want to have or the lower desire partner has more sex than they would really want. Or maybe they split the difference which might be OK if the difference isn't that big, but likely won't be great if there is a big enough divide. This is a total set-up for resentment, pressure, and/or disappointment where neither partner feels good about the compromise.

Committed, long-term relationships present dilemmas like this where there are no easy answers and one or both partners need to reevaluate their assumptions, priorities, and values. Adulthood presents contradictions and messy situations where we need to really think about what is most important and therefore what else we might be willing to be flexible on, if we have to. I empathize with the couples caught in this dilemma of how to reconcile large sex drive differences. Although they may not love the idea of masturbation, they may find that it is the best of the available options that reduces the strife in an otherwise good sex life and relationship. In this case, relationship happiness and perhaps generosity are prioritized over the idea that commitment requires partners to be 100% sexually exclusive.

If you are struggling with how to reconcile self-pleasure with fidelity, you may want to consider these questions:

- Where did your beliefs about masturbation come from?
- Are there circumstances where masturbation is acceptable? If so, when? If not, why not?
- If you keep the belief that masturbation is cheating, what other changes would you need to make in your beliefs, relationship, and/or sex life in order to be happier?
- If you find a way to be flexible on the belief that masturbation is cheating, what other options does that open up in your beliefs, relationship, and/or sex life?
- In what other ways has this relationship created dilemmas that you had to resolve?

At the end of the day, we all need to find a way to reconcile our personal values with our partner's and our happiness with our partner's. This process often isn't easy, but as I discuss in *Chapter 5: Sex Makes You a Better Person*, it is good for us.

Then there are those people who may or may not be morally opposed to masturbation, but feel threatened by their partner's masturbation, as if it is a comment on their own attractiveness or how good they are in bed. It tends to sound something like this: "If you were satisfied with me, then you wouldn't need to do that stuff on your own." (Once again, I will talk about porn in the next chapter, so let's not further complicate things right now.) The survey data doesn't show any relationship between masturbation frequency and respondents' sexual attraction to their partner, partner's sexual skills, or interestingness of their sex life. It's possible that your partner is masturbating because they are dissatisfied with you, but the group averages don't make it seem likely, so don't let your insecurities take them there unless your partner has specifically said that they masturbate because they are dissatisfied with your appearance and/ or sexual skills. (For more on this, see the section on *Sexual Barriers and Masturbation Frequency* in *Chapter 2: How ADHD Impacts*

Sex and Relationships.) Falling into insecurity will be a distraction from identifying and addressing what is really happening here.

If you feel uncomfortable with your partner's masturbating, then talk to them about it. Hold back judgment and seek first to understand before making any decisions. Put your assumptions aside. Ask what it does for them:

- What do they enjoy about masturbation?
- Do their masturbation preferences tell us anything about their other sexual desires?
- Is there anything about their masturbation habits that would be worth incorporating into your joint sexual activities?
- What do they wish you knew about their masturbating?

It may be difficult to hear all this—and difficult for your partner to be honest about it all. You may find it better to do it in bits and pieces, across several conversations. Once you feel like you really understand what masturbation does for them, you may find that some of your assumptions weren't accurate and that that changes how you feel about it. You will probably also find it helpful to match your partner's honesty by being honest about your own feelings about their masturbation—and about your own. Although personally I lean very strongly towards the idea that people should be free to masturbate if they choose to (and definitely feel strongly that people shouldn't feel insecure about their partner masturbating), you and your partner have to decide what works for you. My only hope is that you have a good conversation that enables you to come to an agreement that you can both feel good about.

Masturbation as Path of Least Resistance

The preceding section presumed that your sex life was pretty good, but one or both of you masturbated occasionally. But what if your sex life is struggling? Where does masturbation fit then?

In these cases, masturbation can be used as the path of least resistance to meet one's sexual needs rather than the perhaps more complicated task of addressing what is getting in the way of sex with your partner. Equally important, masturbation can also be the path of least resistance if it is blamed for the sexual problems in the relationship as a scapegoat to avoid dealing with those other issues that are getting in the way—masturbation may be as much the result as the cause of the lack of sex.

If your sex life is disappointing and you are unhappy about your own and/or your partner's masturbation, then you should probably spend some time thinking about how those two things are related. And not just in the obvious ways of how solo activities are getting in the way of joint ones, but more so focusing on what is good and not so good in your shared sex life. For example:

- What gets in the way of having sex more often?
- When you do have sex together, how is it?
- What would make it better?
- What are you afraid to address with your partner? Why?
- What do you think your partner is afraid to address with you?
- What would make it easier to have these difficult conversations?
- How would your relationship benefit in other ways if your sex life improved?

In these cases, it really isn't a masturbation problem but rather an avoidance problem. Fortunately, since it takes two people to avoid something, it only takes one to begin to address it. Often there is some other difficulty at work here that is driving the sexual avoidance, so it's probably more productive to focus on the root cause rather than the end result. You may find it especially helpful to check out the chapters in *Section III: Overcome Specific Issues* to help you think about whether there is anything else going on here. Relationships are complicated and sometimes we need to look beyond the obvious connections to figure out what is causing what.

Masturbate Together

Usually when people talk about masturbation, they are referring to a solo activity. However, it can also be fun to masturbate together—and even informative if it shows you some new ways to touch your partner. Sometimes mutual masturbation is a matter of necessity when intercourse isn't available (e.g., no protection), but it shouldn't be seen as only a second-rate option. Besides the fact that it can be super hot to watch your partner get themselves off, as well as for them to watch you, it can also help you better understand how you each like to be touched, what you think about, and what you like to do before, during, and after orgasm. The better you know yourself and each other, the better things will tend to go when you're doing other things together. There is also a real intimacy in showing your partner how you pleasure yourself.

Sometimes one of you will be up for action but the other won't be in the mood for a big production, but perhaps would be willing to pitch in in some small way. For example, while your partner masturbates, you could lie there next to them, doing some kissing, touching and stroking, or just pressing your body against theirs. Then give them a congratulatory high five when they get the job done. If you are the one masturbating, then show some appreciation for your partner being there and revel in putting on a show. There's nothing like appreciation for what is given to motivate someone to be generous next time.

Take Away Lessons

- Masturbation is a very common activity and often an important part of someone's sex life.

- Some people may feel threatened by their partner's masturbation, for fear that it reflects dissatisfaction with them, or may worry that it will make their partner less sexually available. Generally speaking, neither of these fears tends to be true, so actually ask your partner about it before making assumptions.

- Men are more likely than women to use masturbation to make up for the partnered sexual activities that they aren't having. Even so, masturbation may serve different purposes from partnered activities, so it may be worth some thought and then conversation with your partner about how solo and partnered activities are similar and different.

- Some people will use masturbation as the path of least resistance to get their sexual needs met without having to do the harder work of addressing what is getting in the way of being sexual with their partner. If so, you may be better off just biting that bullet.

11

What About Porn?

It's hard to write a book about sex without a chapter on porn. Despite all the controversy, most people use porn responsibly, but romantic partners still need to agree about it. Since most porn users don't have significant problems with it (including in the survey), I am going to start by talking about how to figure out where porn fits into your personal sexuality and sex life with your partner. I will then talk about more problematic porn use, as well as why porn isn't addictive. Not everyone will agree with that last statement, so I will address the controversy around porn addiction. (Strap on your helmets, everybody!)

It should be noted here, right up front, that when we talk about porn use, we're not only talking about guys. Women are increasingly using porn also and there is more and more porn being made to appeal to women (sometimes also called couples porn, as if women would only look at it with their male partner or if the actors are clearly in a relationship). In the survey, about one in ten men and about half of women said that they don't look at porn—some simple math therefore tells us that nine out of ten men and half of women do look at porn, at least sometimes. More specifically, non-ADHD women looked at porn about once a month and ADHD

215

women about twice a month. Granted, this is a lot less than the guys who watch about twice a week, but it isn't zero. Some women never look at porn, whereas others watch quite a bit, so there is a lot of variability there, but it's probably helpful to not think of porn as only a guy's thing.

In fact, the half of the women in the survey who had looked at porn in the last month tended to feel pretty good about it. Almost half thought it had a positive effect on their relationship and/or sex life, almost half thought it had no real effect either way, and about one in seven thought it had a negative effect. Although fewer women than men looked at porn, they tended to feel more positive about it. I'm not suggesting that women watching more porn is a method to improve your relationship and/or sex life, but rather probably reflects other aspects that make things better.

This next thing probably shouldn't need to be stated, but unfortunately it does because conversations about porn tend to quickly go to the extremes. When I talk about porn, I am referring to legal porn that has adult actors who gave full consent. It doesn't include child porn, unwitting participants, or other illegal varieties that deprive participants of consent. This is partially because those other kinds of porn involve other legal and/or ethical matters, but also because the vast majority of porn that is consumed is of the regular, legal variety. It may be kinky or crazy or weird or hard to know why someone would find it arousing, but it is totally legal. Porn sites have no interest in risking major legal problems for posting clearly illegal videos. Besides the obvious ethical problems of that, it doesn't make any business sense—there is more than enough money to be made with the legal stuff, why would they try to earn a few bucks on something with a tiny audience that could cost them millions in legal fees and fines, shut down their entire business, and land them in jail? This would be like CVS selling illegal steroids out the back door.

We should also probably mention right up front that porn isn't one thing—it encompasses a really broad range. For example, do swimsuit and underwear catalogs count as porn? For some people they do. But even if we only refer to online videos of people having sex, there is still a huge range. To talk about porn as one entity is like talking about TV shows as if they are all the same, which some random channel surfing will quickly disprove. Porn encompasses a broad range of actors, activities, and dynamics. Even someone who really enjoys porn will enjoy some types more than others and almost certainly be completely turned off by other types. Even if two people like the same kinds of porn or even the same scene, they may be focusing on different elements. As with the rest of sex, relationships, and preferences, the nuances matter.

Porn Within Your Relationship

Just as all roads lead to Rome, any discussion about sex these days will eventually lead to porn—along with potentially very strong opinions. Given the easy access to porn on all of our devices, most couples have had to talk about whether porn has a place in their sex life, both while together and solo, and if so, what kind of place. Since porn isn't going away, couples need to be able to talk about it in a way that leads to an agreement that both can live with, especially when there are big differences in how the two partners feel about porn.

In order to have that productive discussion, it helps to start by eliminating some popular misconceptions about porn use so that you and your partner can better address the points you disagree on—accurate information tends to lead to better discussions and decisions. Contrary to some very vocal proponents, porn is not addictive in the same way that alcohol is, does not lead to brain re-wiring, does not lead to sexual violence, and does not inevitably lead to greater and more problematic use. The science simply doesn't support these claims. For these reasons and others, porn addiction was not accepted in the newest version of the official psychiatric diagnostic manual. For more on this, see the following section on *Porn May Be Problematic, But It Isn't Addictive.*

Although there are some who wind up spending more time on it than they intend, the vast majority of porn users don't run into trouble with it. Excessive porn use is usually the result of using porn as a way to manage anxiety, depression, loneliness, relationship stress, sexual problems in the relationship, or other uncomfortable feelings. Therefore, those root causes should be addressed and/or alternative coping skills developed. This may or may not involve a temporary abstinence from porn use. Just focusing on abstaining from porn only treats the effects, not the causes.

None of this says anything about how you personally should feel about your own or your partner's porn use, since that is a matter of preference. The goal of this chapter is to help you clarify your preferences and why you have them, beyond the superficial and obvious, so that you can have a better discussion about porn.

Talk it Out

Part of the problem with the controversy around porn use is that when people talk about porn, several other issues get blended together, which makes for a messy and probably unproductive conversation. Many discussions about porn also contain strong feelings about broader topics, such as:

- Is it acceptable to masturbate, particularly if you have a romantic partner?
- Is it acceptable to have sexual thoughts and desires that don't fit mainstream sexuality (whatever that means)?
- Is it acceptable to enjoy sexual fantasies that differ greatly from what you actually engage in, or even would want to engage in?
- Is it acceptable to have sexual thoughts and desires for someone other than your romantic partner?
- Is it acceptable to have sexual thoughts and desires that you don't share fully with your romantic partner?

All of these are big questions that usually have multi-layered and nuanced answers that influence feelings about the more specific topic of porn. Therefore, you may want to get a deeper understanding of how you each feel by starting with these broader questions. Since these are all matters of opinion, there are no right or wrong answers so much as it is important to figure out what works for each of you individually and to look for points of agreement, as well as to explore what beliefs underlie the points that you disagree on. We learn a lot about sexuality without really stepping back and examining where those ideas came from and whether they still work for us. You may benefit from ongoing discussions that will involve lots of reflection, questioning, and sharing, before the topic of porn even gets brought up. These can be difficult conversations that may involve bringing up sensitive subjects, fears, doubts, and insecurities. You may be challenged to reveal parts of yourself that you haven't before and you may be challenged by what your partner reveals to you. Hang in there and don't rush it—this is important.

Open discussion prevents secrecy and unhappy discoveries— which is problematic regardless of what is being hidden. If you and your partner disagree about porn, then it will probably help to talk with curiosity and honesty about the appeal or lack thereof. If your partner is interested in porn, you could ask them:

- What is it about masturbation that you enjoy—both with and without porn? Are they different?
- Can you describe or show me the porn that you enjoy?
- What is it about that type of porn that turns you on, compared to porn that doesn't?
- Are there themes, activities, or feelings from that porn that we could talk about incorporating into our shared sex life?
- Would you feel comfortable and/or enjoy including me in your porn use sometimes?
- What else do you want to tell me?

If your partner does not enjoy porn or feels uncomfortable with your porn use, then try to understand their position by asking them:

- How do you feel about masturbation and is it different with or without porn?
- How do you feel about having sexual thoughts and desires about someone other than each other?
- How do you feel about porn in general—and (more importantly) why?
- How do you feel about me specifically watching porn—and why do you think I enjoy it?
- How do you feel about the specific kinds of porn that I watch— and are there some kinds of porn that would be more acceptable than others?
- What else do you want to ask me?

All this discussion of sexuality in general and porn in particular builds intimacy and understanding. Your turn-ons may still be different, but you may be able to better appreciate what turns your partner on and why—and what doesn't and why not. It can be interesting and even exciting to learn about each other's sexual fantasies and desires. Good reactions (by both partners) to honest disclosure reduce the guilt and shame that foster secrecy, uncomfortable avoidance, and/or unhappy discoveries.

Talking about porn becomes part of a much larger discussion about turn-ons, fantasies, desires, and intimacy. This greater understanding of each other makes it easier to negotiate an agreement about porn use that you can both feel good about and will therefore be sustainable. And if you do a good job with these bigger discussions, you will probably find that your sex life and relationship overall improve, regardless of what you decide about porn.

The Benefits of Porn

Porn certainly isn't curing cancer, but there are indeed some potential positives about it, at least for those who use it appropriately and feel OK about doing so. One of the biggest is that it is an easy way to feed one's erotic imagination and perhaps find new turn-ons (and likely also some turn-offs, so be careful with your search terms and the sites you click on). It can offer a fun escape from reality and heighten the experience of masturbation or partnered activities. And since a picture (or video) is worth a thousand words, it can also make it easy to show your partner what turns you on—some of which you may want to actually try, some of which you just like to fantasize about. Some people also find it reassuring to see their most secret fantasies portrayed in porn—if there are enough other people who are also turned on by the same thing, then maybe it's OK to have that fantasy.

In the survey, I found that both the most and least sexually satisfied watched the most porn. The least satisfied probably used porn to compensate for the sex they weren't having with their partner. For the most satisfied, porn was a happy addition to what they were doing with their partner. Perhaps because they and their partner feel confident in their shared sex life, they thereby feel less guilty about being sexually attracted to others and could feel free to use porn more. Some partners, even if they themselves don't watch porn, may not care about their partner watching it or may be happy that their partner is masturbating at times when they themselves aren't interested in sex. This would be the same as telling one's partner, "Nah, I'm not interested in Colbert tonight. Go ahead. I'm going to bed." Porn can be used to enhance masturbation, so it feels like less of a loss if partnered activities aren't available—especially if it is done openly and honestly, rather than secretly and without a partner's awareness.

I'm not suggesting that just adding in more porn will improve your overall sexual satisfaction, since obviously the most satisfied folks are doing a bunch of other things that impact both their satisfaction and how they feel about porn, but it may be that working on the things that make porn more acceptable will also have the benefit of improving your overall sexual satisfaction.

It may also be that the most sexually satisfied watch the most porn because they crank up their porn numbers by not only watching by themselves, but also sometimes watching with their partner. I didn't ask in the survey whether people watched it together or alone. My guess, based on the obvious, would be that people who watch it together tend to have more positive feelings about it and find that it adds to the excitement of doing things together. Some partners may not particularly enjoy porn per se, but enjoy their partner's excitement when the partner watches porn—they are aroused by their partner's arousal. This then makes the sexual encounter even more fun for them, too.

When it comes to porn, as in so much else in life, it comes down to how the porn is used, what purposes it is serving, how both partners feel about it, and how it fits into the couple's overall sex life. Watching porn alone can be OK for the relationship if it adds to the couple's erotic energy or reduces unhappiness when one partner is in the mood and the other isn't. By contrast, it can be problematic if it is used as an escape from partnered activities which drains away erotic energy as part of some broader avoidance of dealing with whatever is getting in the way of the couple's shared sex life. If it feels like porn is problematic in some way, then keep reading for ways to get to a better place with it.

Some Things to Keep in Mind

Poor sex ed and (thereby) incomplete sexual literacy makes porn the biggest source of information about sex for most people. Yikes. That's like learning your social skills from watching soap operas. A good foundation of knowledge about sex and relationships makes it possible to understand what is real and fake about the sex shown in porn. Teens and young adults who lack experience and whose sex ed consisted mostly of listing all the terrible things that can happen from sex are most susceptible to learning the wrong lessons from porn—such as, how does sex tend to start, how do participants discuss desires, what tends to be pleasurable, what is normal sexual performance, what do typical body parts look like, etc. Most porn tends to show sex through a very narrow lens that doesn't capture the full range of what people want and do.

The first thing to remember about porn is that it isn't reality, but that's OK. Similarly, most of us can enjoy *Game of Thrones* without being tempted to strap on a sword and raise an army to invade Canada or to solve disagreements in the workplace by poisoning our adversaries. Porn is media, in the same way as all other internet videos, TV, movies, novels, and music. People choose media that takes them out of their reality—are there any TV shows about sorting the laundry? Even so-called reality shows don't reflect most people's reality (hopefully). Therefore, just as we don't expect the rest of our media to reflect reality, we shouldn't expect porn to—but we should also be clear then that it isn't there to be emulated.

As with all other media, there is lots of editing before a porn video is released. It's not like everyone shows up on the set for eight minutes, does a bunch of poking and prodding, and then goes home. All the set up and boring parts get edited out—have you ever seen anyone in porn stop in the middle of sex to go pee? Not to mention any problems that don't show up on the final cut.

Since sex in porn is being filmed, it makes some positions more conducive or necessary than others in order to get the best shots. These may be positions that most people wouldn't find enjoyable, comfortable, or even possible. The actors are pros who have the experience, strength, and flexibility to pull these positions off—and the parts are edited out where they fall over or get to take a rest break. Similarly, most people don't watch professional basketball and then assume that they too should be able to dunk—nor look over at their partner and judge them because their jump shot is so terrible.

By the same token, you are not competing with porn stars' bodies, nor should you feel bad that you don't look like them—most people don't, including those pretty regular looking folks who are also porn stars. For most of us, a real person, there in real life, flaws and all, is way sexier than the hottest on-screen image. A porn star on your screen may be a feast for the eyes and ears, but there is none of that all-important touch and even smell and taste. There is also no interaction—those folks on the screen can't do anything to you and you can't do anything to them. (OK, this is actually becoming less true, as interactive content grows, but let's go with it for now.) There's a lot to be said for the giving and receiving, the begging and taking, of sexual pleasure. It's that interaction and the intimacy it involves that makes sex much better than the simple genital stimulation of it all. Porn can't provide that.

So if you are worried that you can't compete with porn, well, you're right—those porn stars have nothing on you. In the survey, those who watched porn never or daily or something in between rated no longer being sexually attracted to their partner and not feeling the sex will be satisfying as very small barriers to a better sex life. In other words, your partner's porn use is unlikely to be a comment on you or your sex life. For more on this, see the section on *Sexual Barriers and Porn Use* in *Chapter 2: How ADHD Impacts Sex and Relationships*.

The solution to people learning the wrong lessons from porn is not to make porn more realistic, although if you enjoy more realistic porn then knock yourself out. This would be like requiring Hollywood to only make documentaries. Rather, the solution is to promote good sexual literacy so that the people who watch porn can understand what is happening on the screen. For kids and teens, this is part of a broader education about literacy in using media of all kinds: TV/movies, YouTube, social media, news, etc. I would even go so far as to say that a better informed audience would push producers to offer content that is hot as hell but with fewer questionable implicit and explicit messages.

Why Does Most Porn Suck?

As with any media that is mostly free and therefore supported by ad revenue, most porn production is driven by what will get the most searches and clicks. This means clicks to the site and page, as well as clicks on ads within those pages. As with all those other annoying teaser ads that clutter up non-porn web pages and bog down browsers, porn sites are as much about search engine optimization as they are about what's actually on those pages once you show up. Of course, like all other websites, they want to put up good content that keeps you coming back, but they spend a lot of energy on getting eyes there in the first place. One of the implications of this is that the largest porn sites put up a lot of the videos that match the search terms that are entered most often—like other websites, they are keenly aware of search term frequencies. These videos then get the most views so sites put up more of them which becomes a self-reinforcing process. This can lead to a lot of videos that look and feel the same or reinforce the same clichés about desire, gender, and race. It can also lead to quantity over quality, since it's all about getting as many total clicks as possible, not necessarily how long viewers stay.

One of the ways to find better quality (i.e., more interesting) porn is to actually pay for it. When you pay for porn, the producers/websites have an incentive to keep you around, rather than just casually click over in the first place, because they want you to renew and perhaps even tell your friends. Their incentives are different from the free sites where you basically pay with your time (and perhaps frustration) as you click around trying to find something good to watch.

Another advantage to spending a few bucks is that it makes it more likely that you're watching what's called ethical porn which follows certain standards that protect the actors and actresses, including ensuring that they get a fair share of the profits. Don't confuse ethical porn with softcore though—they can get just as crazy. It's kind of like fair-trade food at the supermarket for those who are concerned about fair treatment for all workers.

If Porn is a Personal Problem

I will talk in the next section about how to address porn use if there is a disagreement between partners, but that process will probably be more productive if one first gets some clarity on one's own feelings about porn, especially if the person themselves feels badly about it.

There are situations that most people would agree are problematic (e.g., watching porn at work in a compulsive manner that risks getting fired), but as with so much else of human behavior, there is also a broad overlap between what some people would consider problematic and others wouldn't. There are some people who feel totally OK with watching three hours of porn a night and others who feel mortally ashamed about sneaking peeks at all the cleavage on the covers of the magazines at the grocery store checkout line. Therefore, unless the authorities get involved, what constitutes a problem is defined by you and your partner. This is why studies about problematic porn use don't find a relationship between how much porn or what kinds someone watches and how much they rate it as problematic. The self-rating (or partner rating) of problematic porn use depends not just on what is being done, but more importantly on how one feels about it.

From the survey, I found that except for the men who hadn't watched any porn in the last month, there was absolutely no correlation between porn use frequency and how respondents felt that porn use affected their relationship and/or sex life. Actually, those who find that it has a positive effect tend to use it a little bit more, not surprisingly. Feelings about porn use are nuanced and multidetermined, so at least for most people, how much you watch isn't a big driver of how you feel about it.

One of the ways that porn use becomes problematic is when someone feels bad about the types of porn they're watching, perhaps more so afterwards. This, technically, isn't really a problem with porn, but with accepting what turns them on since the porn selected is the result of the turn-ons. Those who grew up in more sexually restrictive or even sex-negative environments tend to have more guilt or discomfort with their turn-ons. If so, their chosen porn may reveal something about them that they are not yet comfortable with. It's possible to simply avoid those types of porn, but it may ultimately be better to think about why those types of porn, as opposed to others, turn them on and work on accepting that about themselves. (Easier said than done.) This greater self-understanding and self-acceptance makes it easier to come to a sustainable decision about whether to include this porn in their repertoire.

We should also remember here that guilt and regret are not limited to porn choices and that we all make decisions that seemed like a better idea before than after. We can therefore benefit from approaching the specific problem of porn regret with these more general principles of striving to align our choices in the moment with our broader goals and values. (Once again, definitely easier said than done.)

Some people discover turn-ons that they didn't previously have by watching porn. Some critics of porn make the case that the porn is creating these turn-ons, with the clear agenda that some types of sexual expression are not acceptable. I would disagree on two counts. First, as long as it is consensual between two (or more) adults and no one is getting hurt, I am glad that they are enjoying themselves. Second, people are not empty vessels that porn pours bad ideas into. Porn viewers are not passive receptacles, devoid of free will. Although any internet search will bring up some content that isn't exactly what was intended, people look for certain kinds of porn and not others, often rather narrowly. Even if they go to a home page with all sorts of options, they select some videos and ignore many others.

Even if we showed the same video to one hundred people, only some would find it really enjoyable and an even smaller number would be influenced by it. The influence it has depends more on the viewer than it does on the content. If someone is influenced by a particular video, then there must have been something about them, at that point in time, that was primed to be influenced. If we were to somehow measure total impact, the movie *Titanic* probably had a bigger effect than any single porn video, given its massive audience, at least some of which were ready to find doomed luxury liners to be arousing.

Another way that some people run into trouble with porn is by spending more time than they would like to on it. While I didn't ask about this specifically in the survey, since we know that folks with ADHD often lose track of time when intently engaged, we may be able to assume that they may be more likely to also wind up unintentionally spending too much time here, too. While some people would take the position that porn isn't worth spending any time on, if it is mostly just a time management problem, then it should probably be addressed in the same way as any other expanding activity. How would you handle it if the problem was that you were spending too much time on social media? Or working?

It may also be worth pointing out that the question of, "How long do you spend watching porn?" can have several different answers, depending on how you define terms. The broadest answer counts from when that first browser tab is opened, until the last one is closed. But since many porn users spend a fair bit of time clicking around, trying to find something that really works for them, especially on the free aggregator sites, a lot of that time is kind of spent preparing to watch porn. It's kind of like the question of how long does it take to go out to eat—does that consider the time just spent eating or also the time driving to the restaurant, looking at the menu, hearing the specials, asking the waitress's advice, and looking to see what the neighboring tables seem to be eating?

Granted, whether you spend half an hour idly scrolling through thumbnails or captivated in erotic splendor, it's still half an hour that isn't available for other activities, so from a time management perspective it's the same thing. However, some people may feel differently about twenty-five minutes of scrolling and five minutes of splendor than they do about thirty minutes of splendor. In the interests of having a more productive discussion, it tends to help for both people to have the same numbers in mind.

When someone too often spends too long on porn and standard time management strategies don't help much, one might wonder if it is simply a matter of losing track of time or if there are reasons why they are getting stuck here and/or avoiding the next activity. It may be that porn is just a means to an end, the real goal being to avoid the next activity. This reminds me of a great term I heard: procrasturbate—using masturbation to procrastinate. The avoidance may simply be driven by wanting to avoid a boring task, but it may also be more emotionally loaded, such as when the avoided task brings up feelings of uncertainty, guilt, or incompetence. Especially in these more aversive situations, eliminating the porn won't automatically translate into diving into the dreaded task ("Wow, it sure has been a long time since I organized that sock drawer— let's do it!"). Therefore, it's probably more fruitful to address directly what is making the avoided tasks so difficult to deal with. In fact, focusing on eliminating the porn could just become another form of avoidance of getting to the real issues. All of this is an avoidance problem, not a porn problem, and would be the same thing if the person is using Netflix instead.

It's also possible to spend too much time on porn if someone is using it as a way to help them feel better generally, not just about a particular task. It could be a way to manage boredom, loneliness, anxiety, depression, emptiness, inadequacy, frustration, anger, etc. In this case, the real motivation is avoidance of that feeling, rather than a simple desire for the porn itself. It's more about the effect of the porn which is to (temporarily) push away those other uncomfortable feelings in a way that perhaps less intense experiences might not. In these situations, simply removing or reducing the porn use doesn't address the root feelings and therefore isn't likely to either last or help the person improve their life, relationship, or sex life. Therefore, it would be better to instead address whatever is driving that excessive porn use. This might be done on their own or may involve a therapist and/or medication. Once these other issues are addressed, then the person might need to spend some time thinking about what to do with porn going forward.

The final way that some people run into trouble with porn is that they sometimes look at it when they shouldn't. This could be at work, on work devices/networks, around other people, or in other non-private settings. Some people, especially those who are using porn to cope with other uncomfortable feelings, may be compulsive in their porn use where they have trouble stopping themselves from using it, even when their judgment tells them that it is risky. By contrast, others may simply be impulsive about it, where they just don't stop to think about whether this is the right time and place to sneak a quick peek.

While it may blow up in the same way, in that someone gets caught doing something inappropriate for the circumstances, compulsive and impulsive use are completely different and therefore should be addressed differently. If it is mostly impulsive, then it should be addressed in the same ways that other ADHD-driven impulsivity is addressed, by removing temptations and setting barriers to this problematic behavior. For example, this could mean setting a hard rule for oneself to simply never look at porn while at work, no matter what. If the porn use is more compulsive and is causing significant problems, then check out *Porn May Be Problematic, But It Isn't Addictive* at the end of this chapter.

If Porn is a Relationship Problem

For most people, the problems associated with porn use are the arguments that it causes with their romantic partner—how much porn is watched, when, what kinds, or even that it's watched at all. From the survey, 4% of women and 15% of men felt that their porn use has a moderate or large negative effect on their relationship and/or sex life. Meanwhile, 20% of women and 3% of men felt that their *partner's* porn use has a moderate or large negative effect on their relationship and/or sex life. So those numbers are fairly consistent between self-ratings and partner ratings (although we don't actually know if the people who rated their own porn use as problematic also have partners who did, and vice versa). While these numbers are not insignificant, there are plenty of folks for whom porn is either no problem or is positive, but if you or your partner feel it's a problem, then it should be addressed.

The fact that someone feels that porn is having a negative effect on their relationship or sex life could be more about the disagreement and lack of ability to find a workable solution than it is inherently about porn. As a different example, there are some people who would say that bowling is having a negative effect on their relationship or sex life (and probably also some who say that it has a positive effect if they find communal shoes really sexy). While some people may feel ignored when their partner disappears for hours at the bowling alley, there are also those who are just as happy to have some time to themselves and are glad that their partner is having fun.

We don't know from the survey how often respondents think their partners are watching porn—since it is usually a private activity, I didn't think it would helpful for respondents to guess at their partner's porn frequency. We also don't know what kinds of porn people are watching. One of the implications of this is that we don't know how frequency and porn type affect partners' feelings about it. Given that respondents' self-ratings didn't show any correlation between feelings about their own porn use and frequency, we can probably assume that the same applies to partners' feelings about it, which is supported by other research. In other words, on average, the folks who feel that porn has a more negative effect on their relationship and sex life don't necessarily have partners who watch more. Therefore, this is all about personal opinion—if you feel it's a problem, then it needs to be talked about; if you don't think it's a problem, then you are probably better off focusing on the things that bother you more. In other words, this isn't a problem of porn per se, so much as a problem of disagreement and the couple needs to find a way to get more on the same page about it, just as they need to resolve the thousand other things that couples can disagree about.

A simplistic solution to arguments about porn is to just not look at porn (or play golf, or let the kids stay up a little later sometimes, or put political signs in your yard, or . . . .) if it bothers your partner. This total ban may be a good solution if the one who enjoys porn doesn't really care that much about it, so it is easy to give up. But what if that partner kinds of likes porn, uses it responsibly, and doesn't want to give it up? Is it fair then for their partner to have a veto vote on it? Perhaps, but I believe that veto votes should be used sparingly in relationships because they tend to generate resentment which may negatively affect the relationship in other ways, including sneaking the banned activity if it feels arbitrary.

Related to this, in the survey, when I asked respondents to share how they felt about their own and their partner's porn use, I gave them the option to indicate that they don't look at porn or that they don't believe that their partner does. I then compared these two answers (e.g., ADHD men's self-report versus non-ADHD women's beliefs about their ADHD male partners). As I discussed in *Chapter 2: How ADHD Impacts Sex and Relationships*, there are a lot more people watching porn at least sometimes than their partners realize. Women are much more likely than men to incorrectly assume that their partner isn't watching porn, although there are also some women watching porn without their male partner's awareness.

My goal here isn't to force any uncomfortable conversations, but rather to suggest that this unknown porn watching is probably the result of either false agreements ("Fine, I won't look at porn any-more.") or of nonexistent or incomplete discussions that ended in a nonspecific enough agreement to enable some vaguely plausible wiggle room ("Well, you didn't say that I definitely shouldn't look at porn."). This takes one potential problem (disagreement about porn) and adds a second problem of secrecy and/or guilt. It would be the same if one of the partners was spending money without the other's knowledge. Making an agreement and then breaking it is its own problem that then also needs to be addressed.

The other problem with the idea that one person gets to have a veto vote on their partner's porn use (or bowling, or whatever), is that one could just as easily make the opposite argument that if someone wants to do something, then they get to veto their partner's disapproval. These are basically two sides of the same authoritarian coin, both of which are likely to lead to a less satisfying relationship. It's much better to have an honest discussion and negotiation about it.

Some people prefer a Don't Ask, Don't Tell arrangement on certain topics. This includes nonsexual matters (e.g., "Don't tell me what your crazy sister is up to and I won't ask about it either, and we will both be happier."). If it is mostly a nonissue where there aren't strong feelings and there would be no fight if revealed, then this can work. Or if after some full discussions, the couple decides that this really is the best of the available options. However, if there are strong feelings and therefore willful avoidance, this has the potential to be a ticking time bomb. Obviously, the person secretly watching porn may not want to bring it up, for fear of being asked/demanded/guilted into giving it up. But the non-questioning partner may also be fearful of having their suspicions confirmed and therefore turn a blind eye to potential red flags because they aren't up for addressing it. ("Honey, you always seem so relaxed and happy when you come upstairs at the end of the night after spending time on all those work emails and paying bills online.")

Perhaps right now isn't the time to address it, but living under the ax like this is no fun for either person and risks a big blowup if suddenly something happens where the topic can no longer be ignored. In other words, the second problem of the secrecy is revealed and then you're forced to deal with both problems at the same time. These sudden discoveries tend to bring up a lot of strong reactions (i.e., angry, hurt accusations and rationalizing, minimizing defensiveness), making them both upsetting and not the best time to come to any productive resolution. Therefore, it's better to have some explicit conversations about it before you are forced to do so—remove that second topic of secrecy, so you only need to deal with the main topic. Silence requires both people's cooperation, but it only takes one to start the conversation, so you can be that person, regardless of which side of the issue you're on.

It's better to hash out how you both feel about porn, what you would like to see as an outcome, and come to a joint decision that you both can live with and thereby sustain. The topic of porn may be more provocative than figuring out where to go on vacation this summer, but the process is the same as negotiating other disagreements. How did you and your partner resolve these other disagreements? Are there any good lessons there that you can apply here?

In this process, keep in mind that disagreements about porn sometimes also require more fundamental discussions about the acceptability of masturbation and fantasy that involves someone other than your partner or activities that go beyond your usual repertoire. So before you can get to the porn, you might need to back up and talk about some of these other issues (and re-read the previous chapter on masturbation).

You may also want to remember that, like masturbation, sometimes porn serves a different purpose and fulfills a different need from partnered activities. They are both good, but in different ways. There's no competition between them and doing one doesn't say anything about the other—except when it does, which I will talk about next.

Which Came First—The Porn or the Problem?

Sometimes when couples aren't having enough sex with each other, one or both of them is spending too much time watching porn and/or masturbating. Some will take this correlation to imply causation— the porn is interfering with partnered activities, so therefore removing the porn will automatically lead to more sex together. Perhaps sometimes this is true, but the direction of causation usually goes the other way—increased porn use is more likely to *follow* problems in the couple's sex life, rather than cause those problems initially. As Marty Klein, PhD says, no one ever left a satisfying sex life for porn. Given the choice, most people would prefer to have great sex with their partner than to watch great porn.

However, disagreements about porn use can then maintain avoidance of partnered activities if porn becomes the path of least resistance. The obvious way that this happens is that one partner takes the easy way out and uses up their sexual energy on solo activities, but it can also become a situation where the other partner blames all of their sexual troubles on the porn use (and their partner's deficiencies for being interested in that stuff) without looking at what else is going on in their sex life and relationship. Porn can be both an easy substitute and vilified scapegoat, but the reality is that both partners are making choices to do some things and avoid others. Therefore, the better solution is most likely to have some of those conversations that you don't want to have.

Porn use doesn't exist in a vacuum, so if you feel that it is problematic, then you need to look at how it is fitting into what else is going on—what is the porn use affecting, but also what is affecting the porn use? Why has porn become preferred over partnered activities? And why has tolerating porn use and sexual avoidance become preferable over talking about it? To find these answers, it will probably be helpful for both of you to think about these next questions and discuss them. Probably a few times. At least.

- What was happening in your relationship, sex life, and life as a whole before the problematic porn use began?

- Do one or both of you struggle with some sort of problem related to desire or performance, such as pain with sex, erectile difficulties, etc.? (If so, see *Chapter 13: Problems With Performance and Pleasure* and *Chapter 14: Problems With Desire: Not Enough Sex.*)

- How have you and your partner each responded to the problematic porn use? Although perhaps understandable in context, are there better ways to address this?

- If there are times when you and your partner have more sex

together and times when it's less, what seems to contribute to
that variability?

- If there are times when you watch more porn and times when
  you watch less, what seems to contribute to that variability?
- How would you and your partner each want porn to fit within
  your sex life—how often, what kinds, what times, etc.?
- What do you and your partner each want your shared sex life to
  look like?

Don't let porn be the path of least resistance: for not having sex with
your partner or for blaming all your sex (and some relationship)
problems on it. Porn may be a force to be reckoned with, but it's not
that powerful. You're both smarter than that.

I need to make another really important point here. Often when
someone feels badly about their partner's porn use, it's partly
because they feel that they can't compete with porn stars' bodies
or sexual appetites. They feel like their partner's porn use comes
out of a dissatisfaction with them. I totally understand that it can
bring out the insecurities, but doubting oneself is most likely not
the best place to start in addressing this with your partner. For what
it's worth, when I asked in the survey about barriers to a better sex
life, among the smallest barriers were no longer feeling attracted
to one's partner and not feeling like sex would be satisfying. So, at
least on average, most respondents are still turned on by their partners and want to have sex with them. Therefore, you should probably start with the assumption that this is also true for your partner
until you get specific evidence that they feel differently. Unless your
partner actually says, "Honey, I don't feel attracted to you or enjoy
having sex with you," don't assume that they do.

Getting caught up in insecurities will distract you from really taking a look at what is going on with each of you and in your relationship and sex life. It's possible that there are some attraction issues
that need to be addressed but, even if that is part of the problem, it's
really unlikely that that is the whole story, so over-focusing on that
will blind you to these other factors. Feeling like crap about ourselves rarely gives us more insight. If you feel stuck in the insecurity, then muster the courage to ask your partner directly—and then

believe them if they tell you that their porn watching has nothing to do with their attraction towards you.

Porn is a pretty big topic, bigger than this one chapter. If you would like to read more about it and figure out how it fits into your life, I highly recommend Marty Klein, PhD's *His Porn, Her Pain* and David Ley, PhD's *Ethical Porn for Dicks*. Besides being awesomely titled, they both brilliantly explain a very complicated topic.

Porn May Be Problematic, But it isn't Addictive

Porn addiction and sex addiction are thrown around pretty easily these days, particularly when someone gets caught doing something that they shouldn't be—either by their partner or by someone in the media. In these cases, claiming to be a porn or sex addict, or accepting someone else's accusation of it, can feel like a useful explanation for the trouble they brought onto themselves. Also, by labeling the problematic behavior as an addiction, it suggests that twelve step programs and certain treatment modalities should be helpful.

For a deep dive on the science, or lack thereof, of sex and porn addiction, check out David Ley, PhD's *The Myth of Sex Addiction* (2012) as well as his *Ethical Porn for Dicks* (2016), and Marty Klein, PhD's *His Porn, Her Pain* (2016).

I agree that diagnosis should guide treatment, but I disagree that sex or porn can be addicting and therefore I disagree that most of these addiction treatment methods are helpful, or at least worry about some of their side effects. Many (but not all) of these addiction models are not based on an accurate foundation of what constitutes normal variability in human sexual expression and therefore label pretty typical stuff as pathological. If you fantasize about, let alone engage in, anything beyond a rather narrow range of sexual activities, including watching porn, then you are betraying your spouse, undermining marriage, hurting society, and contributing to the abuse of women. And you're probably also going to hell. So some activities are acceptable, but a bunch of others aren't. This can be very shaming which is rarely a helpful part of any treatment program—nor likely to lead to sustainable change.

I would take the counter-position that as long as you and your partner agree on what you're both doing, nobody gets hurt, and you're both enjoying it, then nobody else should get to vote on what you're doing. This gives you and your partner more latitude to come up with a sex life that is satisfying to both of you and therefore much more sustainable. Suppressing normal parts of your sexuality takes a lot of effort. By contrast, dealing directly with what else might be driving any problematic use of sex/porn probably makes for less work in the long run. Also, by removing these other issues, you and your partner are in a better position to create a sex life that focuses on sex and a shared experience rather than distracting yourself from other painful feelings.

Sometimes the sex/porn addiction folks will cite research studies that use brain scans to prove porn's enduring negative effects. Brain scans seem impressive and hard to argue against, but the science really isn't there to support the conclusions that are supposedly shown by the data. Does porn create a temporary change in brain activity, perhaps more in some people than in others? Absolutely. So does tic tac toe. But neither one creates enduring changes. The differences in the brain activity levels between high users of porn and non-users preceded the invention of high-speed internet. To the extent that there is indeed a difference, it is that difference that caused them to be more or less interested in porn in the first place. The brain activity drives the porn use, not vice versa. Those with high sex drives or need for sexual novelty, for example, are probably more interested in porn than those with less. It's like saying that becoming a professional basketball player makes people taller.

The purpose here is not to advocate for porn, so much as it is to help you make a well-reasoned decision about it that is based on facts. Incorrect information, however well intentioned, won't help you and your partner make that good decision. Also, this is not just about porn, but about sex in general. I believe that the assumptions and edicts about sex in general that get wrapped up in these addiction models tend to be too limiting and make it less likely that most people will be able to create an enduringly satisfying sex life that they can feel good about. There are definitely programs and clinicians who work with sex/porn addiction who are exceptions and take a more nuanced view, but generally speaking, they tend to lean to the more restrictive.

Having said all this, there are indeed people who run into serious trouble with sex and porn, for example by engaging in highly risky unprotected sex, multiple infidelities, hours-long porn binges, repeatedly breaking agreements made with their partner/themselves, spending too much money and/or time, losing jobs for their indiscretions, etc. As with everything else that people do, some people take it way too far. So I am not proposing that sex can't be a problem, just that it isn't addictive and that most of these addiction treatment programs aren't the best way to go. Douglas Braun-Harvey, LMFT and Michael Vigorito, LMFT (2015) have created a treatment model for what they call Out of Control Sexual Behavior (OCSB) that helps people identify what is driving their problematic behavior and find healthier alternatives. If you or someone you care about seems to be struggling with their sexual behavior, you can get more information about this treatment approach at www.TheHarveyInstitute. com. You can also look for a qualified therapist on the website for the American Association of Sexuality Educators, Counselors and Therapists (AASECT, www.aasect.org).

If you don't enjoy porn, then you are entitled to that opinion and should never have to watch it. If you don't want your partner watching porn either, then you are entitled to ask them not to, although that will probably involve some discussion, negotiation, and compromise. Porn use is a matter of preference and opinion, but the facts don't support the idea that sex or porn are addictive and therefore inherently bad for its users, their partners, or society. This is why, for a combination of reasons, sex and porn addiction were not accepted as valid diagnoses in the latest edition of the official psychiatric diagnostic manual. Although some people have really strong opinions about sex and porn, the science doesn't support the idea that they are addictive.

Take Away Lessons

- Porn evokes a lot of strong feelings, yet is a relatively common activity for both men and women to enjoy.

- Partners may need to discuss how they each feel about their own porn use as well as each other's, so that a lack of discussion doesn't become a set-up for an unhappy discovery. If they agree that (solo) porn use is acceptable, then they should probably also discuss how those solo activities fit into their shared sex life.

- Those who are already sexually satisfied may use porn as an additional enhancer to an already good sex life.

- Porn is fiction in the way that most other media is fiction. It should therefore not be used as sex ed.

- Most free porn is monetized by collecting clicks and therefore ad revenues. This means that there is a lot of porn out there that is mostly about maximizing clicks. If you prefer porn that is more about a satisfying user experience, you may prefer to pay with dollars than with clicks.

- Some people feel uncomfortable with their porn use, perhaps because they spend more time than they would want or watch things that they then feel badly about. As with the rest of sexuality (and life in general), we each need to figure out where we stand and how to act in a way that we can respect.

- Some people feel uncomfortable with their partner's porn use, which can cause fights in the relationship. There is a lot to be discussed between partners in order to create an agreement that both partners feel OK about and can therefore sustain.

- There are those who claim that porn can be addictive in the way that alcohol is, although the science doesn't back that up. While it's absolutely true that some people use porn in problematic ways, there are other ways of thinking about and addressing the habit that may be more helpful than the addiction model.

Section III
Overcome Specific Issues

Introduction: The Double-Edged Sword of Sex

Wanting something can be a great motivator to works towards it, including by making the necessary personal changes or striving to overcome external barriers. However, wanting something also carries with it the risk of rejection, disappointment, and resentment, especially if we are depending on someone else to be part of the solution. This then raises the question of whether we are better off pursuing what we don't have or finding a way to be happy with what we already have. Philosophers and advertisers may have different answers, although it probably matters whether we're talking about personal freedom or static-free sweaters.

When it comes to sex, we all have our opinions. I would take the position that if sex matters to you, then it matters. There's no right or wrong amount or kind of sex, other than that if you want to have that sex with someone else, then the two of you need to figure out what works. Although great sexual chemistry can have a positive effect on a couple's relationship and each partner's overall happiness, sexual problems or disagreements can be just as bad as the benefits are good. In this way, sex can be a double-edged sword.

In this section, I will talk about various sexual and relationship problems and how to overcome them so you can both get more of what you want. It's not about more is better or that wilder is better (sorry, *Cosmo* and *Men's Health*), but rather that the amount and kind that works for you is better. It's about maximizing the overlap between what you and your partner each want—just as you try to do with every other activity and decision. It's probably less work if you and your partner are generally similar in your desired frequency and specific activities, since there will be less distance to bridge in your negotiations, but couples find ways to come to acceptable agreements even when they start out completely different.

Sometimes the gap to cross doesn't involve your partner, but rather exists between your desired ability to perform and your actual abilities. Problems of performance and desire are not at all uncommon, but also not a death knell for a good sex life. Many can be overcome, improved upon, or worked around. That's what this section is about—getting things back on track.

12

When the Negotiations Break Down

It's not uncommon for the two members of a couple to have some different sexual desires, in both what they want to do and how often they want to do it. Hopefully there is enough overlap that you can create a good sex life together, but even in the happiest couples there will be some differences of opinion or at least desires in the moment. After all, do you and your partner agree about every other thing all the time?

As much as these disagreements can cause strife, there are ways to negotiate out the differences between you and your partner so that you both feel like you get more of what you want, without feeling pressured to do what you don't want to do. If you can negotiate in good faith and come to a mutually satisfying agreement, especially about something as potentially sensitive as sex, that good behavior will benefit your relationship outside of bed, too.

In *Chapter 6: Respectful Communication and Productive Negotiation*, I talked about how couples create a shared sex life. This process can involve some difficult conversations, as can the rest of a relationship, but hopefully there is a good outcome on the other side of that discomfort, especially if both partners make an effort to handle it well. Or at least eventually handle it well. Some strife and getting stuck is pretty standard issue. This chapter is for those situations where a couple is really stuck and the disagreement is causing too much damage to the relationship.

Disagreements About Our Shared Sexual Repertoire

Just as couples can have different preferences about almost everything else, partners can disagree about what sorts of activities are desirable within their shared sex life. Because sex can feel more personal and vulnerable, there is potentially a lot more meaning attached to any differences between the partners' desires. As in, "What's wrong with you that you are/aren't into this?"

Perhaps more so than with other topics, we have a tendency to get moralistic about sexual desires that differ too much from our own desires and make us uncomfortable. That is, it's not just about the activity itself, but what that preference reveals about someone who is into it. As in, "You like vinegar on your french fries? Only sociopaths like that." Maybe it's because our partner's sexual desires can feel like they carry an expectation for us to participate, so it's hard to be an uninvolved by-stander. It can feel like it forces a dilemma—I either need to do something I really don't want to do or I need to tell you that you can't do something you really want to do. It can feel like a situation where one person wins and one loses. It can feel bad to be a grudging participant and it can feel bad to deny our partner. So, potentially, no one wins.

When confronted with this dilemma, it's tempting to bolster your position by taking the moral high ground ("Good people aren't into that," or "You're being uptight and withholding"). What's great about evoking morality is that it eliminates the dilemma. It unequivocally supports your position and invalidates the other person's perspective since there is something wrong with them for holding their position. Slam dunk! The problem is that evoking morality is usually not a convincing argument—few partners see the error of their ways like this. What evoking morality may do is end the discussion, but that is not the same as resolution or agreement. It just drives it underground where it waits to potentially come up again.

Another tactic is to use other people's sex lives as a justification for why you two should or shouldn't do something. While I am all for considering what others are doing as a way to perhaps get some ideas, it doesn't really matter what your friends are doing sexually, unless you are planning to include them in your sex life. First of all, who actually knows what they're doing because people tend to be less than honest about sex (except in seventy-question anonymous online surveys where they lay it all out there, of course)—some people round up, some down. Regardless, even if you surveyed your friends and they not only told you everything but also drew you diagrams and showed you some video off the nanny cam, that still doesn't mean that what they are doing is what you should do. If it works for them, great, but it would be like deciding what to put on your fries by polling your friends—maybe you know too many Belgians who put mayo on their fries and are therefore definitely going to hell.

More than most topics, sex can evoke strong feelings that we don't fully understand in the moment. If that discomfort is too great, it can be difficult to see beyond that visceral reaction to have a productive conversation about the proposed activity, what it means, why it might be of interest, what each partner's concerns might be, etc.

The better approach to resolving these disagreements is to have an honest and fearless conversation—definitely easier said than done, but much more likely to lead to a decision that you both can feel OK about. It may begin with some serious self-reflection:

• Why is/isn't this sexual desire interesting to me?
• Why is it important to me that we do/don't do it?
• Is there anything about this desire that makes me uncomfortable or is hard to admit?
• What is my understanding of why my partner is/isn't interested in this desire?
• What am I willing to give to get what I want here?

- If we did act on this desire, what would that mean about each of us and our relationship? And what if we didn't?
- Is there a compromise that would be acceptable?

The better you understand your own feelings, the more productive a conversation with someone else will be. As you share your perspective, you need to stay open to your partner's perspective by asking them the same questions. There probably won't be any quick and easy answers and you will need to find a way to tolerate that uncertainty until the two of you come to some sort of resolution. Resist the temptation to push for a quick decision since it probably won't serve you best. Besides, if you and your partner have been stuck on this topic for a while, you have already tried all the quick decisions and found they don't work.

Push past the obvious answers and try to go deeper into both the desire and the hesitation: "yeah, but why?" How does it connect to the rest of who you each are, your previous experiences, your personalities, your shared sex life, and your relationship overall? All this background may help you better understand yourself and each other which will serve you well as future issues arise. This may require some serious honesty which requires some serious emotional regulation. Whether we are the person doing the talking or the one doing the listening, we need to keep our heads on and stay present in the discussion.

Especially pay attention to what is happening when one of you feels uncomfortable, anxious, scared, overwhelmed, judgmental, angry, ashamed, etc. What is being evoked there? Most likely something important—maybe really important. Take some deep breaths and center yourself. Tell your partner what they can do to help. Ask for a break if you need it (or your partner does), but then be sure to actually come back. The goal here is not to reduce the discomfort—it's to have a meaningful conversation which sometimes requires us to go into the discomfort. Often, when we get and stay stuck, it's because we avoid the discomfort and then don't get to the deeper truth behind it. We may need to push ourselves, as well as our partner, to stay in the conversation and to bring each of our bests. Regardless of the outcome, it also matters how we got there, so it's important to act with integrity since we are answerable to ourselves, if not our partner, for our behavior.

The balance point in these challenging conversations is to push for what you want, without pushing your partner over; to honor your partner's limits, without selling yourself short; to accept your partner's requests, without sacrificing your integrity. To do this requires the sometimes emotionally complex position of standing strong on your own desires while also honoring your partner's ability to want something different, recognizing that there may be no easy answers but that you will both be happier for it if you can both be decent about how you handle the negotiation.

Disagreements About How Often We Do It

It's not uncommon for the two members of a couple to have at least somewhat different desires for the frequency of sex—and it's not always the man with the higher drive. There's probably a fair amount of biology at work that determines our desired frequency, but there is also a lot of social learning that influences how comfortable we are acting on those sexual desires when they do begin to bubble up. It can also depend on how we feel about our partner, in that specific moment and in general, as well as the times that we feel horny without anyone else in the mix. It can also be very situational, based on how happy or stressed we are, what else is going on in our life, what is happening at that specific moment, etc. In addition, some people can get turned on and really enjoy sex once they get going, but don't find themselves spontaneously desiring sex as often as other people do (more on this later). There is a lot that can influence how often we want to have sex.

Couples with fairly similar drives tend to be more satisfied with their sex lives, because they tend to get about as much sex as they want, without feeling pressured for more than they want. Awesome—sign me up.

But what about those couples who didn't get as lucky—and what about those couples who *really* didn't get as lucky? Large desire discrepancies can place a real strain on relationships and the survey data showed that the more imbalanced the initiation of sex was, the more dissatisfied the partners were—especially with their sex life, but also with their relationship. When one partner was always the initiator, both partners tended to be quite unhappy. This could reflect a significant desire discrepancy, but there might be other reasons why one partner initiates so infrequently (e.g., a belief that good girls don't do that, anger towards their partner, sexual performance concerns, depression, etc.) that may need to be addressed. This imbalance can create a situation where one partner feels pressured and one feels disappointed—again and again. Unlike some nonsexual desire discrepancies, like how often to go out to concerts, that can be resolved with one partner partaking and one passing, sex isn't so easily split up, at least if we're talking about partnered activities in a monogamous relationship.

This can lead to a chase dynamic where the higher desire partner watches their partner with eagle eyes, looking for any signs of potential interest, and often tries to sell them on the idea of getting naked together (maybe they will be interested this time!). Meanwhile, the lower desire partner knows they are being observed and makes a point of not showing any potential signs of interest (where did I put those ratty old pajamas?). Ironically, both partners can feel powerless: the higher desire partner feels at the stingy mercy of their partner's yes whereas the lower desire partner feels forever barraged by overt or subtle requests. Taken to extremes, the higher desire partner may try to initiate even when they're not really that interested, since they don't want to miss out on a potential yes, resulting in a lot more requests. Meanwhile, the lower desire partner gets turned off by the constant pressure and never gets a chance for their natural desire to build, resulting in a lot more nos. This can be pretty miserable for both partners.

Close (or Shrink) the Gap

How often a couple has sex is less important than that they are both happy about it, so it's really more about trying to shrink the difference between their desired frequencies. While I suppose it's possible to accomplish this by the lower desire partner purposely doing annoying things to knock down the higher desire partner's libido, it's probably better to start by trying to increase the lower desire partner's frequency.

This may begin with the deceptively simple question of, *What will make sex worth wanting more of for you?* This may involve the sex itself (more of this, less of that), but it may also involve lots of things that have nothing to do with sex, such as getting more sleep so they aren't passing out when it's time to get excited. I talked at length in *Chapter 4: Role Models: What Can We Learn from the Happiest Couples?* about many lessons learned from the survey about the couples with the best relationships and sex lives. For example, respondents who felt that their partner put in more effort on managing their or their partner's ADHD were more likely to feel sexually generous.

This process may begin with the lower desire partner spending some time thinking about what impacts their desire, both positively and negatively—in this relationship and in previous ones. There may be some good lessons learned from the past for things that you can apply now—e.g., getting into bed early so you have some time to talk and connect without feeling rushed. If you can identify these helpers and hurters, then you can both make a conscious effort to lay that groundwork to make it easier to be sexual. It's sad but true that, when we get caught up in a busy life, we sometimes get a little lazy, despite knowing better. Even for something as fun and important as sex. When you find yourself or your partner slipping down that path of least resistance, make that extra effort to get yourself back on track.

It may be that the solution is not quite so simple and that you and your partner need to spend some time thinking and then talking about what is making sex less desirable. Some discussions about this may help flesh out that understanding, especially if you each approach it with genuine curiosity, rather than an agenda to change anything—yet. The goal here is just to understand, before leaping to do anything about it. The better your understanding, the more likely you are to create solutions that actually work, rather than jumping at the first idea.

Some of what it takes to increase desire may be relatively simple, like using a little bit of lube. But some of it may also involve bigger and deeper matters, such as, "I want to feel like I can say no and have a partner who can handle it, so that when I say yes it's because I really do want it." These are the sorts of things that won't come out if you rush the process and will then continue to trip you up, no matter how much lube you use.

The higher desire partner also has their part to play in all this exploration. For example, why is more sex important to them?

Beyond the obvious that it feels good, what does it mean to them (about themselves, their partner, the relationship) if they have more sex—and what if they don't? What does it mean when their partner says no—or yes? Some people feel like a no isn't just about sex in the moment, but is a rejection of them personally. Or they slide into catastrophic thinking, panicked that things will never get better and they will need to settle for a dissatisfying sex life.

Sometimes discussions about sex become about a lot more than sex. If you just stay on the surface and focus on logistics and the negotiations keep breaking down, it may be because there are some deeper, and as yet unspoken, matters at work that are worth addressing. This may involve some vulnerability and it may challenge your level of intimacy, but if it gets handled well, your relationship will be better off for it. If you're stuck, you need to keep asking yourself and your partner, "What else is going on here? What else do we need to consider and talk about?" It may take a series of conversations to chip away at what is going on. Lots of good behavior on everyone's part will definitely help things along. If these discussions tend to bring out more of the worst than the best in one or both of you and you really can't get to some sort of mutually satisfying resolution, it may be helpful to add a therapist to the mix, preferably one who has some training in sex therapy.

All of this assumes that the lower desire partner still wants to have sex, just not as much as their partner does. For some couples, it isn't a matter of degree, but rather that one partner isn't really all that interested in sex. In this case, you may want to check out *Chapter 14: Problems With Desire: Not Enough Sex.*

Generosity Always Helps

Whether you're the partner who wants more sex overall (or just wants it more right now) or the one who generally wants it less, generosity may be your way out of the disagreement. For example, the person who is less interested may generously offer to do something to give their partner a good time, even though they're not in the mood themselves. However, what is offered may be different from what their partner was hoping for, so that is where their generosity comes in—to graciously be happy about what is being offered, rather than get stuck on what isn't; to enjoy what they are getting, rather than stubbornly wish for more.

At other times when one of the partners is not interested in any sexual activity at that time, then the act of generosity may involve encouraging their partner to freely meet their needs on their own if they choose to. (For more on solo activities, check out *Chapter 10: Taking Some Personal Time: Masturbation.*) The generosity for their partner involves being good about their disappointment, making a shared sexual experience more likely next time, since nothing kills sexual desire better than guilt and resentment. Plus, if you both feel comfortable asking for sex, as well as declining it, confident that you will get a decent response either way, there will probably be more requests and therefore more opportunities to do things together.

Emily Nagoski, PhD has written extensively about how sexual desire can be both spontaneous and responsive. Sometimes desire arises seemingly on its own or quickly from passing sexy thoughts, without much effort. Sometimes though, desire takes longer to build and you may find that you don't start wanting sex until you have already started flirting, kissing, and touching. In other words, sometimes desire follows activity/arousal. This should absolutely not be used as a manipulative justification to push someone to do something they don't want to do, but if you know that you tend to get in the mood if you allow yourself to start down that road, then you can try to start things on good faith, with the idea that you may wind up wanting it. (More on this in the section *Exciters and Inhibitors: The Sexual Gas and Brake* in *Chapter 9: Sex 101 (and 201, and 301. . .).)*

Yet again, generosity here is key. If you feel generous and decide to play along to see if you can kindle some desire, then you still retain the right to change course along the way if the spark never turns into a flame. However, you can increase the odds by educating your partner on what to do to help you find that interest. The generosity on the more interested partner's part is to be good about it if plans change. This good behavior will be rewarded with more opportunities next time to try again.

As in so many other ways, good sex is a collaborative process and generosity tends to be a good thing in relationships.

Difficult Sexual Negotiations

Sexual negotiations can become highly emotional, especially when the two members of the couple have very different desires and they can't find an acceptable middle ground. If not resolved productively, it can lead to resentment, frustration, withdrawal, and hopelessness. It can end a relationship or leave a lasting tension if the couple stays together.

Whereas it's pretty normal to have some disagreements in your sex life, some of those sexual differences can become intractable or cause much more strife. These are those painful situations where at least one member of the couple, but probably both, are really unhappy about the stalemate, but neither knows how to resolve it. There are no easy answers here because, if there had been, then they would have already found them.

Irreconcilable differences early in a relationship will probably lead at least one member of the couple to end it and move on, hopefully allowing both people to find greater happiness elsewhere. However, as a relationship deepens and the couple's lives become increasingly intertwined, it is not as easy to end it— obviously people still do, but the emotional and financial price is much higher when there are kids and mortgages involved. While we wouldn't wish this suffering on anyone, this high price can be a strong incentive to try to make the relationship worth sticking around for. It forces us to do that hard work so that both partners feel that staying is better than going. This means expressing and fighting for our own needs, while also being respectful of our partner's needs.

Undue selfishness, insensitivity, or lack of consideration will probably become a deal breaker for at least one partner eventually. The balancing act in relationships involves getting our own needs met while also meeting our partner's. We can't expect our partner to be more generous or behave better than we ourselves do, so bad behavior may work temporarily, but tends to backfire in the end or in other parts of the relationship.

When it comes to sex, making excessive demands (as defined by the recipient) can be as damaging as excessively denying a partner's requests (as defined by the denied). There are no right or wrong answers when it comes to sex and relationships, nor are there absolutes. What works for one couple may not work for another. *What* a couple does or doesn't do may be less important than *why* they do or don't do it and how they each feel about that.

The risk of ignoring our own or our partner's sexual or relational unhappiness is that it can lead to worse outcomes for both people— one or both people drift out of the relationship; one or both people begin investing that energy elsewhere (e.g., work, hobbies) or into other people. This is another motivator to do that hard work to resolve those disagreements in a way that both people can feel good about. Or at least good enough.

Within ethical and legal constraints, we all have the right to push for what we want from our partner—and to suffer the consequences for pushing too hard. Similarly, we also have the right to deny our partner's requests—and to suffer the consequences for shutting them down. But we need to remember that nothing in a relationship happens in a vacuum—it is influenced by what came before, as well as what else is going on in the relationship. So generosity can be rewarded (and bad behavior can be punished) in more ways than one. Therefore, we have to keep the bigger picture in mind—what price am I willing to pay for this? If it's worth it, then it's worth it, but since life and relationships involve compromise and sacrifice, we have to consider the potential ripple effects.

When you feel at an impasse on one topic, it can be helpful to think about what else is good or bad in the relationship and how important this current topic is to you. This may help you decide how much you want to push for what you want on this topic. It's also worth thinking about how important this is to your partner and whether your sacrifice will be worth it.

Long-term relationships involve tons of negotiations on all sorts of topics, sexual and otherwise. Every couple needs to figure out what works for them, at each stage of the relationship. While there may not be many universals, one certainty is that behaving well during those negotiations, even when taking a strong stand for or against something, makes it much more likely that your partner will also respond well and that you will probably get more of what you want. And if your partner isn't responding well, then perhaps that needs to become the topic of discussion.

If you find that you and your partner keep getting bogged down and you can't find a middle ground that works, it may be worth bringing in a therapist to help you overcome whatever the roadblocks are. This will probably be a couples or sex therapist where you both meet together, but it is also possible to work on your relationship by seeing a therapist alone, if your partner doesn't want to go in together (yet). Some people feel that needing to see a therapist is a bad sign for the relationship, but I would say that it is a good sign for how important the relationship is to you and how committed you are to making things better.

Seriously Irreconcilable Differences

Sometimes couples find themselves stuck in an impasse where neither partner is willing to shift their position. Perhaps they have discussed it *ad nauseum*. Perhaps one partner has tried relentlessly to discuss it but the other partner just won't engage. This can involve lots of nonsexual matters too, but in a couple's sex life, it could involve either how frequently they have sex or what they do during sex. Both people have a strong opinion and there's no easy middle ground.

If you find yourself stuck in one of these situations where you really don't want to give up what you want but can't get your partner to accommodate it, you have a hard choice to make. You need to decide whether it's worth tolerating this one dissatisfaction (or perhaps multiple) in order to get the rest of the benefits of the relationship. No partner will be perfect and no relationship will meet our every wish, but there is perhaps a threshold below which we may feel that we would be happier seeking our fortunes in a new relationship. This can be an extremely difficult choice to make and to pull the trigger on, but it can feel worse not to. If you do so, I encourage you to make the break as respectfully and cleanly as possible. Be honest about your motives and try to be good to each other in the process.

Also, however tempting, resist the urge to stray and start something with someone else before figuring out what to do with this first relationship. Not only can an affair really muddy the waters on what you really want, if you get caught (don't delude yourself that you definitely won't), it can blow up the relationship in an instant. Not only is this hurtful to your partner, it can also crank up the anger and vengeance in the break-up, something that is good for no one, especially any kids involved. An affair also makes it much harder to have an honest discussion about what worked and what didn't in the relationship so that you can both hopefully go forward with a better understanding.

On the other hand, if you assess your relationship, you may decide that there is still more good than bad and that you are willing to forsake this desire in order to keep the rest. If so, you may feel better about it if you can recognize that you had the option to leave but that you made an active choice to stay. You're not the passive victim of circumstances, forced to stay in an unhappy situation, but rather you decided that staying, at least for now, is the best of your available options. Feeling that sense of agency can make it easier to enjoy the parts of the relationship that are working, with less disappointment and resentment.

Podcaster and sex advice columnist Dan Savage has offered a rather radical solution to these intractable situations. If the relationship overall is good and worth keeping but there is a serious sexual disagreement that will likely never be resolved, it may be possible for the couple to essentially farm out some or all of their sex life to someone else by creating a consensually nonmonogamous arrangement. There's a lot to be said about how to do these well, but I cover it briefly in *Chapter 16: Consensual Sex With Other People: Other Arrangements*. The key here is that the arrangement is consensual, as opposed to secretly getting those sexual or emotional needs met by cheating. Making this work is no easy feat, but it may be the only way to keep the good parts of the relationship and eliminate the fighting that is destroying it.

Even if this seems like a crazy idea, it may be worth considering in certain situations. If nothing else, putting this third option out on the table may intensify the conversation about how you each feel about the relationship and what you are willing to do to make it work—or clarify that it just isn't working.

Take Away Lessons

- It's not uncommon for partners to have some differences in what they want sexually. Or when, where, how, and why. In order to keep sex mutually satisfying for the long haul, they need to find a way to resolve these differences productively. It's not uncommon though for couples to get stuck without a mutually satisfying resolution.

- If one partner is struggling to understand why something turns the other on, it may take some real digging and honest communication to be able to feel OK with something that at first felt threatening. The couple may or may not act on that desire, but at least it is no longer a point of insecurity, resentment, or jealousy.

- If one partner has a significantly lower libido than the other, it may be worth thinking about what would make sex more worth wanting for that person. It may also involve occasional generosity to pitch in when not in the mood, as well as generosity to be happy with getting less than what one would ideally want.

- Couples who find themselves really stuck when negotiating a sexual (or nonsexual) matter, need to work hard to have an honest and difficult discussion about how to balance seemingly irreconcilable differences. The better you understand your own feelings and why you have them, the easier it is to hear your partner's feelings without getting defensive or backing down prematurely.

13

Problems With Performance and Pleasure

Despite the fact that the survival of the species is dependent on most members of the population being able to make sex work at least well enough, some people experience difficulties with sex that can interfere with their desire, performance, pleasure, or all three. Almost everyone experiences some transient difficulties, but sometimes these problems don't get better with time. Since these enduring problems can have a large negative effect on individuals' and couples' sex lives, overall relationship satisfaction, and self-esteem, they are worth addressing. Besides, there is too much to gain from a great sexual connection that you don't want to miss out on it.

I didn't ask survey respondents specifically about problems with performance and pleasure, but lots of survey respondents talked about painful intercourse, erectile disorder, and premature ejaculation in the open-ended questions about what would make their sex life better. Some of them found these problems to be major barriers, whereas others felt comfortable working around them. In this chapter, we will talk about how to minimize the impacts of these types of problems, whether that entails reducing their frequency or creating a good sex life despite them.

As with ADHD, there is a wide range of expertise (and comfort) with treating sexual matters, so you may need to do some research to find someone with the necessary expertise. If you would like to see a therapist, look for one who has had some additional training in sex therapy. If you would like to see a physician who has more than general expertise, there are sexual medicine experts who have primary training in another area of medicine, such as urology or gynecology, and then specialize in sexual health. If the standard issue treatments don't work, they will probably be able to figure out a more nuanced understanding and create a more effective treatment plan. You can find provider directories for these more knowledgeable clinicians in Appendix B.

It's definitely true that problems with performance, pleasure, and desire can interact and that each one makes the others more likely. In this chapter, we'll cover performance and pleasure, then go on to desire in the next chapter, because sometimes problems with desire are influenced by problems with performance and/or pleasure. Makes sense.

It's All Connected

It's hard to separate out individual and relationship factors from sexual matters, since they all overlap. For this reason, when sex therapists work with clients who have a romantic partner, they will tend to see both partners, even if it is only one who has a sexual problem. Since, by definition, non-masturbatory sex involves another person, it makes sense to include that other person when trying to understand what is working well and not so well in the client's sex life and relationship. Sometimes they include the partner in order to help the partner better understand the designated client's sexual difficulty and how to respond more productively. For example, talking with the female partner on how to respond to a bout of erectile difficulty (e.g., don't freak out).

Sometimes, though, a sexual problem in one partner may indicate a complementary problem in the other partner. In fact, my sex therapy professor always emphasized the importance of looking at what is going on with both partners because sexual disorders often don't travel alone. For example, a guy with erectile difficulties may have a girlfriend who experiences pain with sex. He feels badly about her discomfort and isn't able to get enough of an erection for sex or loses it midway through because he senses (or worries) that he is hurting her. This interconnectedness makes it all the more important for both partners to be involved in treatment.

This interconnectedness can even take place within a single person. For example, a guy with erectile difficulties may hyperfocus on arousing stimuli in order to maintain his erection but then inadvertently push himself over the orgasmic edge too quickly, causing premature ejaculation. Or if the guy is worried about coming too quickly, he may distract himself from arousing thoughts and sensations and thereby lose his erection. As with so much in life, often things work best somewhere in the middle.

Sex and relationships can get complicated and involve a lot of moving parts, literally and figuratively. If something isn't working as hoped, and your attempted solutions aren't getting the job done, it may be that you need to look more deeply or broadly to see what else is contributing to the problem. This is where skilled specialists, rather than generalists, can be especially helpful.

Genito-Pelvic Pain/Penetration Disorder *can 7. sure*

The latest version of the official psychiatric diagnostic manual, the *DSM-5*, combined two separate female sexual disorders into one. Dyspareunia was pain with intercourse and vaginismus involved contraction of the outer third of the vagina that prevented penetration and intercourse. As you might imagine, these two overlap. These two separate diagnoses were combined into the new mouthful, Genito-Pelvic Pain/Penetration Disorder (GPPPD) and involves one of these four symptoms:

- Difficulty with vaginal penetration during intercourse
- Marked genital or pelvic pain during intercourse attempts
- Significant fear of pain as a result of vaginal penetration

- Tensing or tightening the pelvic floor muscles during attempted vaginal penetration

Some women have a lifelong presence of these symptoms whereas others develop them along the way. The symptoms can be caused or influenced by a variety of factors, including:

- *Physical* Various infections, pelvic inflammatory disease, endometriosis, provoked vestibulodynia (PVD), pelvic floor abnormalities, chemotherapy, and conditions related to menopause can all cause pain with intercourse.
- *Psychological* Expecting and fearing pain during intercourse, being highly attuned to one's physical sensations, anxiety, depression, having negative or ambivalent attitudes generally about sexuality, and feeling powerless to do anything about potential pain can all exacerbate the perceived intensity or effect of pain with intercourse.
- *Relational* Partners who quickly back off from sexual activity at the first possibility of pain can reinforce sexual avoidance and catastrophizing, as can angry responses.

The presence of pain that is impacting your sexual functioning almost always warrants a medical exam by a gynecologist and possibly also a physical therapist who is knowledgeable about these matters. Depending on what is going on, your regular ob/gyn may be more than knowledgeable enough to address it, but if the recommended treatment seems overly involved, if progress is slow or nonexistent, or if you are told that there isn't anything to be done for it, then you probably want a second opinion from someone with more expertise in treating sexual pain. Sometimes a more sophisticated understanding leads to less intrusive yet more effective interventions.

A sex therapist can work with both partners to understand the situation better, explore how it has impacted their sex life, work through exercises to expand their sexual options, and generally get along better. There will likely be some education at the start of therapy, followed by gradual experimentation at home. These experiments (e.g., try inserting just one finger, by yourself) will also help the couple and treatment providers to better identify what is going on physically, what thoughts and feelings get evoked in each partner, how the partners respond to each other, etc. If the presence or intensity of the pain feels mysterious and unpredictable, it can be helpful to keep a pain journal where the couple records various aspects of the situation and then later goes through the entries to try to determine the pattern that is hiding in there.

The goal of treatment obviously is total elimination of pain, but that isn't always possible or perhaps involves treatments that are otherwise undesirable. In these cases, a therapist can help the couple sort through their options and decide what treatments to pursue. They can also work on creating a satisfying sexual repertoire that takes the pain into account but that isn't unnecessarily limited by it. By identifying the specific circumstances that lead to more or less pain, the couple can feel more sexually confident and not at the mercy of sudden and unpredictable pain. This helps them get to a point where they genuinely want sex because they are confident that it will be a positive experience for both of them—worrying about pain is a giant buzz kill. Ultimately the goal is to make sexuality, however the couple chooses to express it, something that they both look forward to eagerly, rather than avoid.

Accomplishing this goal may involve working with both partners on other sexual matters (e.g., erectile difficulties or premature ejaculation in the male partner) as well as working with the couple to not just overcome problems, but to make a good thing better. This can include working on various ways to increase connection, foster exploration of new sexual options, resolve problems or disagreements effectively, etc. As with many other struggles, sometimes those who overcome difficulties actually put themselves into an even better place.

Erectile Disorder: Not the End of the World

Erections sometimes go missing, but it doesn't need to be a big deal nor the end of the fun. Many men find that they sometimes have difficulty getting or maintaining a satisfying erection. This may be more common as they get older, but can occur to men of any age.

Sometimes it is related to normal changes associated with aging. Some of it is also due to the fact that older men tend to have more health problems that can negatively impact their erections—as can certain medications and treatments.

Fortunately, despite all the angst that they can produce, erectile difficulties often respond quite well to medical and/or psychological treatment. The goal is not simply more reliable or firm erections, but the broader one of helping the couple create a mutually enjoyable sex life. Some of this will involve working with both partners to help restore the man's erectile ability, but treatment will probably also involve helping both partners to not tie all of their sexual satisfaction (or self-esteem) to the presence and firmness of the erection. If you do this well, it has the potential to create a sex life that is even more enjoyable than it was before the erectile difficulties began— might as well get some benefit from the suffering.

Just as a good erection results from a combination of physical, psychological, and relationship factors, so too are erectile difficulties potentially influenced by all of these, so we need to look at all three in order to figure out what is getting in the way.

- *Physical* Erectile capacity can be negatively impacted by any of the following: diabetes, hypertension, Peyronie's disease (bent erections), endocrine problems, prostate surgery/radiotherapy, and neurological problems (Alzheimer's, Parkinson's). In addition, antihypertensives, antiandrogens, major tranquilizers, SSRI antidepressants, and the nonstimulant ADHD medication Strattera can all play a role.

What would make your sex life better for your partner?

He can struggle with getting and maintaining erections at times. It's not a physical problem, and most often occurs when he's upset with himself, depressed, and/or gets distracted by something.

Non-ADHD woman, 36, living together,
been together 6–10 years

- *Psychological* Depression, anger, anxiety, low self-esteem, sexual self-doubt or discomfort, and poor body image can all interfere with erectile ability, as well as general enjoyment of sex. Of course, erectile difficulties can also cause or worsen all of these. For some men (and their partners), one random bout of erectile difficulty can cause a downward spiral of performance anxiety where every time thereafter they worry about their ability to get an erection which then undermines their ability to get one which reinforces that worry. . . .

- *Relational* Other relationship or sexual issues can impact a man's ability to get an erection with his partner, as can his partner's sexual functioning (e.g., low or ambivalent desire, pain with intercourse, etc.). Once erectile difficulties begin, they can obviously also impact the other partner and can elicit many feelings, thoughts, and reactions. It is easy for both partners to get over-focused on the current state of the erection (by which I mean freak out) which makes sex much less enjoyable for both and thereby makes erections even more elusive.

If you suspect that other medical conditions, medications, or treatments are impacting your erectile abilities, then speak with your treatment providers and, if necessary, explore your options. Your general practitioner can run a standard battery of blood work to look for the more common contributors, but a urologist may do some more advanced testing (e.g., is too little blood entering the penis or is it leaving too quickly?).

Medications such as Viagra, Cialis, Levitra, and Stendra can help to create more reliable erections for many men. Depending on the causes, there are also other medical treatments such as hormone supplements and erection-inducing injections, as well as devices such as vacuum pumps, internal pump systems, and other more high-tech options, too, if necessary. In addition, improving your general cardiovascular health by exercising, eating better, losing weight, and stopping smoking may also have some positive effect on your erections which is yet another great reason to take good care of your body. These interventions will counteract the physical contributors to erectile difficulties, but won't necessarily fix the psychological or relationship aspects. This explains why, despite erection medications being quite effective, most guys don't refill their first prescription. Suddenly springing a boner on your partner won't magically lead to sexual ecstasy—it didn't work when you were fifteen and it won't work now.

Once erectile difficulties begin, it can impact both members of the couple and how they relate to each other, both sexually and otherwise. When some couples do try to have sex, they wind up approaching it with such uncertainty that it is no longer enjoyable—instead of focusing on all the pleasurable aspects of the experience, all eyes are on the state of the erection, making it much more about performance and monitoring than fun. It becomes like taking your driver's test (which makes parallel parking sound dirty). This process is called spectatoring where the person/couple is so focused on observing what is happening that they are no longer a full participant in the action. If it becomes uncomfortable enough, some couples may avoid sex entirely. Therefore, a sex therapist can help you sort through this fallout and rise above it to create a mutually satisfying sex life. This may begin by helping you and your partner to think through the various treatment options so you can make a well informed and well thought out decision, then make best use of the treatments that you do choose.

The goal of treatment, whether with a therapist or on your own, may involve a return to your previous sex life, but it may instead focus on creating a new one. Overcoming erectile difficulties often begins by avoiding the erection-killing trap where the more hyperfocused you get on the erection, the more it fades away. Ironically, focusing on each other and the pleasurable sensations and letting the erection do what it will do, makes for more reliable erections. The antidote for spectatoring is to shift your focus back to the present moment: what are the sensations on your body? What do you see, hear, smell, and taste? What dirty thoughts were rolling around in your head before the spectatoring pushed them out?

You and your partner can counteract spectatoring by engaging in a couple straightforward exercises at home. They are rather simple to do but, like much else, require some practice to do well. For example, sensate focus exercises can help you both learn to focus more on the enjoyable physical sensations and let distracting thoughts go, by moving slowly and deliberately through a series of touching exercises. There is often a mindfulness component to keep the couple mentally present and in their bodies and to let doubts and distractions slide by. A full description of sensate focus goes beyond what we can cover here, but there are lots of resources online that can give you all the dirty details.

Stop-start exercises help the man and his partner to see that he (they) has more control over his erections than they feared, by getting him up, keeping him up for a bit, letting the erection fade away, then doing it again, and maybe a third time before coming—and then getting his partner off, too, if desired. These successes help both members of the couple to see that they have control over it and therefore not fear its sudden and mysterious disappearance because they have faith that they can get it back up again. This protects against those panic death spirals that will knock a boner down in a millisecond. And although it may seem weird to say that getting a hard-on is a skill, it benefits from regular practice, like any (less fun) skill.

If a guy is able to get good erections in some situations but then not in others, or if he loses good ones along the way, a therapist can help the couple figure out how to reconcile these contradictions. By comparing and contrasting the times when the erection does and doesn't work well, the therapist can help the guy to identify what thoughts or feelings go through his head before, during, and after he loses his erection. If you really pay attention, you will notice that there are indeed some really quick thoughts rattling around in there and that they are the little man behind the curtain who is controlling what happens down below. For example, is he worried about pregnancy? Scared of disappointing his partner? Convinced that reliable erections are a thing of the past? So consumed by any minute change to the status of his erection that he is hardly paying attention to the naked person with whom he is presumably going to use that erection?

Meanwhile, his partner might also find it helpful to talk to that therapist, either together or in her (or his) own session. It's too easy to take a flagging erection as a damning vote on how hot, sexy, or dirty she is. After all, hard-ons just appear all by themselves, right? And, frankly, too often and with too little provocation. So, therefore, if there is a boner malfunction it can only be because the partner isn't sexually interesting enough, right?

The good news about the partner blaming herself is that then they can both share the misery of feeling terrible about what isn't working out—and there's never a shortage of self-blame to go around in these situations. The bad news is that it probably isn't helpful and probably makes things worse. Unless your partner actually says, "Honey, I can't keep it up because you don't turn me on enough," then don't let your insecurities run away with you. The reason is that two people over-invested in the state of the erection doesn't make it work better than if only one is obsessed with it. Quite the opposite, since then both people are focusing more on the boner than on having fun together which makes the whole experience doubly awkward and unsexy. Two adults in a long-term relationship suddenly become two nervous teenagers trying to figure out what to do and hoping they don't mess it up. If you didn't have erection problems before, that will certainly take the wind out of your sails.

A therapist might also address other relationship matters that are impacting the couple's sex life in general and erectile issues specifically (as in, everything else in this book). These other matters may have preceded the erection problems, been caused or exacerbated by them, or have nothing to do with them. In the unlikely event that a guy is having a hard time getting it up or being interested in sex with his partner because she doesn't turn him on enough, then the therapist can help the couple navigate those potentially difficult waters and create a better situation. Incidentally, not being attracted to one's partner and feeling like the sex won't be that good were rated by survey respondents as two of the smallest barriers to a satisfying sex life, so the odds are good that your partner is happy about things when they do happen.

Improving the quality and predictability of erections is helpful, but the equally important other half of treatment involves learning ways to deal with whatever happens. Instead of hanging all of your sexual success or failure (not to mention both people's self-esteem) on how well the guy defies gravity, it can be more satisfying to also learn to compensate for any limitations in your (or your partner's) erectile capacity. After all, more options tend to lead to better outcomes. Besides, many people find that having some variety in what they do tends to keep things more interesting, now and over the long haul, regardless of erectile abilities.

This begins by broadening your definition of a satisfying sexual encounter so that completed intercourse isn't required in order to call it a success. There are plenty of other fun ways to spend that naked time together and many other ways to help your partner have a great time. Many of these other options don't require an erection, so then it doesn't matter whether or not you have one. Unless your hands and tongue also fall off when your erection disappears, there's no excuse to give up. You may even find that focusing on your partner's pleasure (or watching her get herself off) gets you out of your head and magically lets your erection re-appear. Having a trusty vibrator that can serve as a stand-in can be reassuring for both partners and a great addition to your repertoire even if all systems are go. Knowing that you have options keeps the pressure off and reduces spectatoring which eliminates that boner killer.

Ironically, even though these techniques make erections more likely, still the most important thing to keep in mind is to enjoy yourselves and be flexible about your expectations, so that you can still have fun even if the erection makes a temporary exit. If you can do this, you will have learned two important secrets of a happy sex life—flexibility and resilience.

This is especially true for couples where there is a physical cause that significantly alters the guy's erectile ability and there is no amount of therapy or Viagra that can change it. These folks may be left with more drastic options, such as surgery, that are less than ideal. This can have a major impact on the couple's sexual options. The injustice of it all can certainly fuel anger at the universe— totally understandable. The steady march of time brings change, some of which we can only accept, rather than reverse. We are all faced with moments when we need to mourn the passing from one stage of life into the next, to let go of possibilities that no longer exist. Unless you plan on dying young, this is inevitable. The folks who are happiest in their older years, and also all the years before that, are the ones who find a way to come to some acceptance of the parts of their life that they wish were different, while enjoying the parts they like. The older folks who remain satisfied sexually are the ones who continue to have a physical erotic connection, even if it looks different than it did when they were younger.

If you're struggling to find that Zen place in all this and it's tanking not only your sex life but also your general happiness, you may want to talk to an experienced sex therapist who can help you come to some peace with it all. They may also have some creative ideas for how to make the most of what you and your partner can do. I'm all in favor of DIY, but I also value the wisdom of an expert.

Premature Ejaculation: Learn to Slow it Down

Premature ejaculation may be the most common sexual problem for men. It is probably more common among younger men and men with less sexual experience, but can also appear later in men in established relationships. Ejaculation is said to be premature if it happens too quickly (which can be rather subjective and affected by expectations), the man doesn't feel able to slow it down, and he feels badly about it. This can then negatively affect the couple's sex life and overall relationship happiness, but fortunately can respond quite well to treatment.

One of the challenges with ejaculatory control is that vaginas are masterfully engineered to extract orgasms from penises. They provide just the right sensations to all the most sensitive bits, so it can be really easy to lose yourself in the majesty of it all and hit that threshold too quickly. This is great for the survival of the species, but maybe not so good if it gives you a different sexual experience than you or your partner were hoping for.

Just as good sex results from a combination of physical, psychological, and relationship factors, so too is premature ejaculation potentially influenced by all of these, so we need to look at all three in order to figure out what is going on.

- *Physical* Diabetes and cardiovascular disease have both been associated with premature ejaculation, as has withdrawal from opiates and alcohol.
- *Psychological* Depression, anxiety, low self-esteem, and sexual guilt can all make premature ejaculation more likely, as can being out of tune with one's level of sexual arousal. Ironically,

some men struggle with both premature ejaculation and also erectile difficulties—they increase stimulation to ensure they get a good erection but then orgasm too quickly or they try to distract themselves from the sensations so as to not orgasm too quickly but then lose their erection. Satisfying sex usually entails finding somewhere in between.

- *Relational* Sexual and nonsexual relationship factors can also impact the man's sexual functioning. Power struggles, anger at one's partner, poor communication, fear of commitment or intimacy, and feeling pressured to perform can all reduce the man's ejaculatory control. In addition, if the man believes that his female partner does not enjoy sex (which may not actually be true) or if she experiences discomfort during sex or he worries that she might, he may try to get it over with as quickly as possible.

There are currently no medications approved for the treatment of premature ejaculation, but the SSRI antidepressants are sometimes used off-label (i.e., unofficially). The SSRIs are notorious for having the side effect of increasing the time/stimulation necessary to reach orgasm which can be put to good use in the case of premature ejaculation. Numbing creams are available to reduce sensation and thereby slow down orgasm, but they are usually far from ideal (e.g., the man's partner may also get numb). In addition, since the point of sex is to feel what is happening, using something to reduce the sensations seems like kind of a crappy half-solution that surely can't be your best option. If the premature ejaculation is the result of over-stimulation from fears of losing one's erection, then erection medications can be helpful by letting the guy cool his jets a bit since he can trust that the erection will stick around.

However the premature ejaculation started, once a couple has been struggling with it for a while, it can cast a dark shadow on their sex life. If the guy comes too quickly and then one or both partners feel so bad about it that they bail out on the sex right then and there, it can be tempting to avoid sex entirely rather than risk another failure. But to be clear, the real problem here isn't the coming too quickly (and presumably loss of the guy's hard-on for a time), it's the feeling bad about it and then jumping ship. If one or both partners are so filled with guilt, shame, anger, and/or hopelessness that they lose that lovin' feeling, then the potential benefits of sex may not be worth the likely pain. If they do have sex again, they both may be so hypervigilant about him coming too quickly that they can't really relax and enjoy it—which almost certainly doesn't help his partner come before he does.

The antidote here is to teach the guy more control over his orgasm and his partner more faith in that control. One highly effective way to do this is to practice the stop-start technique which involves progressing through a series of exercises at home that teach you greater and greater awareness of your arousal level and response to stimulation so that you can dial it up and down as needed. For example, you may begin by having your partner stroke your erection with a dry hand (no lube) almost to the point of orgasm. She then backs off the stimulation until that urge passes, then starts again. You do this a few times before you finally choose to come—the key word here is choose. And then you definitely give her an orgasm or two, if she wants them. Once you can reliably resist falling over the edge into orgasm with this level of stimulation, then you up the difficulty level by adding lube, then by your partner climbing on top of your erection without moving, then moving slowly, then finally moving quickly. This progression could take days or months and you may add more gradations as needed. As with any skill acquisition, most couples find it most effective when they practice it two or three times a week which makes it the best homework ever.

These exercises are pretty simple, but the trick is to progress upwards fast enough that it is something of a challenge, but slowly enough that you are mostly successful. Mostly—if you blow it once in a while, so to speak, then just try it again next time. No big deal. If you never "fail," then you're probably playing it too safe.

An added bonus of these exercises is that they also help partners be more aware of not only their own level of arousal, but also their partner's, and to thereby communicate better about it. This is no small thing, since good communication and coordination make sex much better for both people.

If you find that you're not making progress in the exercises or that progress here doesn't translate to other activities, then you may be missing some nuances in what you're doing. If so, look up more detailed descriptions online to get some ideas of how to tweak it.

If you find that the stop-start technique isn't getting the job done or if you and/or your partner keep finding really important excuses to not practice it regularly, then you may need to look a little deeper for your solution. Practicing stop-start will help you be more aware of your level of arousal so that you can better manage it, but some men develop rapid ejaculation for reasons other than insufficient arousal awareness and control. There may be other factors "encouraging" him to come quickly—for example, he feels that his partner isn't enjoying sex, just wants to get it over with, finds it painful, etc. If there is truth to any of these worries, then it is worth exploring whether more foreplay, some quality lube, more variety, or different positions might make sex more enjoyable for her. If the discomfort remains or is too pronounced, then a medical examination is almost certainly worthwhile. (For more on painful sex, see the previous section *Genito-Pelvic Pain/Penetration Disorder.*)

You may find that a sex therapist can help you make the necessary refinements, explore what else is going on here, and address other relationship matters that are impacting your sex life. My sex therapy professor told us that she loves treating premature ejaculation because it responds so well to therapy that you can easily be a hero. In addition to helping you slow down the guy's orgasm, a therapist can also help both partners keep their heads on if the guy does come too quickly. Freaking out and feeling bad about oneself or each other rarely makes anything better—nor does worrying about freaking out make the dreaded outcome less likely. Alternatively, a guy who is hell-bent on not coming too quickly may find that the anxiety kills his erection and then he has the opposite problem. A therapist can teach both partners how to stay present in the pleasurable moment so that things stay on track, as well as how to resist reading in a bunch of negative stuff if things do go off track. It happened, no big deal, now what do we want to do? You presumably don't leave the restaurant if they are out of the chicken special—you find something else on the menu and focus on enjoying that. Flexibility and resiliency.

Even if you come too quickly and presumably lose your erection, that doesn't mean that the good times need to end for your partner.

You still have hands, a tongue, possibly some really awesome toys, and some dirty thoughts to share. Don't be a one trick pony where all you've got is a boner and the party is over when that has left the building. Besides, only about a third of women reliably orgasm from intercourse without some other stimulation, so hard-ons aren't the guaranteed success that most guys like to think they are (at least about their own hard-on). If you and/or your partner are enjoying the hard-on, then it's good to keep it around as long as necessary, but let's be clear that your partner's fun shouldn't necessarily end when the boner does.

Either with a therapist or on your own, it may be worth spending some time talking about what you can do in these situations, so that you know you have a game plan—which usually works out better than winging it in the moment. Have these conversations with your clothes on, so there is no pressure to act on anything. Talk broadly about what each of you want from your sex life, as well as specifically about what you would each enjoy doing if the hard-on leaves early. Be direct about what you do and don't like, what you would like from your partner, what you're willing to do for your partner, and what you are not interested in doing. Honesty and specificity here will reduce uncertainty and fumbling later.

If you're extremely creative and great at brainstorming but bad at remembering in the heat of the moment, you may want to write out a list, kind of like a sex menu to order off of. Mounting a whiteboard to the bedroom wall may evoke nightmares of corporate retreats, so a scribbled piece of paper in the bed stand should do it. Or make up a bunch of index cards to flip through and sometimes let it be dealer's choice or random draw. Knowing that you have other options takes the pressure off of both of you, so the encounter can still be a success, even if one orgasm comes sooner than you would wish. As with so many other things in life, a flexible approach with multiple options tends to make the whole thing more enjoyable.

Perhaps not surprisingly, some couples emerge from the adversity of premature ejaculation better off for it. One of the best lessons that you can both learn from this experience is to talk explicitly about and identify all the various ways that you can make your sexual encounters mutually satisfying, regardless of when you each orgasm.

Delayed Ejaculation: Almost, Almost, Almost . . .

While some men reach orgasm too quickly, there are also some who take too long or never get there. As with everything else, there is a bell curve with some people on one end, others on the other end, and most people somewhere in the middle. Delayed ejaculation involves a marked delay or inability to achieve ejaculation despite the presence of adequate sexual stimulation and the desire to ejaculate. This has to be present for most sexual encounters, whether partnered or solo, be distressing, and not within his control.

The occasional difficulty reaching orgasm can happen to anyone. Intentionally holding back orgasm, for whatever reason, does not count as delayed ejaculation, nor if it only occurs in some situations (e.g., intercourse) but not in others (e.g., masturbation) or with some partners but not others. Specific situational factors such as too much alcohol, anger towards one's sexual partner, worries about pregnancy, etc. can all influence the ability to achieve orgasm, but would not count towards a more global diagnosis of delayed ejaculation.

It's also important to remember that there must be sufficient stimulation to achieve orgasm—this means type, intensity, and duration. For example, a handjob with no lube may not cut it. Or perhaps a one-minute blowjob. If a man came too recently and is still within his refractory period (the reloading time) then he may be able to get it up, but it will take much longer to come, if at all. Each guy will have his general threshold for what it takes to get him over the top, but that can vary with the circumstances and change with age, physical conditions, or other life factors.

Some men will find a delay or inability distressing, but others will not. In addition, some partners will find it distressing, but others will not. For example, some partners may secretly (or not so secretly) worry that it reflects a failing on their part to get the guy off because they aren't hot enough or good enough at sex. If the guy feels this pressure of expectation, that may ironically sabotage his ability to enjoy the sex enough to get into that mental zone to orgasm. Alternatively, some partners may worry about pregnancy, perhaps even with adequate birth control, and intentionally or subconsciously convey that to the guy, causing him to hold back. As with so much else in human interactions, there are many possible reactions to the same event.

As with the other sexual dysfunctions, there are a variety of potential causes, all of which can interact:

- *Physical* Diabetes and surgical procedures that affect the relevant genital nerves can cause ejaculatory problems, as can certain medications, most notably the SSRI antidepressants. Aging also makes ejaculatory difficulties more likely.
- *Psychological* Guilt or shame about sex in general or particular sexual activities can interfere with enjoyment and getting sufficiently mentally stimulated to reach orgasm. In addition, just as with erectile difficulties, one or two bouts of inability to orgasm can lead to a self-fulfilling negative expectation. Anxiety or depression, whether unrelated to the sexual difficulties or caused by it, can also impact on it.
- *Relational* Negative feelings towards one's partner, dissatisfaction with one's sex life, discomfort or (perceived) lack of interest from the partner, (perceived) pressure from the partner, and fears of pregnancy can all impact a man's interest and ability to reach orgasm.

Some men experience delayed ejaculation as a lifelong condition, whereas others acquire these difficulties along the way. Once acquired, they may occur in all sexual situations or only in some. Generally speaking, a lifelong condition is harder to treat, but can still be adapted to.

Once a problem begins, it can spill over into other areas of the individual or couple's sex life and relationship, leading to other problems and exacerbating the initial difficulty. It can also lead to avoiding any sexual activity that could lead to problems—which can become all sexual activity. The way out of this death spiral is to begin to figure out exactly what is going on. When did this begin? When does this occur now? What seems to make it more or less likely? When there seems to be trouble ejaculating, what happens next? How do both partners react? If you're not talking about it, why not?

If there appears to be something medical involved, especially if it seemed to change when a medication was changed or after a procedure, then talking to your physician may be helpful. If there appears to be a psychological or relational component (even if there is also a medical cause), you may want to meet with a sex therapist who can help you identify everything that is contributing. This may involve trying some things out at home to see what they reveal. The therapist may teach you some relaxation/mindfulness skills so you (both) can enjoy sexual activity more, explore the negative beliefs that are limiting your experience of sexuality, help you and your partner discuss this and other problems more effectively, etc. The goal of treatment may be to overcome these bouts of delayed ejaculation entirely, but it will probably also aim to increase both of your ability to roll with it and still enjoy a sexual encounter regardless. As with so much else in life, flexibility tends to lead to greater happiness.

Problems With Specific Desires

When it comes to sexual desires, we are a creative species. There is a huge range of what people find sexually arousing or interesting— even just a few minutes clicking around a mainstream porn site will reveal a tremendous array of sexual expression, some of which will likely be much more appealing than others to any one person. Meanwhile, we are all exposed to an endless parade of messages from society, and possibly family and friends, that certain sexual acts are much less acceptable than others—or even shameful or a sign of deviancy.

Although our society has generally become more sexually accepting over the last couple decades, there are still plenty of folks who get caught between what they desire and what they believe they should desire. They struggle with what their desires might mean about them because they can't reconcile their sexual preferences with what they have otherwise learned about sexual desire. This is more common among younger folks who have less life experience and are still trying to figure out lots of other things about themselves, but even well-seasoned adults can still feel uncomfortable with some of their turn-ons.

We don't really understand why certain things turn someone on and others off, but it's probably a combination of childhood and

276 Overcome Specific Issues

adult experiences, exposure to sexually relevant stimuli, lessons learned about sex, and some biology. Why do people have their ice cream preferences? Why do people love some movies but hate others?

Regardless of where these desires come from, it can be difficult to change what someone gets turned on by. Or more precisely, it can be difficult or impossible to remove a turn-on, unless someone just grows out of it or moves on, but that is not a process that can be willed or created by outside intervention. It's much easier to add to our repertoire of what turns us on through exposure or experiences, but even there, you can't make yourself (or someone else) get turned on by activities or dynamics that just don't turn them on. (For more on how to facilitate this process of expanding your or someone else's desires, see *Chapter 6: Respectful Communication and Productive Negotiation*.) Similarly, you can't make someone not like an ice cream flavor they like, but you may be able to get them to enjoy a new flavor. Or maybe get them to enjoy your enjoying it. Or at least get them to appreciate why you like it.

Of course, we should probably pause for a moment to point out that feeling a desire is not the same as acting on it. We all have plenty of activities, both sexual and otherwise, that seem kind of desirable but that we don't act on, for a variety of reasons. I like lots of flavors of ice cream, but don't really eat it that often. It's OK to choose, at least for now, to pass on certain turn-ons. Or to recognize that the fantasy may be fantastic, but know that the reality would never live up.

The bigger problem comes when someone feels bad about themselves (or perhaps their partner) for having certain desires, especially when those desires go against other lessons they have been taught about sex, what it means to be a "good girl" or "respectful guy," or whatever. Part of becoming a sexually mature adult involves coming to some sort of peace with your turn-ons and making good choices (as you define them) about which to act on.

Because sexuality is such a core aspect of our personalities, feeling bad about your turn-ons can have a profound effect on how you feel about yourself more generally as well as in what you reveal to your partner. Some people feel so bad about their turn-ons that they may avoid sex or relationships entirely. Or they only bring part of themselves to the sexual encounter, for fear that their secret will burst forth. This is an unfortunate loss for both themselves and their partner and can create or contribute to other problems with performance or pleasure, described previously.

So what does it mean to have a "weird" or "deviant" sexual preference? Maybe nothing. What does it say about you that you like coconut ice cream? Probably not much. As the steady parade of sex scandals teaches us, what people say can differ a lot from what they do, so if you judge your desires or actions by other people's public words, it's pretty easy to feel bad about yourself. One of the many things that the internet has taught us is that no matter what you're into, sexually or otherwise, there are others who are also into that same thing. It won't take more than a few key word combinations to find some like-minded spirits, if that makes you feel better. Of course, there are also those who get more turned on by the idea that they are being dirty and deviant in their sexual interests and don't want to feel like they are part of the crowd, so sexuality really does cover the range.

There is also the question of who gets to define which sex acts are acceptable and which are "deviant." Social institutions, including religious organizations, school boards, and legislatures, often feel that they have this right. They certainly can have opinions, sometimes very strongly and publicly. The first amendment protects their right to express opinions, but the question of enforcing those opinions on others becomes much more complicated. Personally, I take the position that what consenting adults do is up to them, but not everyone feels that way.

Each of us has to find a way to reconcile not only our internal desires with these external messages, but also the contradictions in all the various messages that we receive. Sex may feel like a more loaded topic, but we have to do this same process for all of the other lifestyle choices that we make. Those whose internal preferences line up better with the primary external messages they have been exposed to probably will have an easier time coming to a satisfying reconciliation. Those whose internal preferences lie further outside of most of their external messages will probably have more work to do to decide what they want to do and how they feel about it. This is probably more likely to happen when their external messages give a narrower range of what is acceptable, since fewer people are likely to naturally fall within that range.

People who are more conflicted about their sexual interests are more likely to struggle with both pleasure and performance. Even if there is some other cause of sexual dysfunction, negative feelings about one's own or one's partner's sexuality will likely make it worse. By contrast, a more accepting stance towards one's sexuality, as well as perhaps a more flexible attitude about what constitutes an acceptable sexual encounter, makes it more likely that the individual and couple will have a satisfying sex life, despite any potential sexual dysfunction.

It may be worth spending some time thinking about your ideas about the acceptability of various sexual activities:

- Are some sexual activities more acceptable than others?
- If so, what makes some more acceptable or less?
- Where did you get those ideas?
- Do these beliefs about sexual acceptability affect the activities that you engage in or how you enjoy them?
- Do these beliefs affect your sexual performance?

Then talk to your partner about these questions and how it plays out for them. You may find it a revealing conversation. The main goal here is to better understand yourself and each other. You may also find that that understanding opens up some more variety in your sex life and/or enables you to better enjoy what you are already doing.

Take Away Lessons

- Problems with sexual performance and/or pleasure are relatively common and often treatable. Or at least work-around-able. The most important first thing to remember is to not freak out—that only makes things worse.

- Problems with performance can create problems with pleasure/pain, and vice versa. Therefore, addressing one may involve also addressing the other. This may involve looking at physical, psychological, and relational factors to determine what is going on and how to improve it.

- Sex should never be painful, so if it is, it needs to be addressed. Treatment may involve reducing the discomfort as well as finding ways to enjoy less painful sexual options.

- Erection problems can have a variety of causes, but can respond quite well to treatment. The more one or both partners pay attention to the status of the erection, the more likely it is to disappear.

- Premature ejaculation can put a damper on a sexual experience, but it doesn't need to if the couple can be flexible in their sexual options. Taking this pressure off may also make it less likely to occur. In addition, some relatively straightforward exercises at home can help both partners learn how to create more staying power.

- By contrast, some guys (or their partners) feel like they take too long to get to orgasm or don't get there at all with a partner. Overcoming this may involve changing techniques or expectations, or possibly medications, but some folks are quite satisfied with a sexual encounter even without the big finish.

- Some people feel badly about their own or their partner's turn-ons and struggle to reconcile those desires/fantasies with the rest of who they are. Not every desire needs to be acted on, but feeling ashamed by them probably doesn't help anything.

14

Problems With Desire: Not Enough Sex

For many couples, sex is a way to reconnect, have some fun together, and recharge for the daily demands of life. Sex can take many forms, but the important thing is that it is a shared and mutually enjoyable erotic experience.

I won't take the position that a couple has to have sex in order to be happy together, because there certainly are couples who prove that you don't—and also couples that keep having sex, despite not otherwise liking each other. However, a good sex life, whatever that looks like for you, does add to how happy you are in the relationship and perhaps overall in your life. It may not be required, but it is a good addition. Having said that, if one partner in a couple is feeling sexually dissatisfied, then that can spill over into lots of other parts of the relationship and for that reason may be worth addressing.

Even when a couple has a great sex life, some people lose that desire. Sometimes they know exactly why their desire dropped, sometimes they don't. Either way, if you would like to, you can

> My first thought when I read the email [to offer quotes for the book] was a feeling of embarrassment and was not going to reply but I do think the lack of a sex life in a relationship is troublesome and difficult to address/change the longer it goes on.
> *ADHD woman, 58, married, been together 21+ years*

work on finding that lost desire. And if you have never had an especially strong sex drive but would like more of one, you may be able to improve that, too.

Within the survey, there were quite a few respondents who were having little or no sex:

- 12% not within the last six months
- 10% had had sex within the last six months
- 16% had had sex once in the last month

We should remember that these are all people in relationships who presumably have a sexually available partner—single folks without a sexual partner didn't take the survey. Put together, almost two out of five respondents were having sex once a month or less. While there are some in that group who are happy with the amount of sex they're (not) having, most people aren't. When asked, in the next question, how often they would want to be sexual with their partner, they said:

- 2% less than once per six months
- 1% once per six months
- 4% once per month
- 7% 2–3x/month
- 15% 1x/week
- 38% 2–3x/week
- 17% 4–6x/week
- 15% daily

> *What would make your sex life better for your partner?*
> I actually don't know as he won't or can't talk about it. We haven't had sex in a few years. I don't know how to deal with this situation at all and as a result I have let it go.
> *Non-ADHD woman, 43, married, been together 11–20 years*

So 38% of respondents were having sex once a month or less, but only 7% wanted to have sex that often. There is a lot of unfulfilled desire out there. In a snapshot, that is why I am writing this book. I want you to have more sex, better sex, and a better relationship overall. If you and your partner are starting to forget what sex is like and would like more frequent reminders, then this chapter is hopefully the beginning of better things. I will also talk about those folks who were never really that interested in sex.

Desire Downers: Many Potential Sexual Drains

If you and your partner aren't having enough sex, it could be a matter of one or both of you having less desire for sex in general or it could be that both of you are still generally interested, but there is something getting in the way of acting on that desire with each other.

Let's begin by taking a look at the usual suspects to see if any of them played a role. Sexual desire is influenced by many factors, so you may need to consider how any or all of these are affecting you. This exploration will involve considering a number of questions to figure out what is most relevant for you. Take your time as you consider your answers and be willing to circle back around. Sexual desire can be negatively influenced by many things, including:

- *Physical conditions*: generally declining health, endocrine disorders (including diabetes and low testosterone or thyroid), cardiovascular disease, cancer, and sleep disorders/deprivation can all impede sexual desire. Some medications (especially the

SSRI antidepressants, but also the nonstimulant ADHD medication Strattera) can also decrease desire, so speak with your physician if you suspect that a medical condition or its treatment are sapping your desire. *my issues*

- *Psychological conditions*: stress, anxiety, depression (including post-partum depression), body image discomfort, substance abuse, sexual abuse, grief, discomfort with one's sexual desires, or excessive worry about being heard or walked in on.

- *Relationship factors*: disagreements or conflict about sexual and/or nonsexual matters, insufficient emotional intimacy (and, ironically, also too much intimacy and comfort), infidelity (real or imagined), reduced attraction, not prioritizing sexual and nonsexual time together, etc.

- *Sexual problem in yourself and/or your partner*: difficulty achieving orgasm, erectile difficulties, premature ejaculation, pain during sex, and negative or limiting sexual beliefs.

Do any of these reasons stand out for you and/or your partner? What do they think? This isn't a definitive list, but it is probably a pretty good place to start.

If none of these jump out at you and you're stumped, then you may want to talk to your physician(s) and/or a therapist who really

---

What would make your sex life better for you?

If he would remember (pay attention to) what I like and don't like . . . it's like nothing is "built on" so you have to make same requests every time—the down side to "It's like the first time . . . EVERY time."

What would make your sex life better for your partner?

I say it seems after 30+ years of marriage, I should reasonably be able predict many outcomes or reactions or "next steps" . . . he says "How COULD you when even I can't predict what I'll say/do/act like/want . . .?"

Non-ADHD Woman, 49, married, been together 21+ years

knows about sexual matters (not all do) to assess how the physical, psychological, and relational are influencing each other. In this process, you may find that there are some hard or uncomfortable truths hiding in that lack of interest. It can be difficult to admit these to a partner, or even oneself, so instead it remains a mystery why you aren't that interested in sex. The obvious pieces don't add up, but it isn't clear what is draining away that desire. Although it may require going through some painful topics, you may find that the process of working on your sex drive will also benefit you and your relationship in other ways.

What Does History Teach Us?

If we're trying to figure out what happened to the sex in your relationship, it can be helpful to look back at the progression of your sex life over the course of the relationship: from the beginning until now; the good, the bad, and the ugly. This will help you identify what was happening before, during, and after the spark fizzled which can be good clues as to what might be contributing. It will also help you identify your sexual and relationship strengths which will be helpful when you try to re-light that spark.

If you used to have a good sex life and would like it again, then start by thinking about when things changed:

• Was it sudden or gradual?
• What preceded that change—in you, in your partner, in your relationship, in your life overall?
• What has happened since then?
• Has your (and your partner's) desire been consistently reduced or does it come and go?
• Has your (and your partner's) desire for solo sexual activity also changed?
• Has a desire change happened with previous partners?
• What meaning do you and your partner each make of this lost desire and how do you each respond to it?

Start gathering these clues to help you identify all the pieces so you can better solve the puzzle. It won't necessarily be easy to make improvements, but you will be in a better position if you understand what is going on. Sometimes the roadblocks involve big, dramatic things like infidelity or other betrayals. Sometimes it is a slow erosion of interest when mundane relationship struggles of daily life aren't addressed sufficiently or when the couple's sex life gets kind of stale. Sometimes it is the casualty of some other sexual problem or life transition. The progression of events over time will likely offer some helpful clues to understanding what is happening today.

You may find that as you begin to address the barriers to that better sex life, that some new elements come up that either weren't there before or that you didn't see before. This is just part of the process. Take heart that you are chipping away at it.

If your sex life with this partner was never as good as you and/or they would have wanted it to be, then you can work on that also. We don't need to be limited by our pasts. Many people actually find that it is within the security of a stable relationship that they can take more sexual risks, so sex can actually improve over time if you are willing to do the work, both in bed and out. Some questions to consider include:

- How is your sex life in this relationship similar to or different from your sex life in prior relationships?
- What gets in the way of a better sex life—earlier in this relationship and now?
- What would you need to give up, change, or do differently in order to have a better sex life?
- What else would change in your relationship if your sex life was better?

This will probably involve some reflection on each of your parts and plenty of conversations (yes, plural). You may also find it useful to read some of the other chapters in this book, as are relevant to your situation, and work on a number of areas. And if you get stuck, or are just impatient and want to really work on things, then seeing a sex therapist could really move things along.

What Are Your Goals?

When it comes to improving your sex life, it's helpful to know what you and your partner each want it to look like. What are you working towards? And is there enough overlap in what you each want? You and your partner don't necessarily need to want exactly the same things sexually, since there are probably lots of other places where you don't want exactly the same things, yet you still manage to get along on those. However, there should be enough common ground that you both feel that you are getting enough of what you want.

What to do when there isn't enough common ground in your goals? For example, if you would like to have sex at least three times a week but your partner can't see doing it more than once a week, that may feel like an insurmountable difference. As I have said elsewhere, satisfaction is a function of experiences versus expectations. That means that we can increase our satisfaction by changing either one or both. The judgment call here is whether we continue to push for more of what we want and choose to suffer the consequences of what that will entail or whether we choose instead to lower our expectations so that we can be happy with what we are getting. At one end, we may commit ourselves to a battle that isn't worth winning. At the other end, we sell our happiness short by settling too soon. The lower desire partner faces a similar dilemma of either standing strong on having sex once a week, knowing that their partner will be unhappy about it, or of sometimes having sex that they don't really want to have, knowing that they will be unhappy about it.

Sometimes couples can split the difference on these disagreements—e.g., a handjob or helping out with a vibrator can be a good enough replacement for greater involvement. But sometimes even these compromises can be difficult to agree on—maybe it feels too much to give, maybe it feels too little to receive. The challenge here will be to keep the conversations rolling, without slipping into complementary extremes (e.g., "You will never be satisfied!" and "You will never want it the way that I do!"). Those black and white, angry accusations make differences feel insurmountable because they are based in unchanging character judgments. This makes it feel pointless to try to negotiate a better compromise. As tempting as it is, in the heat of the moment, to give in to despair, do your best to calm down, keep your head on, and keep talking about what is a potential compromise that you could both be OK with. Having a goal that seems achievable, even if a stretch, is much more motivating than trying to work towards the impossible.

When it comes to goal setting, we should also stop to consider why you each have the goals that you do. Do you actually want to have more/better sex? Or is it mostly because your partner wants you to have more desire and you're tired of the arguments? Do you want to want it or do you mostly want less conflict? While there is always a place for generosity in relationships, it's hard to want something you don't actually want. If this is the case, what would help *you* want it more? What would make sex worth it to you again? This can be a big question with multiple answers, so really think about it and then really talk about it. For more on all this, see the later section, *When Desire is Lacking—And Also the Desire to Desire.*

It's also worth considering why the higher desire partner wants more sex. Beyond the obvious pleasurable sensations, why else do they want more sex? What other purposes does that additional sex serve? And what would it mean if they didn't have that extra sex? In the interest of a more productive conversation, not just fairness, both partners should examine why they want what they want. The better you each understand both of your reasons, the more likely you will be able to find a solution that works for both of you.

You may find that your goals change over time, either up or down or even sideways, which is probably a good thing if you're responding to the progress that you're making. It's probably worth keeping in mind that simply more sex may not be the best goal, unless it's good sex. Often, quality matters more than quantity—and also good quality may increase the quantity a bit.

It's much easier to desire desirable sex, so both partners have a vested interest in keeping their sex life fun and satisfying for both of them, but perhaps especially for the partner who has less interest. What will help that lower desire partner want more sex? If they could have their ideal sex life, then how often would they want to have sex? What could you two do, within the constraints of reality, to make your sex life more closely resemble that ideal? And what can you do mentally to round up the sex life that is actually possible in order to run with it?

This works better if you make your relationship and your sex life a high priority, or at least high-ish, but definitely not the last priority. Keep it interesting by investing the necessary time, mental energy, and creativity into it—and ask your partner to do the same. It's hard to really want anything that's half-assed.

Couples who are able to maintain good sex over the years and decades are able to do so by communicating well with each other about both sexual and nonsexual matters. They are comfortable with their own and their partner's sexual desires and fantasies and are able to negotiate the differences. They are flexible about what the sexual encounter will entail and they avoid performance pressure. Sex becomes more about the shared experience than about some measurable end point. Couples that connect well sexually tend to also be happier overall, so your sex life is worth investing in.

Start Slow

It can feel weird and awkward to start again if you haven't done anything sexual together in a while. That's OK. Sex is kind of like riding a bike—you get all sweaty and possibly greasy. And also you never forget how to do it.

Accept that it is going to be weird and awkward, then push through that self-consciousness and start things up anyway. Break the ice, and tension, by saying how you feel and maybe even laughing a little about it together. Be willing to be uncomfortable but keep going—without doing anything you're not ready for. (This seems like pretty good advice for lots of life circumstances.)

You may find it easier to work your way into it by starting slowly with some easy kissing or gentle touching, perhaps while still fully dressed. Perhaps that is as far as it goes this time. The important thing is that you got things rolling. Then maybe make a date for your next encounter—I know, that feels lame, but anything that is planned is more likely to happen. Maybe next time you do a little more, or perhaps not. Progress should be like working out—you need enough challenge to foster growth without getting injured, so keep working at it. It may feel forced or like homework at first, but it will most likely get more natural as you keep at it and sex once again becomes a part of your routine.

The goal is for these shared encounters to feel like a success, since success breeds success. You will be more likely to want to try it again if the last encounter felt positive or at least positive enough. Having said that, if you play it too safe and move too slowly, you may both be a hundred before you get anywhere. There is also a lot to be said for the ability to cope with failures and keep coming back. Not every time is going to be a winner, so expect some setbacks. Just focus on responding well to it in the moment and then keeping a positive attitude about it next time—this is a good general life skill to have.

If a woman hasn't had penetrative sex in a while, she may need to ease into it slowly, especially if she is post-menopausal. Before jumping into intercourse, you may start by inserting one finger, then two, then a small dildo/vibrator. And, of course, plenty of foreplay and lube is always a good idea. You may even want to start by yourself before letting your partner insert anything, so you have more control over what happens, especially if you are sensitive or it is initially uncomfortable. If it's painful, then definitely stop and change what you're doing. If it continues to be painful, then see a medical professional about it. (See *Genito-Pelvic Pain/Penetration Disorder* in *Chapter 13: Problems with Performance and Pleasure*.)

Maybe Start by Yourself

If one of you isn't yet ready to be sexual together, then you may find it beneficial to start on your own, if you haven't been sexually active in a while. Erections, vaginal lubrication, arousal, and orgasm flood the genitals with fresh blood which helps to keep the tissues healthy. This helps keep everything in good working order. Whether it's solo or partnered activities, those who keep having sex are those who keep having sex. It's kind of a use it or lose it scenario—or at least a try to not get out of shape scenario. It's always easier to stay in shape than get back into shape. So even if your partner isn't up for a workout, you can still do something on your own.

Doing some things by yourself first can reduce the performance pressure when your partner is also involved. You may find it easier to start completely by yourself at first, then perhaps involve your partner in some activities (like kissing), but still maintain control over what happens with your genitals, until you feel ready to do some other things together. Even if the goal is partnered activities, some solo activities first or along the way may help you get there more easily.

What About Asexuality?

Sexual interest is like any other human trait that sits on a bell curve. Some people want a lot of sex, some people want a little sex, and most people are somewhere in between. This can also vary by age and circumstance. Some things can enhance the expression of sexual desire, such as alcohol in the right doses or having a partner who really lights the fire. And some things can decrease the expression of sexual desire, such as depression or a history of trauma or sexual mistreatment.

Then there are those with very little or no sexual desire who are known as asexual. This is thought to be a normal part of that spectrum of human sexuality, just lying at the one end. These are folks who have never had much of an interest in sex—someone who at one time had that desire but doesn't now or hasn't for a long time would not be considered asexual. Nor would someone who otherwise would have a desire to be sexual, but early sexual abuse has made a mess of their feelings about sex, so they don't know how to express sexuality safely and in a way that feels good. People who are asexual may still have a desire for intimate romantic relationships, perhaps some more than others, but those feelings don't include the desire to act on them physically. While they may feel bad about themselves for being different from what is socially expected of them, they don't desire that desire otherwise. By contrast, someone whose depression is tanking their libido may still want to want it, at least intellectually, or can remember a time when they did.

There are some who view asexuality as an orientation and therefore unlikely to change. Although my hope is that everyone reading this book will find that it helps them create a more satisfying sex life (and relationship overall), those who tend more towards asexuality are unlikely to suddenly be convinced. I support the right of each individual to create the life that they want to live, but someone who has very little or no desire for sex may find that this is a frequent and intense source of contention in their relationships, if they partner up with someone who does want sex, at least sometimes. This can be a real dilemma, especially when the relationship is good in other ways: does the asexual partner need to have sex that they don't want to have, just to placate their partner, or does the sexual partner need to forsake something that may be very important to them? No easy answers here.

Some couples find a compromise somewhere in the middle where the asexual partner doesn't necessarily love the sex they are having, but is happy about making their partner happy. Sometimes the other partner supplements with solo activities, as discussed at the end of this chapter. Some other couples allow a certain amount of sex outside of the relationship as a way to keep the parts of the relationship that do work—preferably this is discussed and mutually agreed upon beforehand. (See *Chapter 16: Consensual Sex With Other People: Other Arrangements*.) If either you or your partner are asexual and it is causing way too much strife in your relationship, then you may want to roll up your sleeves and check out *Chapter 12: When the Negotiations Break Down*.

When Desire is Lacking—And Also the Desire to Desire

In addition to folks who are asexual, there are also some other people who just aren't that interested in sex. Some of them aren't currently interested in sex with their partner, for a variety of reasons, but could be interested in having sex with someone else instead. Some people aren't currently that interested in sex with anyone, but had been interested in the past.

Within the survey, one out of fifty said that they were essentially no longer interested in having sex with their partner. I didn't ask whether they were disinterested in sex in general and whether they had never been especially interested in sex. On the plus side, two percent is a pretty low number, but if you're in that two percent, it may feel like a big deal—or not. And if you're the partner of one those two percent, it may feel like a big deal—or not. What we don't know from the survey is whether the folks who no longer want to have sex with their partners feel bad about it (some probably do, some probably don't) or how their partners feel about it (some are probably equally fine with it, some are probably tortured). We also don't know what it would take for these folks to change their minds—some of them might, some of them probably never will.

If both members of the couple aren't that interested in sex, then it isn't a problem, but if one person really wants it and the other one really doesn't, then that can fuel many an argument and a lot of unpleasantness for both partners. In the survey, I asked respondents how important their sexual satisfaction was to their overall relationship satisfaction. For most people, it was pretty important:

- 3% not at all
- 7% slightly
- 18% somewhat
- 33% moderately
- 39% very

Of course, we should keep in mind here that sexual satisfaction is how each individual defines it—for some this will be daily sex that includes the neighbors, but for others it will be monthly missionary in the dark. As long as they're getting their needs met, whatever those may be, they're happy. Those respondents who said that their sexual satisfaction wasn't as important in determining their overall relationship satisfaction could still be very interested in sex, but feel that other factors are more important in determining their overall relationship satisfaction.

Where this leaves us then is that if at least one partner feels strongly about their sexual satisfaction, then it will be difficult for them to be happy in the relationship when those needs aren't being met. And if one partner is unhappy in a relationship, it is only a matter of time before the other partner isn't happy as well. This doesn't mean that their partner is thereby required to meet their every sexual desire in order to keep the relationship humming along—if this were to happen, then that partner would soon be the unhappy one. Rather, it means that both members of the couple have a vested interest in working on that sexual satisfaction. Sometimes this results in the more desirous partner getting more of what they want, but sometimes it results in that partner finding a way to be happy with what they are getting and accepting that those other desires will not be fulfilled, either now or ever. After all, although happy relationships offer certain benefits, they also involve some sacrifices—for example, I have seen many fewer movies with lots of things blowing up since I got married.

If the partner with little desire, or no desire, wants to work on it, then the couple can do so together. However, when one partner doesn't really want sex (or really doesn't want sex) and they are fine with that, then the couple will likely have a real negotiation on their hands. It's hard to work on something if you don't want it and you don't want to want it.

Some people may be disinterested in sex because of depression or from feeling chronically overwhelmed and lose the perspective that they once enjoyed sex and could do so again. The depression and/or stress is indeed tanking their libido now, but is also blinding them to the possibility that things can be different. In these cases, addressing the root cause may help them see more options. If someone has lost their desire for sex due to significant relationship problems, they may be so pessimistic about that improving that they can't see the possibility of ever wanting to have sex with their partner again. Once again, addressing that root cause may change how they feel.

Having said this, it is hard to be motivated to improve something you don't want. However, sometimes we can be skeptical, but work on it anyway, if only to say that we did. Or perhaps we are motivated to improve something else (e.g., depression) and then see what happens with other matters. If you're not interested in having sex again, either with your partner or in general, then you certainly don't have to, but perhaps there are some other benefits in your life and/or relationship to working on whatever might be affecting your sex drive.

If you are the partner of someone who isn't interested in working on this, you may not have much leverage to make them. After all, we can't make anyone do anything if they are really committed to not. Having said that, one of the reasons why people in relationships tend to be happier and do better than singles is that they have partners who push them to work on things and hold them accountable. This sexual disinterest may be one of those places, but progress may not come easily or cheaply. Odds are that you will also have to do some of the work and change some of what you're doing, since it's unlikely that interventions will only involve your partner. If it's worth it, then it's worth it. If it isn't, or if your partner is immovable on this one, at least for now, then you may find that working on acceptance is the surer path to happiness. If you're having a hard time figuring out what to do here, then check out *Chapter 12: When the Negotiations Break Down.*

If You Want to Want it

If you never or rarely feel like having sex, but would like to feel sexual again, then that's something you can work on, both on your own and with your partner. Earlier in this chapter, I listed some common desire downers that could be culprits if you used to have more desire but it has gone away. If any of these are involved, then do what you need to do with those. Some of them may have nothing to do with sex, but are impacting your sex drive nonetheless. The rest of this section will be helpful either in addition or for those folks who tended to not have that strong a desire before, but want to want it more. Again, we don't have to be limited by our pasts.

Some people feel like they never or rarely have sexual thoughts that then build into strong desire. While this is true for some, there are also others who do have small, passing, kind of sexual thoughts that just slip past unnoticed or fizzle out before kindling something bigger. If you feel like you don't have enough sexual thoughts and would like to have more of them, you may find it helpful to notice those little pre-thoughts and coax those little sparks into a flame. For example, it may be helpful to try to notice:

- When do you have sexual thoughts, even little fleeting ones?
- Under what circumstances?
- What kinds of thoughts?

- How do you feel about them?
- What happens next?
- If your sexual thoughts get lost, reflect on why and perhaps try allowing those thoughts to build. What is that experience like?
- What thoughts and feelings do those stronger desires evoke?

This may help you identify what might be preventing those thoughts from building. For example, do you feel uncomfortable, embarrassed, guilty, confused, or worry what might happen if you let some of those desires build? Knowing what is going on here then puts you in a better position to counter that process, if you want to.

On the flipside, you may also find that it helps to put some effort into cultivating desire by engaging in exercises to create sexual thoughts in the first place. You may work on this alone and/or with your partner. Some of these exercises will be purely mental, whereas others will involve trying new things, but at a comfortable pace. These exercises have two goals. First, to practice the skills involved in order to get better at them or more comfortable with the experience. The less obvious goal is that it can help you better understand what is happening by seeing what thoughts or feelings get evoked. It's kind of like how a physical therapist identifies the problem by having you move in different ways to see what triggers pain or reveals a weakness. So these exercises are both an intervention and diagnostic.

For example, you can make a point of taking a moment occasionally to think sexual thoughts and seeing where it takes you. (If your calendar is visible to coworkers, you may want to refrain from entering a recurring appointment for "have dirty thoughts." Or maybe you should.) Just as we can intentionally practice anything else, we can intentionally practice experimenting and playing with sexual thoughts. Start with something easy and comfortable, even if it is just a little bit sexual. Imagine yourself in that situation, think about how it would feel physically and emotionally, and see what thoughts and feelings follow and how your body reacts.

If you find the idea of allowing yourself to have those sexual thoughts makes you uncomfortable, or if you somehow never get around to doing this exercise, then that becomes the exercise—why is that? What feelings does it evoke? What makes it feel like it's not OK? If you really lean into that discomfort, you may find that it reveals or helps clarify what is happening there.

If you get to a point where taking these times to have sexual thoughts feels comfortable, then you and your partner can take turns touching each other in a sensual, but perhaps not overtly sexual, way, such as a hand or foot massage or possibly a back rub. Take your time with it. Focus on the sensations of the moment and how your body responds, as well as what thoughts and feelings it evokes. If you find yourself tensing up or feeling uncomfortable, then reflect upon why and, perhaps, take some deep breaths to help yourself relax back into it. If necessary, take a break before starting again. The goal here is to have a positive experience with touch and closeness, so if it starts heading south, you probably want to either slow down or stop for the day.

You will probably find it easier to relax into the experience and enjoy it more fully if there is no pressure for it to lead to anything specific and either of you can put on the brakes whenever you need to. We want it to be a comfortable experience, yet perhaps also a little challenging so you can move beyond your current limits, as well as perhaps get some insight into what holds you back at other times.

If you find that even some of these first exercises raise too many uncomfortable or even distressing feelings, you may find it helpful to talk to a therapist who can help you gently explore why.

In all this, it's probably helpful to remember that, especially for busy people in long-term relationships, sometimes desire follows sexual activity—sometimes we need to start some erotic activity (with a partner or alone) and let desire build from that stimulation. Even if we're not feeling sexual at first, that desire may build as things progress and we find ourselves enjoying it more and more. This should definitely not be used as a justification to push someone to be sexual when they don't want to, nor to push yourself to compromise your values when there are real reasons why you don't want to be sexual. But if things are generally OK and it's more a matter of lack of desire rather than negative feelings, then sometimes allowing ourselves to go with it can lead to a mutually enjoyable experience. I talk about this responsive desire more in *Exciters* and *Inhibitors: The Sexual Gas and Brake* in *Chapter 10: Sex 101 (and 201 and 301. . .)*.

Where Do Solo Activities Fit?

Masturbation can be an easy way to meet one's sexual desires when a partner isn't interested. This may be especially helpful when the couple has a generally good sex life, but one partner has a higher drive and uses masturbation to make up the difference. (See the section *Masturbation to Make Up the Difference?* in *Chapter 2: How ADHD Impacts Sex and Relationships* for some really interesting gender differences in the survey data.) This works especially well when the higher desire partner appreciates the sexual time together and doesn't feel resentful about when they need to get their sexual needs met on their own and when the lower desire partner recognizes that masturbation makes both of their lives better.

But what about when the higher desire partner needs to get all of their sexual needs met on their own? Some people may not mind this, especially if the relationship is otherwise good, but many would likely miss that shared sexual connection and eventually resent their partner for it. If the couple can't talk productively about their lack of sex and/or one partner's lack of desire, masturbation can easily become the path of least resistance, rather than having those difficult conversations. This may not break the relationship, but it won't help it.

If the higher desire partner can make some peace with their partner's lack of desire and feels like masturbation is an acceptable (if perhaps nonequivalent) substitute, then masturbation can reduce the resentment that eats away at the relationship. Similarly, if the uninterested person respects their partner's continued sexual desires and understands why they would still want to get those needs met, without feeling threatened by the solo activities, then they can view their partner's masturbation as beneficial to the relationship. They may choose to not want to see or know about it (which is a reasonable request, I think), but they are OK with it.

Where things get much messier is when one partner isn't interested in sex, but also doesn't want their partner to be interested or at least to act on those interests. This creates a no-win situation for their partner that makes secret masturbation much more likely—which then makes unhappy discoveries much more likely. And nobody benefits from unhappy discoveries.

Most people would agree that it is an abuse of power to force, explicitly or implicitly, someone to have sex when they don't want to. That's an easy one. However, I would contend that forcing someone, explicitly or implicitly, to not have sex on their own is also an abuse of power, especially if they can't get their sexual needs met with their designated monogamous partner (assuming the couple is monogamous). Not that anyone died from lack of sex, but many believe that some access to sexual pleasure is something of a fundamental human right. Therefore, it seems unfair to tell your partner that they can only get their sexual needs met through you, except that you aren't interested. It is possible to take that position and it's possible that your partner will actually agree to it, but if sex is still important to your partner, then it may be a lot to ask and therefore carry a high price tag in the relationship and ultimately contribute to the end of the relationship, either overtly or indirectly if the partner gets those sexual needs met secretly with someone else.

If one partner is just not interested in sex or just much less interested than their partner, it may be that finding a way to be OK with their partner's masturbation may give the couple a workable solution that eliminates bigger problems. Therefore, if you find yourself in this situation, as either partner, it's probably worth some difficult conversations about masturbation and how you both feel about it. If you aren't having sex together, what would it take to reach a compromise where one or both of you can masturbate instead? And under what conditions—porn, sex toys, etc.? The goal is to reach an agreement that both people can live with and therefore live by, without any sneaking, checking, or resentment.

Take Away Lessons

- Almost two out of five survey respondents were having sex less than once a month, but most of them wanted to have sex more often.

- Low desire for sex can have many intertwined causes, including physical, psychological, and relationship factors. Problems with performance and/or pleasure can also tank desire.

- If you used to have a more active sex life, with this partner or prior ones, then it may be worth looking to see how and why things changed in order to get some clues for what is going on.

- If one or both partners would like to fire up their sex life, it's worth spending some time talking about what each of your goals are and perhaps why those are your goals, as well as how to reconcile any differences.

- If you haven't had sex in a while, it can feel awkward to start again. That's OK. Take your time and move as slowly as you need to in order for it to be fun and comfortable (and maybe a little challenging). The important thing is to have a mutually satisfying encounter that will leave both of you eager for the next time.

- Some people are asexual, meaning that they never had a particularly strong interest in sex. This can give a couple a lot to discuss if the other partner has a strong desire for sex.

- If you (or your partner) are no longer interested in sex, you may want to think about whether you want to want it or whether you are content without it. If you just are no longer interested, it will be hard to feel motivated to change it. But if you would like to feel that spark again, there are things you can do to work on it.

- If one of the partners has very little or no interest in sex, the other partner may be satisfied with masturbation instead. However, since some people have negative feelings about masturbation, it probably bears a discussion about what the higher desire partner's options are. The uninterested partner doesn't get veto power but also the interested partner shouldn't be inconsiderate—it's a discussion.

15

Secret Stuff With Other People: Hookups and Affairs

The goal of this book is to improve your relationship and sex life. Since infidelity can have such a disruptive effect on a relationship, this also means that one of the goals is to make infidelity less likely. And since infidelity is not as rare as most people would like it to be, a goal of this chapter is to help you deal with it if it has been or becomes a part of your relationship. Even if there has never been any infidelity in your relationship, it may still be a good idea to read this chapter so that you can prevent it and deal with it sooner and better if it does occur. There is *a lot* more to say about infidelity than will fit in one chapter, but it should be a good place to start.

In the survey, I asked about both physical and emotional infidelity, since although they overlap, they are also very different experiences and people can have different feelings about each of them. From about a quarter to about a half of respondents admitted to having engaged in one or both of these at some point, although not necessarily in the current relationship. Men were more likely than women to have engaged in a purely physical infidelity, women were more likely than men to have engaged in an emotional infidelity that may or may not have involved a physical component, and those with ADHD were more likely than those without to engage in both types. These are not insignificant numbers.

When it comes to measuring the frequency of infidelity, it really depends how you define terms. Consider how these different questions could get vastly different answers: *Have you ever cheated on a romantic partner?* versus *Have you ever had sex with someone without your romantic partner's consent?* In the second question, I guess a blowjob doesn't count? Or does it? What about kissing a friend goodbye on the lips instead of on the cheek? What about having an emotional affair with someone who you never meet in person? And are we asking about these activities in your current relationship or ever in any relationship? And do you get to define what constitutes infidelity or does your partner? All of these details yield really different numbers, but probably almost everyone would agree that infidelity is more common than most people would wish it to be and that it can be extremely painful for all involved.

We don't need the survey to tell us that monogamy is really hard, especially over very long periods of time. The fact that it is so hard makes it meaningful when we do pull it off—or perhaps even mostly pull it off. After all, if you're posted in a weather station in Antarctica without any potential hookup partners or romantic interests, then it isn't that impressive that you managed to stay faithful.

The challenge of monogamy involves balancing some contradictions and taking the wiser middle path—or at least heading back towards center when we veer off. We shouldn't be careless about our relationship and put ourselves into risky situations or start down slippery slopes that end too easily in really bad places. But the frequency of infidelity also means that we shouldn't be so perfectionistic about it that anything less than 100% fidelity must round down to ending the relationship. We shouldn't risk years of a good relationship with a small period of bad times and worse decisions, but we also shouldn't forget all the good just because of some bad (even though it may feel *really, really* bad in the moment). If there are kids involved, then we really shouldn't risk it, yet also be all the more hesitant to throw it all away.

Relationships are complicated and nuanced and so is dealing with infidelity. It may be that the infidelity is a physical manifestation of a relationship that is already over, in spirit if not in fact. Or it may be a temporary and ill-conceived solution to problems in an otherwise salvageable relationship. Or it may even occur for unrelated reasons in an otherwise very happy relationship. For an extremely wise discussion on the nuances and contradictions of infidelity, check out Esther Perel's *The State of Affairs*.

If the infidelity isn't the death blow, many couples come back stronger after dealing with the infidelity and what led up to it. Just as I wouldn't recommend a cancer scare as a way to re-think your priorities, I certainly wouldn't recommend cheating as a way to kickstart working on your relationship, but it can sure force a lot of issues to the surface if it does happen. There were many survey respondents who wrote that they were currently limping along in the aftermath of an infidelity, trying to figure out what to do. Or sometimes not really trying, but definitely limping; there were also those who came through all that painful work to a much better place.

Fidelity Agreements: What is and isn't Acceptable?

Before we really talk about what constitutes infidelity, we have to talk about how couples decide what constitutes fidelity. Being faithful means that your partner can have faith that you're abiding by your mutual understanding of the rules of the relationship. By

---

Skeletons of wife's long ago affairs never buried nor wounds healed . . . .
What would make your sex life better for you?
It died. Anything that would bring it back to life, starting with renewed trust and intimate communication.
What would make your sex life better for your partner?
Communication broke down long ago. Hopefully similar answer . . . though her individual wellbeing is so frayed many steps needed to get from there to sex.
ADHD man, 61, married, been together 21+ years

contrast, cheating means that you have broken those rules (which your partner may or may not be aware of). This is where the faith comes in: assuming that the rules are being followed when we can't 100% confirm it. Unless you glue a webcam to your partner's forehead, there is always an element of unknown and therefore faith in every relationship. Having faith in our partner protects our sense that everything is how it should be, without fear of secrets or surprises.

This mutual understanding of what is and isn't acceptable within the bounds of a couple's relationship and sex life is called a fidelity agreement. It could involve big, obvious things like whether one is allowed to have sex with someone else, but there are also a million subtleties. For example, is it OK to have a professional lunch with someone of the opposite gender (assuming you're straight)? What about if that professional colleague is someone that you could potentially be attracted to, but you're just talking shop? What if it's a friend and you're not talking business at all? And what if your partner doesn't know this friend? How about looking up or even friending/following exes on social media? How about having emotionally intimate conversations with someone else? What about talking about your sex life with friends—including those you could potentially be (or actually are) attracted to? And the list of possibilities goes on . . . .

When most couples get together, they may have some conversations about the big no-nos: "So, we're not dating/sleeping with anyone else now, right?" But most of us tend to let life point out the necessity of discussing these other questions which too often get triggered when a line is inadvertently crossed: "Wait, you're doing what? I don't know how I feel about that." Or they are very clear indeed about how they feel about it.

When couples don't have sufficient discussion about the specific boundaries of fidelity, much less *why* those are the boundaries, it tends to lead to fidelity agreements that contain too many unspoken assumptions. This can then lead to sudden discoveries where each member feels differently (and strongly) about a particular activity— one feels hurt/betrayed and the other feels persecuted. Once the dust settles, it's time to have some thorough conversations about that situation in order to avoid a fight next time. Life tends to serve up a steady stream of learning opportunities, so what did you each learn from this one? Since you've already had to suffer through a fight, you might as well gain some wisdom from it so you don't need to suffer through it again.

Some questions to consider include:

- What exactly happened in that situation?
- What made it feel problematic?
- Why was the situation perhaps not a threat to the relationship?
- What would have made the situation better? And by contrast, what would have made it worse?
- Have we had similar situations come up in the past that shed light on this situation?

Both of you should think about and discuss all of these questions, regardless of where you fall on the issue. The goal here is not only to explain (i.e., defend) your own position, but to also understand your partner's position. This is the time to get clarity, especially on the gray areas and what to do next time if you're not sure. The goal here is to come to a decision that you can both live with and live by. These kinds of really clear, mutually understood agreements may be especially important when one of you has ADHD and may be more prone to jump to conclusions or forget the details of conversations that were held once, long ago, in passing.

Where couples run into the most trouble is when the two partners have very different ideas about what constitutes a sexual or emotional infidelity—and each is totally convinced that they are right. This will require more discussion in order to come to some agreement, just as couples need to negotiate out all sorts of other topics. One of the places where this can come up is when partners disagree strongly on the use of porn, as discussed in *Chapter 11: What About Porn?*, particularly if there haven't been direct conversations about what is and isn't acceptable to use.

Even if a couple does do the hard work of really exploring their own limits and using empathy to understand the other person's limits, relationships evolve over time and therefore so do the partners' fidelity needs. Rapid changes in technology also change the relationship/sexuality landscape. For example, before the internet, checking up on exes was much harder to do, so it wasn't frequently a topic of discussion. Therefore, good fidelity agreements are flexible, adaptive, and reviewed when needed. Fixed rules become obsolete as each partner's fidelity needs evolve or new situations arise, so it is more important to honor the spirit of the agreement than the letter. If you find yourself standing on a technicality, then you probably know that you kind of crossed a line. When in doubt, ask—and always ask before acting.

Within these discussions, it's important to convey that your partner can be honest with you. You can do this by reacting well to what they tell you, especially when the two of you disagree strongly. These good reactions will make your partner more likely to bring something up later, especially if they feel that they are getting close to a line that they don't want to cross. Or at least it makes it harder for them to justify withholding information by claiming that you would have freaked out about it. You probably won't want to hear what they have to say, but it will almost certainly be better to hear it then than to let things develop further and then find out about it.

Preventing Infidelity

People go outside of their fidelity agreements for a lot of different reasons. Sometimes it's a response to dissatisfaction with their partner, relationship, and/or sex life, but sometimes it has nothing to do with any of those—for example, if getting older is causing an existential crisis and the person uses an affair to feel young, desirable, and alive again. Or the illicitness of the affair adds a sense of excitement to a life that has become way too predictable and safe. Sometimes the indiscretion is impulsive in the moment, like when someone gets drunk on a business trip and hooks up with a random stranger. Sometimes it is totally premeditated when someone goes online specifically to find someone to start a relationship with. And some people slip into it sideways, when those chats with a social media friend become longer, more frequent, and increasingly intimate.

However it starts, there is often a tendency to justify or minimize the cheating, in the same way that we justify other behavior that we know we shouldn't be doing (hey, everybody lies on their taxes a little bit, right?). People will minimize the significance of what they are doing or the odds of getting caught, or convince themselves that it is OK to do it. Just as people get a little crazy when they fall in love, people starting affairs can get a little crazy too and feel driven to pursue it. This doesn't excuse them of responsibility for their actions, but it may explain why generally reasonable people can do such unreasonable things—think of all the celebrities, politicians, and professional athletes who get tons of media attention but somehow convince themselves that they can get away with running around in secret. For some people, infidelity involves way too much gas and nowhere near enough brakes—straight into a wall.

There are a thousand reasons why people stray. Let's start with the ones that a romantic partner may potentially have the most direct ability to influence, then cover some of those factors that may have nothing to do with the relationship.

Address Relationship and Sexual Problems

It's definitely not true that infidelity only occurs in unhappy relationships or in response to sexual problems. However, they do make it much more likely. This is just another reason to address problems before things get worse. This leads to two related bits of blunt advice:

- If your partner's fidelity is important to you, then your partner's relationship and sexual satisfaction should be, too.
- If your fidelity is important to you, then your relationship and sexual satisfaction should be, too.

Relationship problems can involve too much negativity (arguing, criticizing, controlling, irresponsibility, shaming, etc.) or not enough positives (support, connection, intimacy, fun, etc.). My hope is that this survey and book will make it easier to work on all of those. Understanding and better managing ADHD, and whatever else may be going on, will make it easier for both of you to be happier in the relationship and overall.

Sexual problems may involve problems with performance, such as erectile disorder, premature ejaculation, painful intercourse,

> It's hard to feel things so deeply and be with someone you love and who loves you and still not feel seen and "ok" as you are. I have intense romantic and sexual expression that I want to share more with my wife and I hope we can while we're both healthy. . . . I don't wish to feel pushed to a point where I feel compelled to look outside the marriage.
> *ADHD man, 56, married, been together 11–20 years*

difficulty with orgasm, etc. or with desire, either in terms of frequency or what constitutes your sexual repertoire. Many of these issues were addressed in the other chapters in this section, so check them out if they are relevant. Since all of these issues can make infidelity, or at least the temptation to stray, more likely, that is yet another reason to address them.

Because of the interconnected nature of all of these, problems in one area make problems in the others more likely, and thereby difficult to resolve. If you and your partner have been stuck for a while and don't seem to be making progress, then it may be worth bringing a professional into the mix to move things along. Unfortunately, most therapists, even couples therapists, have received little to no training in sexual matters, so if this is part of the picture, it's probably worth finding someone who is more capable of addressing it. One good place to start is the professional directory at www.aasect.org.

Some people use infidelity to help them tolerate an unsatisfying situation where they don't feel like they can get their needs met more directly. They can keep the good parts of the relationship without having to address the problem areas—kind of have their cake and eat it, too. Sometimes the affair partner becomes the third leg of the stool that stabilizes the relationship and enables it to go on, despite the problems that exist. The other primary partner may even collude a bit with the situation, by ignoring subtle (or not so subtle) signs that there is something going on. While this is a risky solution because it can blow the relationship apart if discovered, it can keep the relationship together (at least temporarily) and is therefore less disruptive for the partner and children. Of course, a less risky solution like working on the problems in the relationship is probably preferred—and is a lot easier to do when there isn't a third party stirring up feelings and muddying the waters of what the wandering partner really wants. Or if a discovered third party evokes a mountain of hurt and rage in the other partner.

I don't think that trying to prevent a negative, like infidelity, is as motivating as working towards a positive, like feeling good in yourself and in your relationship, so not having to worry about infidelity should be the cherry on top, not the sundae. If you find that you're spending way too much energy worrying about your own or your partner's fidelity, then you probably need to take a hard look at your relationship, sex life, partner, and/or yourself. That excessive worry suggests that something is not as it should be (although sometimes the only problem is unnecessary worrying). You deserve more peace of mind than that, so do the hard work to get there.

Know Your Slippery Slopes

In addition to general relationship and sexual problems, there are lots of ways to put or find yourself outside the bounds of your relationship, but each of us is probably more vulnerable to some than to others. Some of this is driven by our personality, but may also evolve as our life circumstances change—what seems tempting when you have kids and a mortgage may be different than when you had roommates and a crummy apartment. Therefore, since forewarned is forearmed, it may be worth spending some time identifying your slipperiest slopes. You may want to spend some time really thinking about these questions:

- Would you be most tempted by a purely physical hookup, an emotional affair, or a combination?
- What kind of a person would you be most tempted by? Is there anyone currently in your life that you have at least some small feelings for or could potentially be tempted by?
- What situational factors would contribute most to your straying?
- What situational factors would have the greatest protective effect against your straying?

- What relationship factors or situations would contribute most to your straying?
- What relationship factors or situations would have the greatest protective effect against your straying?
- If you were to stray, how would that affect your partner, relationship, family, friends, and life?

These are big questions, so spend some time really reflecting upon them. If you're up for it, have your partner think about these same questions and then spend some time talking about each of your answers. Total honesty here may trigger feelings of jealousy or fuel the fires of worry by identifying specifically what the risks are, so these may be difficult conversations to have—or to live with afterwards. The reward for that discomfort is that actual infidelity is probably less likely after having discussed it. However uncomfortable the conversations may be, actual infidelity would be much more uncomfortable, so do the hard work to get all the way through these conversations to a productive end.

Within these discussions (yes, that's plural), you should probably also discuss what each of you should do in the event that there is something about your partner's behavior that is making you uncomfortable. How should (and shouldn't) this be addressed? Hint: It probably goes something like this: "So I have been noticing something and it kind of makes me uncomfortable, so I just want to run it by you and get it out in the open." Having talked about this already makes it easier to bring it up later if your Spidey sense starts tingling—and to bring it up earlier when perhaps less has transpired and it's therefore easier to address.

You should probably also discuss what each of you should do if you find yourself as the one who is beginning to get into questionable waters. What would your partner want you to do? How would they want you to bring it up? While the obvious request of "just stop feeling and doing that stuff" is easy to say, if it was as easy as that, couples therapists would be a lot less busy. Rather than simply white-knuckling your resistance to the current temptation, it may be helpful to think about why this person or situation is so tempting to you, perhaps especially at this time in your life. Does it tell you anything useful? Understanding the need that is being met will help you (and possibly your partner) not only avoid unhappy entanglements, but possibly also benefit your relationship and/or sex life overall.

Having conversations about potential infidelity doesn't mean that your relationship is troubled. To the contrary, it shows wisdom about the realities of temptation and that talking about these feelings makes us less likely to act on them. It's better to face the things that make us uncomfortable and deal with them directly, rather than wish that they didn't exist.

I sometimes say that ADHD is a disorder of actualizing good intentions, so if you too often act on impulse and then regret it afterwards, you may want to be especially attentive to your slippery situations and remove yourself sooner than later. You may also find that medication gives you a bit more willpower to resist temptation.

Surviving Infidelity

Most people say that they would leave if their partner cheated on them—or kick the partner out, or kill them . . . .

It's easy to take a firm, non-negotiable position on that topic—at least before it happens. If you've been dating for a month, then that's an easy trigger to pull. But when you are living together or married, are completely financially intertwined, and perhaps have kids still at home, it becomes a much less easy answer. Or maybe you just really love this person and don't want to give up everything that is good about the relationship. When actually confronted with the complicated realities of this terrible discovery, most people choose to stay and work on things—after feeling alternately homicidal and suicidal, shamed and self-righteous, powerless and empowered . . . .

The specific nature of the infidelity probably also matters quite a bit—we can't really talk about infidelity as if it is one thing. For example, an ongoing emotional and sexual affair will probably be viewed differently from a single drunken make-out session or a brief intimate conversation with an ex over social media. The effect that the infidelity has on each partner will depend on what that specific type of infidelity means to each one. So, if you were to poll your friends on what to do about a specific situation, you may get a lot of different opinions—only some of which may be helpful for you. This doesn't mean that you shouldn't seek advice from others, but expect some variability in the answers and do what's best for you. Also, remind your confidants that this is your choice and that although they get to have an opinion, you are the only one who gets to vote.

The state of the relationship at the time of the infidelity also has a big effect on how the discovering partner feels about it. It may be the last nail in the coffin of a dying relationship in which case it forces the inevitable. Other couples may be struggling, but still feel connected and want to stay together, or at least try to work on things, so the possibility of reconciliation exists. And others are happy in the relationship and now need to figure out what to do with this bolt out of the blue. Whether you're the one who strayed or the one who discovered it, you both need to figure out what you want to do now.

To Tell or Not to Tell?

Should you tell your partner about a past infidelity? What about a current one that is still ongoing?

These are really hard questions and don't have cut and dry answers. It comes down to two ethical principles that become mutually exclusive once an infidelity occurs. The first is that of self-determination: we all have the right to make our own choices and therefore to have full knowledge to inform those choices. If you had an affair, your partner probably wants to know about it so they can make their own decisions about what to do with that information. But this isn't a trivial situation of picking up a pizza where they may want some input on the toppings. While your partner would probably want to take this affair information into account, this information will likely come with a lot of pain which they won't be happy about.

This brings us to the second ethical principle: do no harm. In this case, you should ensure that your partner is spared the pain and never finds out about the affair. If you feel guilty about what you have done (which shows you have a conscience), then it shouldn't be your partner's job to absolve you of that guilt (which would be compoundingly selfish). Leave them in their blissful ignorance and focus instead on improving your relationship so that both of you will be happier.

So there's the contradiction. Self-determination suggests that infidelity should be disclosed, but do no harm suggests that you shouldn't. Perhaps fortunately, there is a wrinkle on this that may help you make that choice. While we all like to think that we're James Bond and will never get caught, the reality is that many infidelities are discovered, sometimes in really random, highly unlikely kinds of ways. As an example, during my first year of grad school, I went to a small resort in Mexico with my family, kind of in the middle of nowhere. As I was sitting by the pool, a guy I sort of knew from college walked in. There was nothing illicit going on, but sometimes the incredibly unlikely long-shots do happen, no matter how careful you are. Unfortunately, it's human nature to tend to let our guard down as time marches on, so we become less careful. Which creates all those situations where someone gets surprisingly sloppy and their partner unsurprisingly catches them.

The overlap between the two ethical principles is that, if your partner may inadvertently find out about the infidelity, it is almost certainly better for them to hear it from you than in some other way—it may not be doing no harm, but perhaps less harm. It may only be a five percent discount, but it may slightly reduce the feelings of deception and subsequent distrust, especially if it is sooner rather than later and also freely chosen rather than forced because you know that it will definitely come out anyway (e.g., someone else found out and said they would tell next week if you didn't). Also, if you disclose the infidelity, you can choose the time and place so that it is less painful for both of you, whereas if your partner discovers it on their own, who knows what the circumstances could be. You're really rolling the dice there. If the odds are high that your partner will find out, then it's almost certainly better to be the one to tell them and probably sooner than later, since events may beat you to it if you delay.

If you are absolutely, totally convinced that your partner will never find out about your infidelity, then that leaves you stuck in this ethical dilemma and you need to figure out what to do.

Part of this may involve a really hard second look at those odds—sometimes we fool ourselves or forget about little red flags. If you aren't sure what the likelihood is, then you need to spend some time on it. We can probably say that infidelities are more likely to be discovered when they occur closer to home, with someone in your social circles, with someone who your partner knows, happen more often, occur over a longer period of time, and more people know about it. Regardless, random discoveries can occur, so you never know.

Of course, all of this assumes that the infidelities are in the past—it may be a whole different ballgame if it is ongoing, especially if you don't know if you want to end it or which partner you want to keep. My obvious advice to those contemplating an affair is that it is almost always better to end the first relationship before starting a second one. It makes it easier to see whether you want to keep the first relationship, doesn't hurt your partner as much, and keeps things much simpler ethically and legally. Unfortunately, once you're in the midst of an infidelity, it is much harder to sort all of this out and can really distort how you feel about your primary partner and that relationship. If you do decide to leave, you may come to regret that later, especially because affair partners often look much less interesting when they become the primary partner. Also, if you need to unwind your primary relationship, that will probably be much easier to do without your partner feeling betrayed, and therefore vengeful, if they find out about the infidelity, not to mention how others (e.g., children, family, and friends) may feel about you if you make this messier exit.

First, Calm the Storm

The sudden discovery of infidelity can be like lighting a powder keg. Some people have suspected it for a while and just needed proof whereas others are caught completely unawares. Sometimes the straying partner confesses preemptively, but often the other partner finds some evidence that is hard to explain away and the confession is forced. Even then, some straying partners continue to deny even in the face of painfully obvious evidence. Technology has made it both easier and harder to hide our tracks, including when straying.

Usually the first stage of affair recovery involves weathering the emotional storms where the betrayed partner feels hurt, angry, confused, embarrassed, indignant, and pretty much everything else. In nuclear proportions. The straying partner may feel guilty, embarrassed, ashamed, defensive, justified, and maybe even relieved—and pretty much everything else. It can be a real roller coaster ride as the couple swings back and forth and all over the place, trying to make sense of what happened and figure out what comes next. Do I stay? Can I live with myself if I do? Or do I cut my losses? How would this affect the rest of our family and friends? Who do I blame for this? Should I tell anyone? Do we need to go to therapy? Do I need to call a lawyer? How about an STD test? Or a credit check?

There's a lot to be said about how to survive this time, but a lot of it probably boils down to three basic points:

• Take care of yourself, physically and emotionally, during this difficult time.

• Remind yourself that, no matter how terrible it feels or dark it looks, things do tend to get better with time. One way or the other.

• Don't make any big decisions in the midst of this emotional storm. There will be more than enough time for that later.

The straying partner has the responsibility to apologize, empathize, make some serious amends, and reassure the hurt partner, but not to the point of being a literal or emotional punching bag. The hurt partner will likely demand information about what exactly happened, how, when, where, and perhaps most importantly why. This is completely understandable and can help them better understand what happened and what it means. However, it can also come to a point where more information (e.g., sexual activities engaged in, reading all the emails) is not actually helpful and only gives them more things that cannot be unseen or unheard.

Often the hurt partner is bothered most not by what happened, but by the betrayal of it all and that the straying partner knew what they were doing yet pretended that everything was OK. This shatters the hurt partner's faith in their partner and their ability to trust their relationship smoke detectors. They thought everything was fine but it definitely wasn't, so how can they know in the future if there is a problem—or believe that there isn't? It's like a veteran coming home from war and jumping at every loud noise, never knowing when to relax. This hypervigilance response and the intrusive thoughts that accompany it are totally expectable, but most people find that it tends to dissipate with time, even though in the beginning it doesn't feel like it ever could.

If the whole situation feels more emotional and out of control than either of you feels comfortable with, then it may be helpful to meet with a therapist who can guide you through this tumultuous process. It's probably best to start with a couples therapist, but one or both of you may also wind up meeting with an individual therapist. This will likely be difficult and sometimes even painful work, but it will probably leave you better off for it, whether you ultimately choose to stay or go.

It can be tempting for the hurt partner to seek support from family and friends to cope with this difficult situation. This is a good idea for many reasons, but infidelity is a topic that most people tend to have extremely strong opinions on. In addition, it can also irrevocably change these family and friends' feelings towards the straying partner which can make things weird and awkward if you decide to stay together—as many people do. Therefore, as angry as you are at your partner at this time and maybe even as much as they deserve it, you may be better served by thinking a bit about who you disclose to. If you have kids together, then you may also want to consider how disclosure to certain people will affect them, directly or indirectly. If you do tell someone about your partner's infidelity, you may want to tell them that you value their support and opinion, but at the end of it all, it will be your decision about whether to stay or go.

One last point to make here is that the discovery of infidelity can have the possibly counter-intuitive effect of firing up both partners' libidos. Even in the midst of all the pain and guilt, raging and crying, the couple can be screwing with a white-hot passion that they haven't felt in decades, or ever. It's like soaking gunpowder in rocket fuel and lighting it with a hand grenade. That eagerness can feel primal and unstoppable—and completely maddening and confusing in the midst of so much pain. Maybe it's an attempt to reconnect and reestablish the primary relationship. Maybe it's a psychological defense against all the hurt. Maybe it's a desperate attempt to prevent future indiscretions. Regardless, it's common, so if you find yourself in this situation and are wondering what the hell is wrong with you, the answer is nothing. There is likely way too much else to feel bad about—don't add this to the pile. If it feels OK while it's happening and you don't feel too bad about it afterwards, then enjoy the respite from all the rest of the chaos.

Learn From it

An interesting contradiction about infidelity is that it can be one of the most painful things to happen in a relationship, yet can also result in some positive changes that make the relationship better. Recovering from infidelity, for both partners, forces some real examination of the relationship and oneself. It shows you what you need to work on and also what parts of the relationship you aren't willing to give up. It also forces you to examine whether it's worth staying or not, once you add it all up—so if you do decide to stay together, then it is an active choice to do so, rather than passively continuing to get into bed each night next to the same person you woke up with.

The way I see it is that if you have already suffered through the infidelity discovery (or the keeping it secret), then you might as well get the benefit of some good life lessons. The price has already been paid, you've already earned it, so you might as well learn something from it. No point suffering for nothing.

Therefore, after you get over the initial shock and/or explosion once an infidelity is revealed, it's worth both of you spending some time to really think about what happened here:

- What was happening in each of your lives when the infidelity began?
- What was happening in the relationship?
- What would have prevented it?

- What maintained the infidelity, if it was ongoing?
- What purpose did the infidelity serve? What needs were being met?
- What was done to hide the infidelity? And what red flags were being ignored?
- What are the lessons learned from the infidelity?
- How do we each prevent this from happening again?

You will also need to have a lot of conversations about all this, some of which may involve individual and/or couples therapists to calm the fires and really understand what happened and where to go with it. At the end of it all, you may still decide to part ways, recognizing that the infidelity was the last straw—or a sign that things were already too far gone. Parting may be what is best for one or both of you. Even so, it will still be better to come to some understanding of what happened and how it fits into the entirety of the relationship so you can part more amicably, or at least less contentiously. This may save you lots of heartache and also some legal fees, not to mention less ongoing strife if you still need to parent together. Even if you do part ways, this probably won't be your last relationship, so there are still good lessons to be learned here and then applied elsewhere.

Restore Trust

Infidelity can be a double whammy for the partner who discovers it. The first and obvious hit is whatever actions were engaged in. This often drives the initial reaction. The lingering effect of infidelity though involves its impact on trust by disrupting their belief that when things seem OK in the relationship, that they actually are. With the exception of the situations where someone immediately comes clean to their partner, infidelity involves ongoing deception—for example, after spending time with that third party, the partner comes home and acts as if everything is normal in the relationship. All the usual rules still apply. Yet they know that something very big has changed, but their partner doesn't yet know that.

318 Overcome Specific Issues

This undermines their partner's ability to assume that no news is indeed good news and to trust that things really are as they seem. As a result, once this deception is revealed, it's easy to wonder and to worry and maybe even to look a little paranoid.

The counterbalance to this distrust is that the straying partner strives to be as transparent and predictable as possible. Trust is restored by being open, avoiding suspicious behavior, being where you should be, answering questions directly, ensuring that words and actions line up, and sharing anything that needs to be shared before you're found out.

Of course, this presumes that the infidelity is over—but sometimes it isn't. Sometimes people have difficulty giving up the affair partner or can't decide which relationship to keep. This dilemma can be painful and maddening for both partners—and the affair partner, too. I can't say that the answer is always to go back to your primary partner, but many relationships that start as infidelity don't survive once they become the primary relationship. This is because the dynamics are completely different when it's a secret, hidden, extra relationship compared to when it's the main event. Also, affair sex tends to be different from married sex and can be difficult to maintain. Affairs are like going somewhere on vacation— mostly fun and without much responsibility, but if you moved to Barcelona, then it would become a lot like your life now. Teetering between staying and going can be torturous for everyone involved and I would encourage both of you to take your time, try to act with integrity, and make the decision that is best in the long run.

Assuming the straying partner ends the affair and re-commits to their primary partner, it can still be difficult for the hurt partner to maintain faith that the affair is really over or that some new person hasn't entered the picture. It can create a situation where the hurt partner is torn between protecting themselves from getting hurt again versus living a life without fear and enjoying the relationship again. Finding a happy median here involves balancing the need for transparency with the need to move on.

Obsessively checking in on your partner can become its own curse and keeps the infidelity front and center in your mind and in your relationship. If after some reasonable initial period of time (however you define that), you still feel a need to check in frequently on your partner's activities, then perhaps you need to ask yourself what is missing for you and how else you can get that feeling of trust back. If you feel like you will never get it, that you will never be able to move on from the infidelity because it was too egregious, then it may be worth some hard thinking about why you are still in this relationship and whether it is serving either of you to stay. That's a difficult choice to contemplate, but it is possible that the relationship is so damaged that it can't recover. The goal of affair recovery isn't simply to keep the relationship—it's to have a relationship worth keeping, whether it's this one or the next one.

This brings up some existential issues that we probably need a philosopher to help us figure out. Love involves risk—whether it's a friend, a romantic partner, or a child. To want is to risk disappointment, to have is to risk loss. To love is to risk pain. Sometimes that pain comes with unpreventable death, sometimes it comes with preventable choices. Ending this relationship with your straying partner is no guarantee that your next partner won't also hurt you, somehow, some way. Foregoing future relationships does protect you against future hurt, but also means sacrificing a lot of joy and may therefore be too high a price to pay for security. Therefore, the potentially safest bet when it comes to not getting hurt again may be to learn as much as you can about what happened this time so that the painful parts of history don't repeat themselves, whether with this current partner or another one.

Restore Normalcy

While the goal of affair recovery may be to move the relationship to a better place, there will be times when you are tired of all this goddamn affair stuff and just want to watch TV together like other boring couples. The process of affair recovery can be exhausting and all-consuming. It's important work, but as with exercise, you also need your rest times in between workouts in order to rebuild. Affair recovery is part marathon (just keep going) and part interval workout (sprint, then jog, then sprint again). Hopefully as things progress and you both settle in a bit, there will be less sprinting and more jogging. Make a point of creating some fun, easy times along the way and also of enjoying those random little moments.

Also, don't be surprised if there are weird and awkward moments along the way (Really?! *Another* infidelity reference on TV?). One or both of you may get triggered by what happens or where you go. And it may take some time to feel totally comfortable sexually again. None of this means that there is a problem. It just means that this is the process. If something is coming up that needs to be addressed, then address it ("So, maybe I'm over-reacting, but I feel uncomfortable about this.") Be specific and direct and be empathetic and supportive. If the frequency of these weird and awkward moments seems to be decreasing, then you're probably on the right track. If they're spiking, then maybe that's a signal that something needs to be addressed.

You may find it helpful along the way to have affair-free zones where you both agree to not deal with affair stuff for an evening and to just live some life together. It's like that advice of spending time together as a couple where you don't talk about kids, bills, or work. This isn't an avoidance, but rather a rest period which will put you in a better place to work on it next time.

Remember that no matter how weird and awkward it can feel at times, as with other big transitions, things do tend to settle back in and life returns to normal or possibly a new normal. Hang in there and do what you need to do to survive day by day so that you can make it for the long haul.

Take Away Lessons

- Sexual and emotional infidelity are more common than most people would want them to be. For some couples, the infidelity is an intentional death blow to a struggling relationship, whereas for others it unintentionally ends things. And yet others come back stronger after working their way through a lot of difficult issues.

- Some infidelities occur because the partners did not have a sufficiently explicit conversation about what was and wasn't acceptable in the relationship. It's important to have these conversations before anything happens and at least one partner feels betrayed.

- There are many reasons why people knowingly go outside of their relationship. Sometimes it reflects problems in the primary relationship where it's easier to seek happiness elsewhere. But sometimes they are happy with their partner and sex life and still get involved with someone else. Therefore, if your partner strayed, then don't assume that it says something about you unless they tell you it does.

- Since infidelity can be so destructive to a relationship, it is important to know what your slippery slopes are so that you can either avoid them or pull yourself away early when it's easier.

- Once an infidelity occurs, it may or may not be better to tell your partner. It depends on the circumstances of the infidelity and whether you want to work on things in your primary relationship. Hard and fast rules here miss a lot of the important nuances.

- If an infidelity is discovered, it can turn both partners' worlds upside-down with lots of hurt feelings on both sides. As hurt and crazy as you may feel at this time, remember that the intense pain of this moment does settle down and people do get past it, so focus on getting through moment by moment and don't make any big decisions yet.

- Although not recommended as a way to kickstart a flagging relationship, there are couples who rise from the ashes much better off. If you're able to really explore what led up to the infidelity and how you each handled it, you may find that there are a lot of useful lessons to be learned, whether you stay together or not.

- The couples who do stay together (or at least for now), need to find a way to restore trust without making the relationship into a police state. Then they need to find a way to make things normal again, even if that means creating a new normal.

16

Consensual Sex With Other People: Other Arrangements

Let me start by saying that I don't love that this chapter is in a section that is mostly about overcoming problems, even if one of those problems is being single, but it didn't really fit anywhere else and I didn't want a one-chapter section entitled *Seriously Advanced Stuff for Experts* or something. So here we are. On the other hand, it probably is fitting that it is almost the last chapter because you really need to have worked on everything else if consensual nonmonogamy is going to work out well. And since these arrangements seem to be gaining in interest, I thought it would be worth saying a few things about them.

Most couples have monogamous relationships, meaning that sexual and/or romantic contact with others is not permitted. At least, that's the plan. There are those, however, who have a more open arrangement, meaning that some sexual and/or romantic contact with others is allowed within the context of their committed relationship. It goes by lots of names and we will discuss some of the variations, but it all falls under the general category of consensual

> *What would make your sex life better for you?*
> More frequent and kinkier sex, also sex with others.
> *What would make your sex life better for your partner?*
> Finding people to swing with.
> *ADHD woman, 34, married, been together 6–10 years*

nonmonogamy. The key word here is that it is consensual, as opposed to infidelity which is by definition nonconsensual. They are also called open relationships, as opposed to relationships that are closed to outside sexual or romantic partners.

This is still an uncommon arrangement, but it seems to be on the rise, both in practice and in general interest. Within the survey, the results followed the broader trends: men were more interested in trying it and had had more previous experiences with it than women, and ADHD more than non-ADHD. Both gender and ADHD status had a big effect. When asked about their level of interest in consensually nonmonogamous sexual activities, from two to seven percent of respondents answering the question said that they and their partner have engaged in these activities (meaning, their current relationship). Those numbers jump up to eighteen to thirty percent have done so at some point in time, which matches some other research. This could mean that some people dated two people at the same time. In order to really explore what activities were engaged in and what the arrangement was, we would need to ask more detailed follow-up questions, but this highlights the fact that this is not a trivial minority. And, going by internet search numbers, interest in it has been increasing over the last decade, so it may be worth talking here about what people are wondering about.

Here are some interesting and possibly revealing findings from the survey data:

- Two thirds of married folks weren't interested in considering a consensually nonmonogamous arrangement—somewhat less for those who are dating but don't live together. So obviously the remainder had at least some slight interest.

- Those who are dating but don't live together are slightly more likely to consider a consensually nonmonogamous arrangement and to have engaged in these activities with their current partner (6% of daters versus 5% of marrieds). This makes sense since there is likely less emotional commitment, as well as legal and financial entanglements, when dating than when married, so there is less to risk if it doesn't work out.

- Those with a "strong interest" in trying a consensually nonmonogamous arrangement (if their partner was interested) were significantly less satisfied in their relationship and sex life, whether dating or married. This makes sense if they feel like it is a potential solution to a bad situation—whether it is or not is a different question.

- Those who have engaged in some sort of consensual nonmonogamy with their current partner had the highest relationship and sexual satisfactions. This shouldn't be interpreted to mean that opening up your relationship will automatically improve things, but it does show that some people can do well with nonmonogamy. Undoubtedly these are couples who are doing a good job on lots of other parts of their relationship and sex life.

A consensually nonmonogamous arrangement can evoke many strong feelings, from those who swear by it as the only way to long-term happiness within a committed relationship to those who couldn't even imagine considering this crazy stuff. These arrangements can be like a complicated piece of electronics: they offer lots of exciting features, but they can also provoke lots of cursing and yelling, and can crash and lose all of your data (i.e., positive feelings between you and your partner). So they are definitely not something to dabble in. If you're going to try it, you should definitely do it right and know what you are getting yourself into. No impulse buys, please.

Covering the Range

Consensual nonmonogamy comes in lots of flavors. It can be primarily about sex or the emotional relationship or both. A three-way, where a couple has sex together with another person, is maybe one of the simpler versions. But even here there are variations: are both partners equally involved or is one of them doing most of the interacting with the third person? Or maybe the other partner is just watching and not physically involved at all.

Then there is swinging or swapping, where two couples switch partners. This could be in the same room, where the watching is part of the fun, as well as in different rooms and even at different times. Or maybe the couples only have sex with their own partner but they are all doing it in the same room, so they can watch the other couple and be watched.

Some couples allow the partners to have sex with others. This could be a regular hookup partner or different people. Or maybe it is not acceptable locally, but is while out of town. Or maybe only with a same-sex partner (or an opposite sex partner for gay and lesbian couples). Some people get turned on hearing about their partner's adventures, which brings more sexual energy into their relationship, whereas others prefer more of a Don't Ask, Don't Tell policy. The couple negotiates what is and isn't acceptable, such as who they can have sex with (e.g., friends?) as well as what activities are acceptable (e.g., kissing?) and how often they can have sex with the same person. As with monogamous couples, they need to negotiate and define what constitutes fidelity, it's just that they have a broader definition. And, as with monogamous couples, people sometimes cheat by knowingly going outside those bounds, leading to heartache, some intense conversations, and possibly a need to re-negotiate what is acceptable.

Then there are those who prefer an emotional connection with more than one person. This may or may not include sex. If there is an emotional or romantic component, then it is called polyamory, meaning many loves. Usually one partner is designated as their primary and then the other(s) as secondary. This can get extremely complicated if there is a large number of people involved and requires lots of discussion, negotiation, and honesty. The people who do it (or at least do it well) swear that it is worth the effort.

The idea with open relationships is that it allows both partners to be happier and get their needs met better, without having to sneak around to do it. Sometimes the goal is to reduce resentment when one partner wants to keep the relationship, but also wants to get some different needs met elsewhere. Sometimes the goal is to bring some of that romantic and/or sexual energy back into the primary relationship so that it becomes more fulfilling. As with everything else in relationships, people engage in these arrangements for a variety of reasons and their motivations can evolve over time, as can their feelings about it.

When a couple has an open relationship, each partner may participate in different ways. For example, one partner may have sexual and/or romantic relationships with others but the other partner prefers not to. Or maybe one partner only does a little with others. And both partners are OK with that arrangement.

There are no pre-written rules for these relationships, so each couple has to figure out what works for them. Then they need to re-negotiate as circumstances change. It may be worth keeping in mind that this is also true of monogamous relationships—yes, there are certain strong suggestions for how the couple should arrange the relationship, but there is also a range and everyone needs to figure out exactly what works for them.

We don't yet have enough research to answer whether monogamy or nonmonogamy is the better arrangement (at the level of group averages), nor which individuals or couples may do better with each arrangement. There are definitely individuals and couples who bring themselves a load of trouble with nonmonogamy, but there are also those who swear that opening their relationship made it better and more sustainable. Besides, given the high rates of divorce and marital dissatisfaction in monogamous couples, the nonmonogamous folks feel that the risk is worth the reward if it improves the relationship. Nonmonogamy isn't the path to greater relationship and sexual fulfillment for all couples, but there are well adjusted, happy people who say that opening up their relationship made it better, not worse, so we can't say that it definitely can't work.

The Fantasy Versus the Reality

Most people have sexual and romantic fantasies that involve people other than their partner. It could be real people in their lives (like a sexy coworker), media personalities, or completely imaginary people. Playing with those fantasies can be good, dirty fun. Some people like to share and hear their partner's fantasies, whereas others prefer to keep some or all of them private.

Given the near ubiquity of fantasies about others, it is easy to see why nonmonogamy would be appealing. Especially because fantasy brings only the best parts and none of the problems. As with moving to the Caribbean in dark and dreary January, the reality of nonmonogamy is much more complex and takes a lot more work to do well, even if it involves less sweeping up sand.

If you are considering it, you and your partner will need to have *lots* of conversations about it ahead of time (i.e., no heat of the moment, drunken, and/or impulsive hookups). You will need to really think about why this is appealing and what you hope to get from it and then be clear about that from your partner's perspective, too. You will need to have lots of discussions about various what-ifs (e.g., what if one of us starts developing stronger feelings for that other person? What if one of us breaks the new agreement and goes beyond what we decided is acceptable?). This is no time to let yourself believe that everything will be OK just because you want to jump into it. If you have doubts, explore and voice them—and if you feel your partner has doubts, then explore those, too. Take your time on this process so that whatever needs to come out, comes out—beforehand, that is, because it will definitely come out afterwards if you don't.

One of the biggest topics is what to do about jealousy—which is a pretty important topic for monogamous folks to talk about, too. Remaining attentive and considerate to each other can reduce some of the jealousy, but it's important that both partners feel like they can freely bring it up if it comes up. It's also important to remember that, no matter how reasonable and logical you are in discussing it beforehand, the green-eyed monster has a tendency to make up its own mind in the moment, so you definitely want an agreed-upon plan about what to do about it if it does rear its ugly head. It's also worth keeping in mind that jealousy is a common topic in every relationship and that monogamous couples also have to deal with it. For example, someone may feel that friends, work, or the kids are getting too much of their partner's time and attention and that it is taking away from the time and attention that they feel they should get.

You may also find it helpful to talk to a therapist who has some expertise in helping couples negotiate these arrangements. This can be a challenge, depending on where you live, but someone who does sex therapy in general may be more open to working with you on this, even if they don't specialize in it. By contrast, in my opinion most couples therapists will likely be biased against it and will likely instead steer the conversation towards exploring the attachment pathology or something else that is interfering with your ability to be monogamous. Therapists who specialize in sex or porn addiction are also generally more likely to be more conservative in their views and biased against it. Obviously every therapist has to decide which clients they feel they can be helpful to, but starting out with a bias tends to not serve clients best. You can see if there is a certified sex therapist in your area by looking up the provider directory at aasect.org. Some therapists will see nonlocal clients by phone or video chat, but the ethics of this are still being sorted out. There are also people who bill themselves as sex coaches (seriously) who don't have the same restrictions about practicing across state lines, but you really need to check their credentials and background because anyone and their dog can call themselves a coach.

Whether you do or don't meet with a therapist, there are a number of books out there and lots of online resources to help you decide if this is right for you and, if so, how to set it up well. Since this can be an extremely consequential decision, you probably want to get multiple perspectives on it and really do that homework of self-reflection and discussion before acting.

Not the Solution for Relationship Problems

Even the folks who are big advocates for nonmonogamy will quickly say that it should not be used as the solution for relationship problems. Rather, it should be something that makes a good relationship even better. Just as getting married or pregnant is more likely to exacerbate, rather than fix, a struggling relationship, adding others into the mix won't work any magic.

Longstanding sexual or relationship problems should be resolved before you complicate things. This is especially true if one or both of you is growing increasingly distant and you're hoping that add-ing new people will add some life to a fading relationship. If so, it is almost certainly better to do that hard work of assessing whether you really want this relationship. If so, how do you save it? If not, how do you end it as gracefully as possible? Involving other people is more likely to blow it up in a ball of fire than to grease the tracks for a smooth exit. Don't fool yourself, and don't allow your partner to fool themselves, that this will cushion the blow.

Maybe the Solution for a Specific Problem

Sometimes opening up a relationship can be the solution to a spe-cific and irreconcilable problem within an otherwise fulfilling rela-tionship. For example, someone who is totally bisexual, or maybe just leans that way, may have a hard time not getting those same-sex needs met (or heterosexual if they are in a same-sex relationship). They may want some solo or shared experiences with someone of the same sex. Their partner may recognize that this isn't something that they can provide themselves and therefore not feel threatened by it, or even recognize that some flexibility here actually preserves what is otherwise a good relationship. And maybe they also enjoy the whole process.

Some people also have specific sexual or emotional desires that their partner either can't meet or doesn't want to. This is a situa-tion where the couple can't split it down the middle and neither person can let go of their position. One partner really wants to do something and the other really doesn't. For example, someone who wants to be disciplined by a dominatrix. They may be otherwise very happy in their shared sex life but, as with folks with same-sex desires, aren't getting this one itch scratched. Their partner may find a way to prefer that they segregate off that one part of their sexuality. It's kind of like watching a movie by yourself rather than forsaking it or forcing your partner to watch it with you—both people are happier. Obviously, having sex with someone else will involve a lot more discussion than a movie.

Some couples with very large differences in their desired sexual frequency, including if one partner is no longer interested, may also find that there is less chasing and denying if they outsource some or all of that sex to someone else. Both partners get more of what they want, while keeping the good parts of the relationship.

All of these arrangements require diligence on the part of both partners to ensure that they continue to invest in their shared sex life and relationship. It can be easy to take the path of least resistance and let these outside activities draw more and more of the involved partner's energy, as well as let the uninvolved partner off the hook in other ways. But staying engaged in your relationship and sex life is a fairly universal requirement, so none of us can ignore that.

In order to successfully outsource the solution to one specific problem, the couple will have needed to do lots of good work to address most of the other problems in their relationship. This solid foundation keeps the relationship standing strong.

Communication—And Lots of it

If you are considering some sort of nonmonogamous arrangement, you need to have lots of conversations—with yourself, with your partner, and possibly with a therapist—to be really clear about what you're doing and why. And probably with anyone else you are involving—even if it is a one-night stand in a distant city, you should still be honest with the other person about your relationship status and what they can expect out of this situation. These conversations need to happen before, during, and after. There are some who joke that polyamory is just another name for people with a communication fetish—if you think that a relationship of two people requires a lot of talking, it grows exponentially with every other person you involve.

Consensual nonmonogamy isn't a new concept (and nonconsensual nonmonogamy (cheating) definitely isn't a new concept), but it seems to be more on people's radars of late. More people are thinking about it and more people are actually doing it. As with every trend, we need to see where this goes and we will learn more about it from those who try it. Regardless of what others are doing, you and your partner need to figure out whether this is something that might work for you at this time.

Take Away Lessons

- Although most couples have monogamous relationships (or at least that's the plan), there are some who decide to allow some sexual and/or romantic activities with others. There appears to be increasing interest in these types of consensual arrangements.

- Consensual nonmonogamy covers a broad range of activities and arrangements.

- The fantasy of consensual nonmonogamy can be very exciting, but doing it well requires a lot of individual thought and couple conversation to be sure that the reality works out well. This involves being clear about the reasons to try it, the goals, the limits, and what to do if someone feels uncomfortable.

- Almost every proponent of these arrangements will say that it should not be used as a way to resolve problems in a relationship, but rather should be a way to make a good relationship better.

17

Lessons for Dating: Begin With the End in Mind

Although this book is primarily for those who are currently in a relationship, there is a lot of wisdom from these relationships that can be shared with those out on the dating scene to find good partners and create a happy relationship. You may be younger and not have much relationship experience or older and back in the dating scene, perhaps after a decades-long hiatus. You may buy this book while in a relationship, then later come back to this chapter if that relationships ends.

Lessons From Your Past

The past prepares us for the future, at least if we are willing to extract those lessons and apply them forward. What have your past relationships taught you? What did you do well? What do you need to work on? What are you looking for in a partner? What are your non-negotiables that you aren't willing to flex on?

What kinds of partners have you tended to seek out in the past and does that still work for you? Or are you at a different stage of life and therefore your needs have changed? For example, if you're not big on details, shall we say, then you may have sought out people who just can't get enough of details, but is that the person you still want to be and the relationship you want to have again? It's OK if you do, but is there a price associated with that kind of relationship that you would prefer to pay less of?

We get better at relationships by getting more experience with them. There's nothing like an intimate relationship to reveal parts of yourself that you didn't know so well before—sometimes these are positive qualities, but sometimes not so much. Romantic relationships also teach us empathy about other people's experience and how to address disagreements and balance both partners' needs. These are lessons that can only be learned from the doing, although being intentional about examining why you do what you do, your partner's perspective, and how the relationship is going will enable you to learn the most valuable lessons. Experience alone doesn't necessarily teach us anything—it takes some effort to learn the right lessons.

It's easy to look back and lament "if I knew then what I know now . . ." but we couldn't know what we know now without having gone through it. Since we can't rewind time, our next best option is to figure out what are the lessons learned from that past suffering so we don't have to do it again. It's kind of like having already paid the tuition, we might as well learn a few things. Looking back on twenty years of marriage, there is a lot that I would change about those early years (and also some from those middle years, and some from those more recent years . . .), but at least I am applying those hard-earned lessons to make things better now. And I hope that, at fifty years of marriage, to still be learning. Besides, life keeps changing, so you need to evolve along with it.

Those who rush into the next relationship blaming their ex for all the troubles in the last relationship are likely to find themselves unhappy in many of the same ways. This is because they are likely to seek out and attract similar partners and then behave in similar ways. Kinda boring to just repeat the last relationship, right? Wouldn't it be more interesting to find new mistakes to make?

What Role Did ADHD Play?

There are more than enough things for any couple to struggle over, but if ADHD contributed to the demise of your last relationship, it may be worth taking a specific look at that. The older you are, the more likely you were to have spent more years pre-diagnosis and therefore untreated. Not that you and your partner weren't aware of ADHD, you just didn't have an accurate understanding of why you did some of the things that you did. It's easy to think back on how some events would have worked out differently if you had known earlier—and easy to be sad or angry about the fact that they didn't. You may blame yourself, your partner, your parents, and/or previous clinicians for not picking up on ADHD sooner. Sometimes it really should have been diagnosed earlier, but sometimes it just isn't likely that that could have happened.

Once ADHD was diagnosed, to what extent did you and your partner put in the effort to educate yourselves and apply that new knowledge to make your lives and relationship better? If the answer is not so much, then that might be something to seriously consider going forward. Again, relationship happiness involves much more than just ADHD, but slacking on this will likely cause problems. More broadly, those who slack on addressing ADHD are likely to slack on addressing other topics, too.

Lessons From the Survey

The survey revealed a lot about the differences between the most and least happy couples—check out *Chapter 4: Role Models: What Can We Learn From the Happiest Couples?* This is useful not just for people who are currently in a relationship, but also for those who are looking for a new partner. We might even go so far as to say that it's even more useful for singles because it's probably easier to create a satisfying relationship if you start with a good partner, rather than trying to change the one you've got.

The big take-away from the survey is that those who put in the effort to be a good partner, in a variety of ways, are most likely to be happy. Good partners tend to evoke good behavior from their partner, so they both win.

Part of this involves putting in the effort to manage ADHD well, including finding new clinicians if the current ones aren't getting the job done. Both partners should be willing to work on this, as well as whatever else life brings. To what extent is a new potential partner a team player, not just in word, but also in deed?

You also want to consider how much a new partner makes sex, and the relationship overall, a priority. This may be easy in that new relationship glow, but what about when that starts to fade? Are they still invested once that dopamine surge settles down? Are they still sexually generous? Accepting without judgment? Can you ask for what you want, sexually and otherwise? And, of course, vice versa for all of these.

There is certainly much more to a romantic relationship than sex, but do you and a new partner have enough overlap in your desired frequency and activities? A big difference could become an ongoing strain on the relationship. And since differences of opinion will arise in any couple, are the two of you able to effectively resolve disagreements about sex and other important topics? Can you both balance standing up for yourself with also being flexible when necessary? Have you had an honest discussion about masturbation and porn so that it isn't a ticking time bomb, awaiting an unhappy discovery?

What Are You Looking For?

Feelings can certainly change over time, but when it comes to dating, it's helpful to have some sort of an idea of what you are looking for. Are you just looking for a casual, good time with perhaps a few different people at once? Are you looking to get married and pregnant? It's all good, but you're more likely to find what you want if you know what you're looking for. It also makes it less likely that you will find yourself in something that you don't want, which is probably bad for all involved. So, take some time and really think about who and what you are looking for—what are the most important qualities or elements? What are the deal breakers?

Being clear about what you want not only helps you assess the various people you encounter, but also makes it easier for potential partners to decide whether what you each want is compatible.

Granted, none of this is a legal commitment, but people will tend to be more forgiving of a genuine change in feelings than they will of feeling deceived.

What Do You Deserve?

How you were treated in your last relationship, in all of your relationships, or in your life overall can have a big effect on what kind of a relationship you seek out this time. For example, someone who spent most of their life with untreated ADHD may unconsciously expect that it's an inevitability that a new romantic partner will often be angry or disappointed with them. Given their life history, this is unfortunately not completely unreasonable, but it can extend out to accepting behavior from a new partner that isn't warranted, especially if they have worked hard on getting their act together. Or perhaps someone whose last partner had ADHD but made little effort to manage it well may be overly willing to accept that they need to be the responsible one in the next relationship, even to their own detriment.

Taking some time between relationships can help us sort through what is reasonable to ask for the next time around. So can talking to friends about the relationship and how they saw things between you and your ex. Your friends aren't more right in their impressions than you are, but they may be able to add a useful perspective. You may also find it helpful to see a therapist to dig further into the details.

Whether you were the one with or without ADHD, one rule of relationships remains true: those who deal with their own issues are in a better position to seek a partner with fewer issues and to ask them to manage those issues. In the survey, the couples who were the happiest and had the best sex life were the ones where both partners worked hard on the ADHD—and presumably everything else, too.

Dating Apps for the Impatient and Impulsive

ADHD coach and author Caroline Maguire told her publisher that she wouldn't do Twitter because people with poor impulse control shouldn't be given the power to instantly share their every thought far and wide. Incidentally, this is also why she doesn't keep chocolate chips in the house. Perhaps that advice applies equally well to dating apps, which can be even more emotionally provocative than strangers' character-limited musings. (Read "character" however you prefer.)

Dating apps can be a total double-edged sword, even if you do have a great ability to hit pause. They can feel both necessary and evil. And like everything else on the interwebs, they're both. The good news is that they allow you to meet people that you never otherwise would have. The bad news is that it can be overwhelming to sort through everyone to find the ones who are actually worth meeting. Let's talk about how to get more of the good out of these apps and get less tangled up in the bad.

Truth in Labeling

When it comes to dating, and a lot more, I'm a big proponent of truth in labeling, meaning being clear about who you are and what you are looking for. The truth will come out anyway, so you might as well cut to the chase from the get-go. This will spare you future disappointment when a potential partner finds out that they got bait and switched. If you're looking for The One, then say that. If you're looking for something fun and easy, then say that. If you wish you were taller, then don't only post up-angle photos. Although we all want to put our best foot forward, starting a relationship with a lie should be a red flag for the other person to run for the hills.

Fish in the Right Waters

There are all sorts of dating apps and services out there, but they are not all created equal. Some cater to the devout, some to the seriously kinky crowd (not that those are necessarily mutually exclusive). Depending on what you are looking for, who you are, and where you live, some of those apps may be better for you than others. Do a little research to figure out which will best meet your needs, then try a few (or less) and see what happens. Resist the urge to jump quickly to some new app, but also don't waste too much time in empty waters. Ask your friends about which apps they have had the most success with and perhaps start there.

Invest the Time

Setting up a desirable profile may feel like homework, but it could get you much more than a good grade. Unless an actual teacher replies to you and corrects it. Think about how you want to present yourself and take the time to create a full and compelling profile that shows who you are and what you are looking for. Then show it to some friends for a peer review. Sex advice columnist and podcaster Dan Savage told a story about a listener who asked him (well, chased him down) for some feedback on why he wasn't getting more responses to his dating profile. The guy was really into martial arts and had a number of pictures of himself with swords which had the unintended effect of making him look like an ax murderer. So, some focus grouping may be helpful.

Once your profile is ready for prime time, you need to invest some time checking out other people's profiles and replying to who messages you. If you tend to have a hard time remembering details about lots of different people (wait, is he the one who loves or hates long walks on the beach?), then you may find it less stressful to talk to fewer contenders at one time, rather than hitting up as many people as possible. And if you find yourself forgetting something about someone you're talking to, just own it: "Sorry, I'm not always great with these kinds of details. Remind me again where you grew up?" Honesty is probably better than obvious fumbling to cover it up.

Resist FOMO . . .

The seemingly endless parade of profiles can make it hard to commit to any one person, if there is always a hope that someone even better is behind the next swipe—fear of missing out (FOMO). Technically speaking, there is always that possibility. If you're sensitive to dopamine hits, then dating apps will give you endless obsessive fun. This can run the risk though of making it harder to appreciate the person(s) you are actually going out with. It can be hard for the reality of this person in front of you to compete with the fantasy of what might be possible from the next person that you haven't met yet. If you tend to be impatient, it can be really easy to burn through a lot of first dates and constantly moving on to the next swipe.

If you find that wondering about all those other fish in the sea is interfering with enjoying and getting to know the person in front of you, try to make a conscious effort to notice what is interesting and worthwhile about who you are currently talking to. Some people make their good qualities really obvious, but some take a bit more digging to discover them. This is not to say that everyone you meet will be a great match for you, but you want to at least take enough time to make an informed choice about it. Impulsively jumping to the next person may get you a lot of first dates, but probably not a lot of third dates.

. . . But Know When to Move On

Odds are that you will need to talk to and go out with a bunch of people before finding someone who is a good fit for you. That probably means that you will find some people who are OK, but ultimately not what you're looking for. And maybe a few who are definitely not what you're looking for. When it isn't so obvious, it can be difficult to know whether to try to make things work or to move on. This is a judgment call, which means that it will sometimes be fuzzy and subjective. Unless the other person is absolutely terrible, you will likely have mixed feelings about the relationship— part of you may want to stay, part to leave.

Sometimes talking things through with a friend can help you make that choice, but you need to be careful of how you describe the relationship because that will have a really big impact on the kind of advice that you will get. And also consider the source, since some people will tend to give certain kinds of advice or value some potential partner traits over others.

You may also want to consider your past relationships and whether you have tended to stay too long or bail out too quickly. If there is a trend there, especially if you later regret how you handled things, you may want to really consider that and correct it as needed.

To Tell or Not to Tell?

I've had clients ask me when they should disclose their ADHD (or whatever) to a new partner. As always, it depends. There are no hard and fast rules (e.g., third date). If this is someone that you're just having some casual fun with, you probably have less of a moral obligation to disclose anything. On the other hand, if your new or potential partner would be impacted by this new information if the relationship got serious, they will probably have more of a desire to know about it since they have something at stake.

Although there is no official due date at which point you need to reveal something personal like ADHD, I would caution you against waiting too long until feelings on one or both sides have grown. Regardless of how your partner feels about what you're disclosing, they might feel like you purposely misled them by withholding information that they should have been given earlier. Having said that, people who tend to react well and be non-judgmental tend to be told more things.

When it comes these sorts of disclosures, I often advise clients to initially talk symptoms before diagnoses. For example, I had a client who told her new boyfriend, "I will never be on time." She wasn't dismissive of it and she does feel bad when she keeps him waiting, but she wanted him to have the right expectations and not invent his own reasons (e.g., she's inconsiderate). The goal here is to explain symptoms that the other person already sees—no secrets being divulged here. The other person's reaction can be revealing of how they would handle bigger disclosures. Again, we're shooting for non-reactive and non-judgmental.

If someone doesn't react well to a disclosure, then perhaps that needs to become the topic of conversation. And perhaps you may want to consider whether you are a good match. If things go well, then it probably does become reasonable for a new-ish partner to be told about your ADHD, what you do about it, how it still affects you, and how it might affect them. Most people tend to be more forgiving if they feel that the other person is putting in the effort on it. Ultimately, remember that everyone has some sort of issues and baggage, so don't get down on yourself about ADHD—and perhaps reconsider staying with someone who causes you to feel badly.

Survive and Thrive

Dating, especially when you've only had a date or two with some-one, can be confusing and disappointing. People can disappear suddenly and without reason, especially if you met them online and your lives don't overlap. This just is what it is, but remember that everyone has to go through some disappointments and maybe broken hearts before they find a relationship that works. If you're not sure what happened that caused someone to end things, then ask. You may not hear back, but there's no harm in asking. Tell them that you would like some honest feedback so you know better what to do in the next relationship. If what they tell you is similar to what you've heard from others, then there is probably something to that advice. As I've said multiple times, the goal is to learn from your relationships, including the ones that ended too quickly.

On the flipside, if you're the one doing the ending, try to do it respectfully. Let the other person know that it isn't working out and perhaps explain why, at least if you feel it would be helpful for them to know. Dating is hard enough—let's be good to each other.

Take Away Lessons

- If you are back on the dating scene, it is probably worth reflecting back on your prior relationships and what they have taught you. What is most important to you in a partner? What would you do different? How did ADHD impact the relationship and how did you each respond?

- The survey results tell us that those who put in effort to be a good partner, in multiple ways, tend to have more mutually satisfying relationships. So, hold yourself to high standards—and new partners, too.

- It really helps to be clear about what you are looking for in a new relationship and potential partner. Past relationship struggles, related to ADHD or otherwise, can impact what we feel we can expect and ask for. We don't get everything we want, but you may want to reflect on whether you are settling.

- Dating apps can be a blessing and a curse. They can be an invaluable tool to meet people you never otherwise would, but they can also make you despair about humanity. Being really clear about who you are and what you want, trying new apps if necessary, putting in the necessary time, and knowing when to move on can all help you get more of the benefits and less of the misery.

- If you have ADHD (or whatever), at some point you will need to tell a new partner, if only because they will figure it out themselves anyway. There are no hard and fast rules on when this should be, but their response may provide some useful information on what to expect from them as a partner.

18

Final Thoughts

Most of my time is spent seeing therapy clients in my office, mostly folks with ADHD and their romantic partners and family members. Obviously, no one shows up in my office to brag about how awesome they're doing, so I see a lot of unhappiness. I see the many ways that ADHD can impact how someone functions in the world, how they feel about themselves, and how they interact with others. I see how romantic partners and family members respond to this, in better and worse ways. Of course, I also see lots of good and bad moves from my couples where neither partner has ADHD. The good news in all this is that generally speaking, people tend to be happier when they leave therapy, even if they were really unhappy when they arrived.

I'm a big proponent of medication for ADHD for those who need it because it can be quite helpful in managing the symptoms of ADHD. At the end of the day though, I'm not really interested in ADHD symptoms—I'm interested in how this person is functioning in their life. Are they happy? Do they have interesting work and hobbies? Do they have meaningful relationships? Do they respect themselves? In other words, what I would hope for any client and any other person I met. Helping them better manage their ADHD may be necessary for them to achieve these bigger, loftier goals. If so, let's focus on that. But that's not where the story ends.

I was recently presenting a training for therapists on how to work with clients with ADHD. As I made my way through various therapy techniques and finally got to the last section on relationships and sex, I kept coming back to the idea that the goal of treatment is to help our clients live better lives and that, for many, that culminates in having a rewarding relationship and sex life where both partners get their needs met and they treat each other well. Ultimately, everything else I covered was all in the service of this goal. This is no easy task for any couple and ADHD can certainly add some additional challenges, but that makes the benefits of that emotional and sexual connection all the more important.

Sex of any kind can be a wonderful experience, but hot sex in a committed relationship can elevate the whole relationship. It takes us out of the mundane, temporarily allows us to push away other concerns, and highlights the best of what we have to offer each other. The rest of the world drops away and it's just you and me, at our most honest and exposed. Imperfections be damned. Luxuriate in the glory of it all.

With that in mind, I'd like to end a book on ADHD by saying that, even though I treat a lot of people with ADHD, I don't treat ADHD. Rather, I help people with ADHD and their family members live better lives. My hope is that this book helps you and your partner live a better life—and also your kids, and their kids.

I'd like to give the final words in this book to one of the survey respondents. This feels fitting.

> This may sound a little weird. . . . I truly worry about the sex lives of my children. Both of my children have been diagnosed with ADHD. My beautiful, 18-year-old daughter and very handsome 14-year-old son both exhibit the same behaviors regarding the opposite sex that I exhibited when I was their age. I hope that a book such as yours can possibly help them in their future relationships.

Appendix A: The ADHD Relationship Sex Survey

Section 1. Thanks for Your Help on This Important Topic

The purpose of this survey is to better understand the sex lives and relationships of couples where one partner has ADHD (sometimes called ADD—we use ADHD to refer to both) and one partner does not have ADHD.

1. Are you in a romantic relationship where one of you has ADHD and the other one does not? (If neither of you has ADHD or both of you has ADHD, please answer No and then exit the survey.)
   - Yes (one partner has ADHD, one partner does not). ✓
   - No (Neither partner has ADHD or both partners have ADHD).

Section 2. Demographic Information

2. What is your age?
   - 17 or younger (sorry, we're limiting this survey to adults—come back later!)
   - 18–23
   - 24–29 ✓
   - 30–39

345

- 40–49
- 50–59
- 60 or older

3. What is your gender?
   - Female
   - Male ✓

4. Which of the following best describes your current relationship status?
   - Dating, living separately
   - Living together but not engaged or married
   - Engaged but not living together
   - Engaged and living together ✓
   - Married/civil union

5. How long have you and your current partner been together as a couple (from first date)?
   - 0–2 years
   - 3–5 years
   - 6–10 years ✓
   - 11–20 years
   - 21 years or more

6. This relationship consists of
   - One man, one woman ✓
   - Two men
   - Two women

7. Do you have any children of the following ages currently living with you at least part time? [check all that apply]
   - 0–3 years old
   - 4–12 years old
   - 13–18 years old
   - 19 years old or older

Section 3. ADHD Questions

8. Who in the relationship has ADHD (as diagnosed by a relevant professional)?
   - Myself ✓
   - My partner

9. Which of the following treatments for ADHD have you and/or your partner used within the last year? [check all that apply]
   - Educating ourselves about ADHD through books, magazines, websites, webinars, meetings, etc. ✓
   - Medication (stimulants or non-stimulants) ✓
   - Psychological therapy ✓
   - Coaching
   - Professional organizer
   - Lifestyle management: exercise, sleep, diet, stress management, etc. ✓
   - Other

10. To what extent do you feel that you have worked on your or your partner's ADHD?
    - No real effort
    - Some slight effort
    - Some moderate effort
    - Quite a bit of effort
    - Lots of effort ✓

11. To what extent do you feel that your partner has worked on your or your partner's ADHD?
    - No real effort
    - Some slight effort
    - Some moderate effort
    - Quite a bit of effort
    - Lots of effort ✓

12. To what extent do you feel that treatment overall has been effective in managing your or your partner's ADHD symptoms?
   - Has made things worse
   - Not effective or hard to say
   - Slightly effective
   - Somewhat effective
   - Very effective ✓

Section 4. Relationship Questions

13. Over this past month, how satisfied overall have you been with this current romantic relationship? - no sex allowed haha
   - Very dissatisfied ✗
   - Somewhat dissatisfied
   - Slightly dissatisfied
   - Neither satisfied nor dissatisfied
   - Slightly satisfied
   - Somewhat satisfied
   - Very satisfied ✓

14. During the first year of this current relationship, how satisfied overall were you with this romantic relationship?
   - Very dissatisfied
   - Somewhat dissatisfied
   - Slightly dissatisfied
   - Neither satisfied nor dissatisfied
   - Slightly satisfied
   - Somewhat satisfied
   - Very satisfied ✓

15. Over this past month, how satisfied have you been with your sex life? - no sex allowed
   - Very dissatisfied ✓
   - Somewhat dissatisfied
   - Slightly dissatisfied

- Neither satisfied nor dissatisfied
- Slightly satisfied
- Somewhat satisfied
- Very satisfied

16. During the first year of this relationship, how satisfied were you with your sex life?
    - Very dissatisfied
    - Somewhat dissatisfied
    - Slightly dissatisfied
    - Neither satisfied nor dissatisfied ✓
    - Slightly satisfied
    - Somewhat satisfied
    - Very satisfied

17. How important is your sexual satisfaction to your overall relationship satisfaction?
    - Not at all
    - Slightly
    - Somewhat
    - Moderately ✓
    - Very

Section 5. Sex Questions

When we use the term "sexual activity," we are using the term broadly to include any form of physical erotic activity. This includes kissing, touching, oral sex, intercourse, using sex toys, and any other activity that one or both of you considers sexual. It may or may not result in orgasm.

18. How often have you and your partner engaged in sexual activity together during this past month (may or may not include intercourse)?
    - Not within the last six months
    - Within the last six months
    - Once this month ✓

- 2–3 days/mo
- 1 day/wk
- 2–3 days/wk
- 4–6 days/wk
- Daily

19. How often would you want to engage in sexual activity with your partner (may or may not include intercourse)?
    - Less than once per six months
    - Once per six months
    - Once/month
    - 2–3 days/mo
    - 1 day/wk
    - 2–3 days/wk ✓
    - 4–6 days/wk
    - Daily

20. Who tends to initiate sexual activity (may or may not include intercourse)?
    - Always me
    - Usually me
    - A little bit more me
    - Pretty even
    - A little bit more my partner
    - Usually my partner
    - Always my partner ✓

21. How quickly do you become interested in sexual activity (may or may not include intercourse)?
    - I need very little warming up (emotionally, relationally, and/or physically) to get in the mood
    - I need at least some warming up (emotionally, relationally, and/or physically) to get in the mood
    - I need a moderate amount of warming up (emotionally, relationally, and/or physically) to get in the mood

- I need quite a bit of warming up (emotionally, relationally, and/or physically) to get in the mood ✔
- I need a lot of warming up (emotionally, relationally, and/ or physically) to get in the mood

22. How often do you get distracted (for more than a quick moment) during sexual activity (may or may not include intercourse)?
    - Never
    - Rarely
    - Infrequently
    - Sometimes
    - Frequently
    - Most times ✓
    - Every time

23. To what extent does prescription stimulant medication for ADHD (taken by you or your partner) affect your enjoyment of a sexual encounter (assuming that the medication is active during the sexual encounter)?
    - Neither of us takes prescription stimulant medication or it is never active during sexual encounters
    - Large negative effect
    - Moderate negative effect
    - Small negative effect
    - Hard to say or no effect ✓   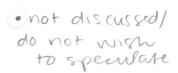 not discussed/ do not wish to speculate
    - Small positive effect
    - Moderate positive effect
    - Large positive effect

24. How comfortable do you feel making specific sexual requests of your partner (not just generally initiating sexual activity)?
    - Very comfortable
    - Somewhat comfortable
    - Slightly comfortable

- Neither comfortable nor uncomfortable
- Slightly uncomfortable
- Somewhat uncomfortable
- Very uncomfortable ✓

25. How comfortable do you feel fulfilling your partner's specific sexual requests (not just generally responding to sexual initiations)?
    - Very comfortable
    - Somewhat comfortable
    - Slightly comfortable ✓
    - Neither comfortable nor uncomfortable
    - Slightly uncomfortable
    - Somewhat uncomfortable
    - Very uncomfortable

26. How comfortable do you feel sharing your sexual fantasies and turn-ons with your partner, including those that you may or may not want to act on?
    - Very comfortable
    - Somewhat comfortable
    - Slightly comfortable
    - Neither comfortable nor uncomfortable
    - Slightly uncomfortable
    - Somewhat uncomfortable ✓
    - Very uncomfortable

27. To what extent do you enjoy talking during sexual activity?
    - I really enjoy it
    - I usually enjoy it
    - I sometimes enjoy it
    - I could take it or leave it
    - I find it can be distracting
    - I find it can be somewhat problematic
    - I find it bothersome or quite problematic ✓

28. In general, to what extent do you prefer to engage in the same sexual activities during all or most sexual encounters versus prefer to have a larger repertoire of sexual activities to choose from for each sexual encounter?
   - Strongly prefer to engage in the same sexual activities
   - Somewhat prefer to engage in the same sexual activities
   - Slightly prefer to engage in the same sexual activities ✓
   - Fairly evenly split between consistency and variety
   - Slightly prefer a larger repertoire of sexual activities
   - Somewhat prefer a larger repertoire of sexual activities
   - Strongly prefer a larger repertoire of sexual activities

29. In general, to what extent do you have a desire for engaging in familiar sexual activities versus a desire for experimenting with new sexual activities?
   - Strongly prefer sticking with familiar sexual activities
   - Somewhat prefer sticking with familiar sexual activities
   - Slightly prefer sticking with familiar sexual activities
   - Fairly even split between familiarity and novelty ✓
   - Slightly prefer trying new sexual activities
   - Somewhat prefer trying new sexual activities
   - Strongly prefer trying new sexual activities.

30. To what extent do you feel that your partner reads you well and knows how to please you sexually?
   - Not at all
   - To a small degree
   - To a moderate degree
   - To a large degree ✓
   - To a very large degree

31. When it's time to focus on your sexual pleasure, to what extent do you feel that your partner makes that a priority and puts in the necessary effort?
   - Not at all
   - To a small degree

- To a moderate degree
- To a large degree
- To a very large degree ✓

32. When it's time to focus on your partner's sexual pleasure, to what extent do you make that a priority and put in the necessary effort?

- Not at all
- To a small degree
- To a moderate degree ✓
- To a large degree
- To a very large degree

33. To what extent are you willing to be sexually generous and give your partner sexual pleasure when you are not feeling sexually interested?

- Not at all
- To a small degree ✓
- To a moderate degree
- To a large degree
- To a very large degree

34. To what extent is your partner willing to be sexually generous and give you sexual pleasure when s/he is not feeling sexually interested?

- Not at all
- To a small degree
- To a moderate degree
- To a large degree
- To a very large degree ✓

35. How often have you masturbated over this past month?

- Not this month
- Once this month
- 2–3 days/mo
- 1 day/wk

- 2–3 days/wk ✓
- 4–6 days/wk
- Daily

36. How often have you viewed pornography over this past month (alone or with your partner, to orgasm or not)?
    - Not this month
    - Once this month
    - 2–3 days/mo
    - 1 day/wk
    - 2–3 days/wk ✓
    - 4–6 days/wk
    - Daily

37. If you look at pornography, how do you feel about it?
    - I don't look at pornography
    - It has a large negative effect on my relationship and/or sex life
    - It has a moderate negative effect on my relationship and/or sex life
    - It has a small negative effect on my relationship and/or sex life
    - It has no real effect on my relationship and/or sex life ✓
    - It has a small positive effect on my relationship and/or sex life
    - It has a moderate positive effect on my relationship and/or sex life
    - It has a large positive effect on my relationship and/or sex life

38. If your partner looks at pornography, how do you feel about it?
    - To my knowledge, my partner doesn't look at pornography
    - It has a large negative effect on our relationship and/or sex life

if we arent having frequent sex

if we are having frequent sex ✓

- It has a moderate negative effect on our relationship and/or sex life
- It has a small negative effect on our relationship and/or sex life
- It has no real effect on our relationship and/or sex life ✓
- It has a small positive effect on our relationship and/or sex life
- It has a moderate positive effect on our relationship and/or sex life
- It has a large positive effect on our relationship and/or sex life

39. Have you ever engaged in sexual activities of a primarily physical nature without emotional involvement with someone other than your partner without your partner's prior knowledge or consent? This may have been during your current relationship or a prior one.
    - Yes
    - No ✓

40. Have you ever engaged in an emotional relationship (possibly physical, but definitely involved an emotional connection that would have made your partner uncomfortable) with someone other than your partner without your partner's prior knowledge or consent? This may have been during your current relationship or a prior one.
    - Yes
    - No ✓

41. How adventurous/kinky would you say you are?
    - Not at all adventurous/kinky
    - Slightly adventurous/kinky ✓
    - Somewhat adventurous/kinky
    - Fairly adventurous/kinky
    - Very adventurous/kinky

42. Have you ever engaged in consensual nonmonogamous sexual activities (e.g., threesome, swinging, swapping, open relationship, polyamory, etc.)? This may have been during your current relationship or a prior one.
    - Yes
    - No ✓

43. If your partner was OK with it, would you be interested in consensual nonmonogamous sexual activities (e.g., threesome, swinging, swapping, open relationship, polyamory, etc.)?
    - No interest ✓
    - Slight interest
    - Moderate interest
    - Strong interest
    - My partner and I have engaged in consensual nonmonogamous sexual activities

44. How often do you find certain kinds of touch that would otherwise be enjoyable or neutral, to be uncomfortable or not pleasurable?
    - Never
    - Few sexual encounters
    - Some sexual encounters ✓
    - Many sexual encounters
    - Every sexual encounter

45. There are many possible barriers to a more satisfying sex life, some of which are listed below. You will probably find that some of them apply more to you and/or your partner than others do. Please rate the extent to which each of these below has been a barrier to more frequent and/or enjoyable sexual activity over this past month.

	Not a barrier	Small barrier	Moderate barrier	Large barrier	Very large barrier	Extreme barrier
I don't wish to communicate that everything is good between us by having sex	✓					
Distractibility throws off the rhythm of sex			✓		E	
I'm too angry with my partner to want sex	✓		E			
My partner is too angry with me for us to have sex	✓					
Our feelings about each other are too complicated or too negative for sex to feel comfortable	✓		M			
I don't think that the sex will be satisfying, so I don't even bother	✓		E			

I am no longer sexually attracted to my partner	✓				
I am disinterested in sex in general, not just with this partner	✓				
My partner seems like another child, lessening his or her appeal	✓				
My partner bosses me around too much, lessening his or her appeal					
One or both of us are too busy with other things to have time for sex			✓		m
There would be more time for sex if time was used more efficiently I am too tired to have sex		✓			

(continued)

Continued

	Not a barrier	Small barrier	Moderate barrier	Large barrier	Very large barrier	Extreme barrier
It can be difficult to switch gears from other demands and be sexual			✓ m		✓	
I resent that my partner doesn't pay enough attention to me unless he/she wants sex	✓		m			
Sex has become kind of predictable and boring	✓	m				
My partner acts disinterested in having sex with me, even when I ask		✓			m	
I don't feel ~~loved~~ *desired* enough to want to have sex with my partner	✓		m			
We haven't had sex for so long, I feel uncomfortable to try it now	✓		m			

Statement						
My partner asks too much of me sexually	✓					
My partner does not understand my sexual needs or can't please me sexually	✓					
I feel uncomfortable sharing my sexual desires with my partner			✓			
I don't understand my partner's sexual needs or can't please him/her sexually	✓					
Prescription medication use impedes at least one partner's ability or desire to have sex	✓					
Recreational drug or alcohol use impedes at least one partner's ability or desire to have sex			✓			

46. To what extent do you feel that your or your partner's ADHD adds barriers to sexual activity in addition to what most couples face?
    - Contributes to a better sex life
    - Hard to say or no effect
    - Small negative effect
    - Moderate negative effect ✓
    - Large negative effect
47. What would make your sex life better for you?
48. What would make your sex life better for your partner?
49. Is there anything else that you would like us to know?

Appendix B:
Provider Directories

Finding the right service providers can be challenging in both ADHD and sexuality, but these directories are a good place to get some names and then research further from there. Being listed in a directory isn't a guarantee of quality, but at least they are interested.

ADHD

chadd.org (Children and Adults with ADHD)
add.org (ADD Association)
ADHDcoaches.org (ADHD Coaches Organization)
ChallengingDisorganization.org (Institute for Challenging Disorganization)
napo.net (National Association of Productivity and Organizing Professionals)
PsychologyToday.com

Sexuality

aasect.org (American Association of Sexuality Educators, Counselors, and Therapists)
sstarnet.org (Society for Sex Therapy & Research)
issm.info (International Society for Sexual Medicine)
isswsh.org (International Society for the Study of Women's Sexual Health)
PsychologyToday.com

Appendix C:
Recommended Reading

There are many good books out there that have influenced my thinking and may benefit yours.

ADHD

Russell Barkley: *When an Adult You Love Has ADHD: Professional Advice for Parents, Partners, and Siblings*

Edward Hallowell & Sue George Hallowell: *Married to Distraction: Restoring Intimacy and Strengthening Your Marriage in an Age of Interruption*

Melissa Orlov: *The ADHD Effect on Marriage: Understand and Rebuild Your Relationship in Six Steps*

Melissa Orlov & Nancie Kohlenberger: *The Couple's Guide to Thriving with ADHD*

Gina Pera: *Is It You, Me, or Adult A.D.D.? Stopping the Roller Coaster When Someone You Love Has Attention Deficit Disorder*

J. Russell Ramsay & Anthony Rostain: *The Adult ADHD Tool Kit*

Linda Roggli: *Confessions of an ADDiva: Midlife in the Non-Linear Lane*

Stephanie Sarkis: *ADD and Your Money: A Guide to Personal Finance for Adults With Attention Deficit Disorder*

Sari Solden & Michelle Frank: *A Radical Guide for Women with ADHD: Embrace Neurodiversity, Live Boldy, and Break Through Barriers*

Susan Tschudi: *Loving Someone With Attention Deficit Disorder: A Practical Guide to Understanding Your Partner, Improving Your Communication, and Strengthening You*

Ari Tuckman: *More Attention, Less Deficit: Success Strategies for Adults With ADHD*

Ari Tuckman: *Understand Your Brain, Get More Done: The ADHD Executive Functions Workbook*

Sexuality

Laurie Betito: *The Sex Bible for People Over 50*

Lori Brotto: *Better Sex Through Mindfulness: How Women Can Cultivate Desire*

Paul Joannides: *Guide to Getting It On: Unzipped*

Ian Kerner: *She Comes First: The Thinking Man's Guide to Pleasuring a Woman*

Marty Klein: *His Porn, Her Pain: Confronting America's Porn-Panic With Honest Talk about Sex*

Marty Klein: *Sexual Intelligence: What We Really Want From Sex—and How to Get It*

Justin Lehmiller: *Tell Me What You Want: The Science of Sexual Desire and How It Can Help You Improve Your Sex Life*

David Ley: *Ethical Porn for Dicks: A Man's Guide to Responsible Viewing Pleasure*

Barry McCarthy & Emily McCarthy: *Rekindling Desire, 2nd ed.*

Jack Morin: *The Erotic Mind: Unlocking the Inner Sources of Passion and Fulfillment*

Emily Nagoski: *Come as You Are: The Surprising New Science That Will Transform Your Sex Life*

Esther Perel: *The State of Affairs: Rethinking Infidelity*

David Schnarch: *Intimacy & Desire: Awaken the Passion in Your Relationship*

Literature Cited

Barkley, R. (2005). *ADHD and the nature of self-control.* New York: Guilford Press.

Braun-Harvey, D. & Vigorito, M.A. (2015). *Treating out of control sexual behavior: Rethinking sex addiction.* New York: Springer Publishing Company.

Herbenick, D., Bowling, J., Fu, T-C. (Jane), Dodge, B., Guerra-Reyes, L. & Sanders, S. (2017). Sexual diversity in the United States: Results from a nationally representative probability sample of adult women and men. *PLoS One* 12(7): e0181198. https://DOI.org/10.1371/journal.pone.0181198

Klein, M. (2016). *His porn, her pain: Confronting America's PornPanic with honest talk about sex.* Santa Barbara, CA: Praeger.

Ley, D. (2012). *The myth of sex addiction.* Lanham, MD: Rowman & Littlefield.

Ley, D. (2016). *Ethical porn for dicks: A man's guide to responsible viewing pleasure.* Berkeley, CA: ThreeL Media.

McCarthy, B. & McCarthy, E. (2013). *Rekindling desire,* 2nd ed. New York: Routledge.

McCarthy, B. & McCarthy, E. (2014). *Therapy with men after sixty: A challenging life phase.* New York: Routledge.

Nagoski, E. (2015). *Come as you are: The surprising new science that will transform your sex life.* New York: Simon & Schuster.

Index

Made in United States
Orlando, FL
17 December 2022

26929305R00213